TRAINS *of* THOUGHT

The Criticism of T. S. Eliot (1949)

Stendhal et la voie oblique (1954)

The Intellectual Hero (1961)

The Novels of Flaubert (1966)

Stendhal: Fiction and the Themes of Freedom (1968)

Flaubert (1971)

The Romantic Prison: The French Tradition (1978)

Victor Hugo and the Visionary Novel (1984)

The Hidden Reader: Stendhal, Balzac, Hugo, Baudelaire, Flaubert (1988)

In Praise of Antiheroes: Figures and Themes in Modern European

Literature (1999)

TRAINS *of* THOUGHT

Memories of a Stateless Youth

VICTOR BROMBERT

W. W. Norton & Company • New York • London

An early version of the prologue appeared as "Trains of Thought," *Ontario Review* 46, Spring/Summer 1997, pp. 75–90.

Frontispiece: Summer of 1936, with my parents in Marienbad. Prologue: Summer of 1936, at the age of twelve, in the garden of the hotel in Marienbad. Part opener I: On the rue Eugène Manuel in Paris, where we lived. Part opener II: Fall of 1940. On the rue de la Buffa in Nice. Part opener III: Spring of 1943. After my induction into the army. Epilogue: As an undergraduate at Yale.

For information about permission to reproduce selections from this book, write to Permissions, W. W. Norton & Company, Inc., 500 Fifth Avenue, New York, NY 10110

The text and diplay of this book are composed in Fournier
Composition by Molly Heron
Manufacturing by The Haddon Craftsmen, Inc.
Book design by Chris Welch
Production manager: Julia Druskin

Library of Congress Cataloging-in-Publication Data

Brombert, Victor H.
Trains of thought : memories of a stateless youth / Victor Brombert.
p. cm.
ISBN 0-393-05115-3
1. Brombert, Victor H. 2. Stateless persons—Biography. 3. World War, 1939–1945—Personal narratives, American. I. Title.

CT275.B746 A3 2002
940.54'8173—dc21   2002067081

W. W. Norton & Company, Inc., 500 Fifth Avenue, New York, N.Y. 10110
www.wwnorton.com

W. W. Norton & Company Ltd., Castle House, 75/76 Wells Street, London W1T 3QT

1 2 3 4 5 6 7 8 9 0

To Bettina,
    the cherished future and present
    behind every one of these pages about the past—
        and
To Lauren and Marc,
    for whom this book was written
        —with love

Prends garde à la douceur des choses . . .

Beware of the sweetness of things . . .
—Paul-Jean Toulet

CONTENTS

Prologue

Trains and Stations

At the beginning was the train. It seems to me that I have always been on one. At times I almost believe that I was born on a train. I even imagined that I was conceived in a sleeper, between two European cities, or crossing some frontier. It later amused me to learn that certain specialized bordellos in Paris had rooms that simulated the rocking and the sounds of a moving train.

As a child I stored sensations inseparable from the compartment's cradling motion: lights gliding along the ceiling, other lights flicking by the window, the shapes of cranes and water pumps against the night sky, the sounds of jarring and couplings when the train has halted in some station. There were so many other train sensations—but how to be sure that they are truly the child's impressions, that they were not inscribed into memory at a later time? When exactly did I register the sound of the probing hammer against the axle or the brake, the more accented beat in the tunnels, the almost organic creakings when the train stood still, the human panting of the locomotive? I knew nothing yet, for sure, of the throbbing and panting of the locomotive in Italo Svevo's *Confessions of Zeno*, associated with the death of the father. I later discovered on my own how choking a son's sense of guilt can be.

The shuttle between past and present weaves a network of locomotion; trains of thought crisscross the inner landscape and connect with the child kept alive. Perhaps the shuttle train of memory is guided partially by an act of will. Was it not to perpetuate the child in me that I stayed awake all night on the sleeper between Pisa and Paris—the train that carried me toward Bettina with my desire alive, yet worried that it would desert me upon arrival? I kept lifting the blind and looking out the window, excited by what lay ahead, but also by the child in me determined to stay awake all night so as not to miss one instant of joy. In truth, I always liked to have my sleep interrupted, to fall in and out of sleep over and over again. Some books I learned to love (though not in the tyrannical lycée) echoed my feelings. Montaigne, I was amused to learn, claimed to have instructed his manservant to wake him up repeatedly at night so that not even sleep would escape his consciousness.

The feminine charge of the sleeper compartment was strong, though the double-decker bunks introduced into the paneled privacy a certain angular hardness. The word "erotic" was not within the child's grasp, but the feeling was there. Occasionally now, in some European town at night, I like to walk to the station and watch a train roll slowly by or come to a brief rest on its mysterious journey, its blinds drawn. I read the magic names of the cities on the markers (Amsterdam-Venezia; München-Paris) and imagine glamorous women in provocative poses. *La madone des sleeping* was the title of Maurice Dekobra's best-seller in the 1930s. I had known early intimacy on trains, but that was with my mother, or my sister, Nora, or my nanny, Lotte (whom I persistently called Loppe), and who on one occasion complained that I had wet my bunk above hers—on purpose.

The closeness of a woman's presence surrounded by mobile patterns of light was also an integral part of many late-afternoon sofa sessions with my grandmother in the darkened living room. The lights came from the rare cars in the street, and on one occasion a loud noise, followed by cries, made us jump up. It was an accident, and the upturned delivery lorry with its three wheels still turning blended in my mind with the newspaper image of a derailed locomotive lying pitifully on its side, its underbelly showing. There is also the memory of the steamroller on a country road surrounded by the summery smell of tar. Vehicles appear and disappear on the screen of memory. I have an image of myself inside my mother's very green Graham Paige, an unusual foreign car in a European city. I did not like the color green, and Mama had a way of driving too slowly, constantly drifting toward the left side of the road. The train remained the ideal reality—the train and the monumental railroad station with its lofty glass and steel sheds. Every boy, I would read much later, dreams of being a locomotive engineer. I simply wanted to be the locomotive itself.

I still see myself on the Promenade des Anglais in Nice, running back and forth ahead of my mother, with my fists clenched, imitating the sound of the locomotive, moving my forearms as though they were the parallel driving rods of the huge wheels. The warm midwinter sun projected the elongated shades of the palm trees across the Promenade, and the seven-year-old boy, absorbed by the shuttle, felt vaguely surprised and happy to have been taken out of school because of the death of his little sister.

What went through my mother's grieving mind, I now wonder, as she watched me run ahead of her and then return, puffing audibly, with the same endless movement of the arms, totally caught up in my mimetic game? Perhaps she thought it was as frivolous as when at home I connected the silver knife rests and dragged them smoothly across the patterned dining room carpet.

But no game could rival in intensity the elation of being inside a real train. Toy trains never held my attention, and the more sophisticated they were, the less I was entranced. For what, other than the actual train experience, could offer me in profusion the sensations I yearned for: the anxiety of departure, the ceremony of farewells on the station's platform, the contrast between the relative privacy of the compartment, where my parents settled after much shuffling of baggage, and the thoroughfare nature of the corridor to which I soon escaped. The smell of the hard-boiled eggs and the taste of the tea kept lukewarm in the old thermos bottle blended with the smell of the locomotive smoke that wafted through the barely ajar window. In those days of soot and smoke it was customary on railroad journeys to wear special travel clothes. I loved to slide the compartment door open and closed and stand in the corridor, facing the window, with my foot on the radiator in imitation of adults. The wind-slap of a passing train hurtling in the opposite direction produced thrilling tremors. I watched automobiles on a more or less parallel road, making mental bets as to whether the train would win the improvised race. A tunnel would interrupt the sport.

Moving from our coach to the *wagon-restaurant* was a minor adventure. With unsteady steps, my parents and I crossed the loud and shaking concertina connectors, the covered gangways leading from one coach to another. Seated in the diner in front of starched tablecloths and napkins, I paid little attention to the food. I relished the effects of speed and mobility on my lateral vision, creating beyond the window frame a choreography of lines and shapes evolving at different speeds, punctuated by the visualized rhythm of the stark telegraph poles intercepting the horizontal sway of wires: the foreground tearing by to the point of distortion and fuzziness, the middle distance gently gliding by, while the distant background—the faraway steeples, the hills, the clouds— seemed to accompany us on our journey. Years later, I would respond keenly to Marcel Proust's description of the three steeples in their changing light and shifting positions, revealing and at the same time concealing their reality, and ultimately transforming them into the dancing maidens of a legend. My trains of thought would become a shuttle between what I remembered and what I read.

While munching the baguette on which I spread inordinate amounts of butter and mustard, I scanned nonsense sentences to the hammering rhythm of the wheels on the rails—two short beats followed by a longer accent, or the reverse, one long beat followed by two short ones. At times, the dactyls or anapests of that poetic meter of the railway were replaced, but only as a brief transition, by the more stately iambic beat. On these journeys with my parents I had no idea there was such a thing called "metrics." But I would not be surprised that my later delight in the metrical variety of English verse had something to do with the sounds I heard while eating Dover sole on French trains carrying us to the Côte d'Azur, to Switzerland, or to Germany.

Walking back to our compartment against the train's direction brought an elating sense of opposing motions, rendering very physical the sense of freedom I associated with train travel. Then came the doze, the half-sleep, the mindless stare at the pictures of distant cities on the walls of the compartment, the guessing game about the fellow passengers whom one would never see again, the slowing down in some station, the asthmatic spasms of a locomotive in search of its freight cars, the secret wish not to reach one's destination. But there was also the dream of getting off at some station with a girl my age, perhaps even with a stranger-woman who had for a moment, absentmindedly no doubt, looked at me: "O, you whom I might have loved . . ." The very name of Baudelaire was unknown to me, but these brief encounters in compartments that brought people into fleeting proximity surely prepared me to understand what it means to be a poet of modern life.

The gentle shock of couplings and the clash of buffers awakened me from my reverie when new coaches were added in some station. But nothing compared with the peculiar silence of suspenseful stays at frontiers, where the vaguely threatening ritual of passport control took place. Together with the change of personnel and the sounds of a foreign language, there was the scrutiny of documents. My parents' nervousness—they talked in whispers as customs officials approached—was communicated to me. I did not altogether dislike the feeling, nor did I ever shake off a sense of guilt and fear vis-à-vis uniformed authority. My early political education in the 1930s had much to do with border controls, visas, and the sound of sternly polite questions asked across the threshold of a compartment that for an interval of time ceased feeling cozy.

Sometimes there was worse. I must have been eleven or twelve years old when we crossed Germany on our way to Marienbad, a spa in the Sudetenland. At the Czech frontier I saw men with swastika armbands drag a couple off the train. Fellow passengers whispered, "*Devisenschieber.*" "What is *Devisenschieber?*" I asked my father. My parents hushed me, but my father added something about smuggling currency out of the country—a heinous crime, I later learned, that the Nazis associated with Jews trying to bring valuables to the safety of foreign banks. Such episodes did not discourage my parents from occasional journeys to Marienbad. They were both firm believers in spas, and my mother was on the French championship bridge team that competed at the resort. Soon, however, in 1938, the Sudetenland would be annexed by Hitler to the ecstatic glee of the German-speaking local population, though even now I cannot imagine the gentle, elderly tennis coach who initiated me into the secrets of the backhand giving the "*Sieg Heil*" salute.

My train education was interwoven with private fantasies derived from mystery stories and films about spies operating on trains. The "gentleman-*cambrioleur*" Arsène Lupin, the protagonist of a series of novels by Maurice Leblanc, was my favorite hero. He combined the most sophisticated skills as burglar with a romantic disposition, generosity toward the needy, refined taste in clothes, and an ironic elegance of manners. And he was a French patriot! Hints of national pride colored Arsène Lupin's exploits, and I felt vaguely happy and victorious every time he triumphed over obtuse English or German adversaries.

Trains also brought to mind images of the Great War. I had stared at such images in illustrated books. Our schoolteachers talked much about scenes of departure for the front. My parents wanted me to read antiwar books such as Roland Dorgelès's *Wooden Crosses*, Henri Barbusse's *Under Fire*, and most of all Erich Maria Remarque's *All Quiet on the Western Front*. The volumes, in their uniform oilskin covers, were delivered to our Passy apartment by the Russian émigré with an Oriental face who came every few weeks with a beat-up old valise filled with books for the family. But these pacifist novels brought by the heavily laden ambulant book-lender, far from deadening my martial curiosity, had the opposite effect, making me see war as a very special, now unavailable, initiation into a world of courage, sacrifice, and brotherhood. Pictures of enthusiastic, flag-waving *poilus* leaving for the trenches on crowded, old-fashioned cars with wooden footboards filled me with awe and a twinge of envy.

I could not know then that only a few years later other trains would carry people to even more terrible destinations, sometimes in sealed cattle cars. I might have ended up, as did my Aunt Anya and Danielle Wolf (the taste of whose lips blends in my memory with the nocturnal sea smells of Trouville), in one of the terminal stations called Treblinka, Sobibor, or Auschwitz. The horrors of Nazi Europe can hardly be recalled without the sinister whistle of the locomotives and the relentless rhythm of the rails. Claude Lanzmann's film *Shoah* is punctuated by these haunting syncopations. *Europa* is another film projecting the nightmarish images of a rail odyssey into the Nazi past. My family got out of the hell of Europe in 1941 with not much time to spare, almost by miracle. Soon after, when the Soviet counteroffensive outside of Moscow made clear that a final German victory was no longer a reachable goal, Hitler became more determined than ever to carry out at least one final solution—the total extermination of Europe's Jews. Inexorably, the death trains rolled to the east. Fortunately, in France, there were still officials willing to be bribed. My father had learned how to convert hostile functionaries into temporarily auspicious intercessors, and dollar bills helped enormously.

Trains could also mean escape or salvation, as with that night train to Switzerland when uniformed Nazi agents were searching for Jews, and the conductor (perhaps he was a good old Sozial-Demokrat) played dumb. Or again, that train from the Spanish border to Madrid, which was so crowded that I found myself separated from my parents by two full coaches. I can still smell that compartment, transformed into a sweatbox by the sweltering heat. We were on our way to the United States, though unsuspecting as yet how long, circuitous, and difficult our crossing of the ocean was to be.

But in the 1930s, before the *drôle de guerre* and the collapse of France in 1940, trains meant the luxury of vacations, often spoiled, it is true, especially in midwinter or at Easter, by the fear of the school report that would be waiting on our return. The initials of the PLM line (Paris-Lyon-Méditerranée), on which we most often traveled, filled me with anticipatory delight. Trips down south were punctuated through the night by the dimly lit magic names of stations when the train came to a halt with creaking sounds: Dijon, Valence, Montélimar, Orange, Fréjus—until, fully awake, we were greeted by sunny bays, the reddish hue of the Esterel range, on our way to Nice and to my beloved palm trees.

I associate those years with the smooth gliding in and out of stations, the cries of vendors selling lemonade and warm sausages from the platforms, the happy music of the railway, and the porters with wine on their breath and leather straps around their shoulders reaching for baggage through the open window of the compartment. But this period also meant for the pampered boy and self-centered adolescent a precious tuning in to the discordant political sounds, and a vague intuition that history was more than reading illustrated textbooks describing Joan of Arc's supernatural visions, Louis XIV's glorious reign at Versailles, or Napoleon's brilliant military campaigns. History, I began to suspect, was not merely a past to resurrect and revere, but an oppressive present, an inevitable unfolding of events, very much like the fateful forward motion of the trains I loved so much.

Of course, I did not yet know what a collective fate meant. But there were daily reminders of the ascendancy of Hitler, his megalomaniacal successes, the sharp divisions of French society after the advent of the leftist Popular Front in 1936 (whenever Léon Blum, the elegantly mustached socialist prime minister, appeared in newsreels there were loud jeers and boos interspersed with cries of *"sale juif"*—dirty Jew), the brutal progression of the Spanish Civil War, the annexation of Austria following the resignation of Kurt Schuschnigg, the shame of the appeasement policies leading to the Munich agreement when Édouard Daladier and Neville Chamberlain sold out Czechoslovakia. In newsreels—just before Fred Astaire and Ginger Rogers tapped their way through the latest American film on the Champs-Elysées—we watched as Chamberlain and Daladier were greeted with thoughtless ovations upon their return from Munich. There was the shame of weakness and betrayal, but also the relief that war had been averted. There was even a certain fascination with the hysterical voice of the Führer. Some of us who knew German entertained our friends at school by imitating, to the point of hoarseness, the frantic crescendo of Hitler's speeches. But there was also a malaise in these mocking performances.

The malaise at times took a concrete form. I see myself once again in transit, during a lengthy stopover at the Cologne railway station, walking with my father to the *buffet* for a glass of beer. The *buffet* smelled like a beer hall, my father commented, as he downed his glass. It was hot, and I suddenly felt like a grownup as I shared a man's pleasure with my father. But I was also aware of hostile Germanic faces all around us, the many uniforms, and my father's almost physical discomfort as the pleasure of the cool German beer faded. We left the *buffet* in haste.

Railway travel also brought more intimate revelations, unfolding unknown horizons through the picture frame of the compartment window—locomoted epiphanies, such as when, in that month of February after little Nora's death on the operating table, my mother took me out of school to share with her an intensely private existence of mourning in full view of the Mediterranean. All during the journey, I could still hear my mother's intermittent sobs as she had explained to me that my five-year-old sister had been taken up to heaven by angels. I, too, had sobbed lying in bed next to her, because of her weeping. But what sensation, what emotion could rival the discovery as the train, on that bleak winter day filled with images of death, came down from snow-covered Switzerland toward Genoa, suddenly revealing the shimmering sea and the sharply outlined promontories, and then, in quick succession, tunnels, cypresses, fishing villages, more bays and capes, flowers and cactus plants, rapidly hiding and then again unveiling a spectacle of beauty that made me ache for fear of losing it—all this to the accompaniment of a sunny language I had previously heard only sung in the extracts from *Cavalleria rusticana* and *The Barber of Seville* on the old, breakable records I played over and over again on my parents' gramophone. My passion for Italy, years later, truly began on that Mediterranean train ride, overcast only by a sense of loss and grief, in the presence of a voluble and irrepressibly mirthful family who offered to share aromatic food with us.

After San Remo, at Ventimiglia, we had to change to a slower train, and then the coastline became even more varied and arresting, and the sea more blue, and there were other names of places I had never heard of before, names I could barely make out in print, for I had only recently begun to read—Menton, Monaco, Beaulieu, Villefranche-sur-mer—and then, in very large letters, our destination, Nice, where for several days my mother and I still felt the rocking of the train, even when walking in the street. It was while walking hand-in-hand on the rue de France that we suddenly smiled at each other with complicity, as we began to hurry back to our hotel room, having taken a fig-tasting laxative that, in those days, was recommended practice after a long trip.

Many of these early memories blend with books and pictures I later discovered, making me search for their secret power or charm or, better still, making me want to appropriate them. Over the years, I have loved to discuss authors who write about the poetry and mystery of trains. If for no other reason, I fully enjoyed Michel Butor's novel *The Modification*, all of which takes place on a train from Paris to Rome and is pervaded by a mesh of network-images of fate, suggesting projections, retrospections, unavoidable concatenations. The distance between myth and the workings of the protagonist's psyche is never great. And how much I sympathized, on first reading, with Proust's alter ego Marcel, riding on a train at sunrise, trying feverishly to possess the fleeting landscape from both the east and the west sides of the compartment, as he rushes from window to window in an attempt to gather the fragments of his shifting vision into a total view. I loved to dwell on this passage.

The poetry of the railroad also had its darker side, for there was the turmoil of departures, the terror recurrent in dreams of missing the train or of being pursued by a gigantic locomotive, the nightmare of derailments or of being trapped in a tunnel—all, no doubt, suggesting fears of unleashed, potentially catastrophic forces. Years later, when I discovered Émile Zola's novel *The Human Beast,* I was hardly surprised that a locomotive could become a personalized monster and a symbol of uncontrollable human passions. I was entranced by Zola's description of the Gare Saint-Lazare, which I knew so well, where the sounds of bumpers, whistles, and horns mingled with the clanking of metal turntables, the screech of brakes, mysterious tremors, lugubrious moans. For the adolescent, reading about these sounds was an act of recognition: they were childhood memories. Zola was merely putting them into words, as he dwelled on how the green, yellow, and white lights blinked threateningly next to fiery red signals and blinding jets of steam. The rear lights of trains did indeed seem like open wounds. Nor did it come as a surprise when, later still, as I began to read less haphazardly, I realized that violence and death were often associated in books with trains and railroad stations. In *Anna Karenina,* repeated railroad images foreshadow the violent end of Tolstoy's heroine under the wheels of a train. (I had fallen in love with her, and I suffered.) As for the much less lovable Ivan Ilych, in Tolstoy's shorter story, he symbolically experiences in his death throes the common, yet always strange sensation of a train going backward, while in fact it is moving forward.

Literature was full of my favorite images. Other children, it would seem, carried into adulthood and into their art a similar fascination with trains, at times even linking railway images to their artistic activity. Verlaine, in one of his poems, likens the telegraph wires seen from the train to the lines of a paragraph. And I was delighted to discover, not long ago, that Stephen Spender, in his poem "The Express," spins out a prolonged metaphor of the train beginning to roll with a "manifesto" and a "black statement" of pistons, leading past the grim "page" of the cemetery with its engraved tombstones, soaring with the "meter" of its wheels, singing as it progresses swiftly through the landscape on metal "lines." For Thoreau, the sound of the train was nothing less than the vibration of the "universal lyre." The train metaphor becomes cosmic.

I can still stand for a long time on the hard floor of a museum, staring at canvases with even the slightest hint of a railway setting or a train crossing on a distant viaduct. Many a time I have attempted to understand the secret of Manet's painting in which a fashionably dressed little girl stares into the extensive railyard below the Pont de l'Europe, the bridge spanning the tracks that lead out of the Gare Saint-Lazare. The iron bars separating the girl from what she so intently looks at leave one guessing. What does she see, what does she dream about while the woman with the small dog in her lap and the open book in her hand looks straight at the viewer? What the little girl sees or is trying to see is largely shrouded by plumes of whitish smoke and is beyond the viewer's field of vision. Is it the cyclops-eyed beam of an oncoming locomotive, and the movement of its huge, pumping pistons? Is it the play of signals, the passage of a train with people waving from the windows? Does the girl yearn for departure, does she dream of an undefined freedom? The prisonlike bars through which she surveys the scene, with her back turned, might suggest such longings.

The Saint-Lazare railroad station, from where, once a year, we took the train for Normandy, had been a favorite of the Impressionist painters, who usually went less far—to Louveciennes, to Argenteuil, to Pontoise, places that they made famous. Perhaps it is less their vision that I now cherish than my own memories of summer freedom when we left for Cabourg or Deauville, after the dreaded school examinations in July, when the heat and the smell of the summer fruit that filled the streets of Paris distracted me during cramming sessions near the open window. Whenever I look at Monet's painting of the smoke-filled shed of the Saint-Lazare station with its multiple shades of light beyond the standing train, its locomotive facing the buffer stop as passengers crowd the platform, I experience shock waves of recognition. I see myself climbing onto the train, tennis racquet in hand, elated by the departure for the seaside, the thought of the friends who returned every season, the bicycle rides, the outings, the games we played on rainy days—yet at the same time depressed by the knowledge that I had once again flunked geometry or algebra, and that I would have to suffer my mother's daily naggings as well as the torture of long hours of private tutoring to prepare for the make-up exam in the fall.

Pictures of trains meant more than departures and arrivals. They provided links between disparate experiences. In my mind there existed firm, though arbitrary family ties between artists as different from one another as were Monet, Pissarro, or van Gogh, whose yellow house in Arles is depicted by him in a melancholy manner, despite the glaring sunlight, as a distant train rumbles across an equally yellow overpass, its thick, twirling spiral of smoke leaving a long trail against the relentlessly blue sky. Van Gogh's wheat fields themselves are crossed by trains that seem indifferent to the presence of a lonely horse and buggy and women busy reaping. But I never doubted that between these representations there was a meaningful rapport.

I even collected train postcards (some of them given to me by friends or students who knew of my hobby); occasionally I take them out of their torn folder and inspect them. There is the one advertising the Calais-Interlaken-Engadine express, featuring on its face, without apparent order, a sanatorium-like hotel with a Swiss flag beneath steep glaciers, a sleeper train about to enter a tunnel with smartly dressed figures on the rear platform, a timetable listing all the stops, some gorges and waterfalls, and, at the very center, the mirror surface of a lake with sailboats, surrounded by pine-covered hills and shimmering peaks in the background. In the same folder there is a photograph by André Kertész: a 1928 view of the towering Meudon railway viaduct above the chaos of the construction site, and a sordid street that provides the narrow perspective on the locomotive crossing high up in the sky. Another shows a peaceful English landscape by Pissarro, with a train moving slowly out of a country station, its large, square, red front bumpers coming straight at the viewer. But the most unusual and disturbing is a postcard of a photograph by O. Winston Link captioned "Mr. & Mrs. Pope watch the last steam-powered passenger train pass their home." The Popes stand on their ornate porch, at night, looking away from the camera, he with his arm around her waist—two absorbed figures, alone together, aware perhaps that something ominous is speeding by.

What made me collect and keep these heterogeneous images of trains? Art, publicity, personal memories—all were mingled. But the very confusion gave me a hint. Perhaps the train image was a steady reminder that life and art, the various levels of experience, could not be disentangled and detached from each other, that in my consciousness a ceaseless shuttle went back and forth between orders of reality, and that I could never accept the notion of a gap, of a fundamental rift between the dream projections of my memory and those engendered by books and pictures. The shuttle meant that art and life were not to be divorced, that in fact they nurtured each other. The lesson became clearer over the years and explained, perhaps, why I could admire Flaubert or Kafka, who both opted for art over and against life, but felt more at home with Stendhal or Svevo, whose insecurity, paradoxes, indirections, and fundamental irony betrayed an unwillingness to make a final choice between writing and living.

How I loved Svevo's short story "Brief Sentimental Journey," in which Signor Aghios, on a train ride between Milan and Trieste, deeply sympathizes with a little girl all in tears because, once inside the train, she can no longer see the train from the outside. For a fortnight she had thought of nothing but this first railway journey. She had wanted everything: to be on the train, to see the train in motion—and herself riding in it. Signor Aghios sympathizes with her frustration. He too would like to see it all, and all at the same time, unreasonable though this may be. He knows that ideal travel means supreme consciousness. It abolishes all lines of demarcation between inside and outside, between the eye as seeing and as seen.

The story of Signor Aghios, the man who cogitated even in his slumber, confirmed what I had always suspected—that train images exist as broader metaphors, that there is a special disposition, something like a "train sensibility," ready to respond to the anonymous crowds at stations, the thrill of departures, the music of the rails—so reassuring, repetitive, assertive, deafening, but also capable of inducing slumber through its monotonous lullaby. And with the lullaby, the night fatigue, and the lethargy came the desire not to arrive anywhere, the yearning for an endless journey.

The history of trains, as I learned from books, is a central chapter of social history. The reign of timetables and speed produced new tensions between our subjective time and the official time symbolized by the huge clock on the tower of railroad stations, themselves emblems of modernity, vast cathedrals of the age of steam, marrying iron and glass, bringing into often jarring association the soaring glass and iron sheds leading out to the world of the future, and the reassuring, past-oriented monumentality of the grand concourse and the façade.

But these were abstract concepts. What mattered to me were sensations more personal and more elusive: the imagined sense of freedom of a traveler without baggage, the guilt of the passenger without a ticket, the awareness of the rails as a figure of necessity, the possible brief encounter, reveries of mystery and sex, the frustrated curiosity of the eye as the train slowly moves through suburbs, gliding by rows of houses and windows behind which were acted out, in my imagination, endless fantasies of human promiscuity.

Trains of thought . . . They included the trains I never took, nor probably would ever take. In Istanbul, not long ago, I ambled to the railroad station just in time to watch the noisy, chaotic departure (made more picturesque by kicks and fistfights) of the train for Moscow, deciphering the Bulgarian markers on the coaches that listed the stopovers—Sofia, Bucharest, Kiev. The voyages I never made were like the digressions of my mind. But who is to tell what a digression is? I reflected on the word "train," with its connotations of drawing, pulling, connecting. Digressions, I knew, were really connections. The many trains of my thoughts referred to past journeys, real and imagined, but also to journeys into the past. The traveler was always in several places at the same time. Does memory conduct the trains of our thoughts toward a coherent network? I was not sure. Traveling inside one's mind was often like traveling in a foreign country.

Even real train rides could have an aura of unreality. It was like watching the replay of a film, when, at the end of our year in Rome, Bettina and I watched the Italy we had come to know glide by as in a dream—Orvieto, Chiusi, Cortona, Castiglion Fiorentino, Arezzo, Florence, Bologna, Parma, Milan. Or when in Mexico, Madamina (one of Bettina's other names) ate all those mangoes, while I took pictures through the window of the huge organ-pipe cactus. A woman warned us that mangoes were *fruta caliente*, "hot" fruit, but too late for us to avoid their laxative effect. Shortly after, on the night train between Coatzacoalcos and Palenque, in the middle of the jungle when the train ran out of steam and all the lights and the ventilation system went out, and we gasped for air on the train's platform, unreality enfolded us in the form of enormous moths that swarmed like malevolent bats. We even took trains for the wrong destination as when, in Brig, I distract-edly drove our car onto the auto train for Saint Gall, and there was no way of backing out. But does one always know where one wants to go?

So it is with these pages. . . . I do not agree with a friend of mine that there comes a time when one wants to make sense of one's life. I prefer the instability of the shuttle. I would like the landscape to continue rolling by, yet I also wish to arrest its motion. Is it possible to possess one's experience rather than to make sense of it? Can one possess one's sensations, past and present, and yet allow them to mingle, and love their flux? I write next to a window, though not facing it, and daydream between the lines I write. I suspect that the reason I put pen to paper is that I yearn to reconstitute the parts of a composite self, the fragments of a world that has in large part disappeared. The stations of my life stretch across the map of Europe, and then across the Atlantic. But the deeper reason, once again, may have to do with the distant rumble of trains. At night, I can hear the reassuring yet gloomy wail of the Dinky, the shuttle train, coming home from Princeton Junction.

Long before I had ever heard of Princeton Junction, my future was determined on a train speeding in that direction. It happened on an impulse. In January 1946, I was returning from Boston to New York in a crowded, overheated coach. I had recently been discharged from the army at Fort Dix and, before returning to my parents' apartment in Manhattan, had spent my first night of freedom in a large hotel in Tren-ton, New Jersey, basking in the luxury of a private bathroom. And now, a few weeks later, I was returning once again to my parents in New York. I felt doubly liberated—from the army, but also from my parents. I had decided to avail myself of the GI Bill of Rights. Books and classrooms filled my vision of the future. I was eager to complete my higher education, which had been postponed for five years, ever since I took the *baccalauréat* exam on the run, one might say, in Bordeaux, in the early summer of 1940, with the German army sweeping southward, strafing thousands of refugees on the road.

On that train between Boston and New York, so unlike the European trains I was used to, every war episode seemed distant and irrelevant: the escape across Spain; the six-week-long ocean crossing on the banana freighter *Navemar* (we, the 1,200 refugees, were the bananas in the hold of that cargo boat, greeted by the American press as "the floating concentration camp"); Omaha Beach with the 2nd Armored Division, known as "Hell on Wheels," where, digging my nails into the soil under a night strafing, I promised to myself (it was the closest I could come to a prayer) that if I survived, I would never in my life complain again; the breakthrough at Saint-Lô, when the sky was dark with our planes and the lunar landscape trembled, and I discovered that I was decidedly not a hero; the liberation of Paris, when, half-drunk, I crisscrossed the familiar yet eerie city in my jeep and learned, as in a dream, from an old, invalid woman in an apartment near the place de la République that Dany had disappeared into a camp together with her infant child; the *garçonnière* on the rue des Vignes where Yvette gave me lessons in love-making; the Battle of the Bulge in the blinding snow, and the harsh voice of General Norman Cota, at early dawn, near a desolate field, when he screamed at the remnants of the 28th Infantry Division that he would personally shoot "any bastard who runs," then ordering me to gather "my men" (I did not even know who they were), to dig in, to let the Tiger tanks roll over us, and to "take care" of the infantry that followed. All we had were a few rifles and carbines.

All this seemed quite far removed and even unreal on that train between Boston and New York. I was returning from an interview at Harvard. I could not foresee that the same Eastern seaboard railway line connecting Boston to New York via New Haven would someday, many years later, carry me to Princeton Junction. But what I already knew was that there happened to be different "stations" in my life, some of them edifices of metropolitan grandeur, others more intimate places of transit, but all of them providing connections, in either direction, between the child, the boy, the adolescent, the adult, and now . . . . Revisiting these stations, in my mind or in reality, often puzzled me. How did the little liar, the little thief, the lazy student, the wretched son learn to live with himself and with others? How did he gradually come to translate weaknesses into the semblance of strength? Some of the stations are dark. Anguish clings to them like the smoke and grime that have eaten into their very substance.

And now, when trying to fall asleep, as I hear the tooting of the Dinky that connects the Junction to the home station, I do not know what makes me think of the sinister locomotive whistle coming through the Shanghai fog at the end of *Man's Fate*, and those wounded prisoners about to be thrown alive into the boiler of the locomotive. André Malraux's muffled train whistle has a very special resonance, as I reflect on all that has happened, and on what I myself was spared.

Part

I

THE 16th
ARRONDISSEMENT

Chapter 1

THEY CALLED HIM JASCHA

I t may have been drizzling, as on so many winter days. I do not
remember where we took the bus on this expedition to the rue de
Provence. Was it at La Muette, close to where Jacques lived, or on
the place de Passy, not far from my parents' apartment? All I recall is
that we got off near the Gare Saint-Lazare and then walked somewhat
furtively to our destination, looking up to check street numbers.
Jacques preceded me. After all, he was a year older, and it was he who
had all the information. I envied him, and not only for his carefree gait.
His father had encouraged him, had given him the address—and the
money.

The fourteen-year-old boy that I was then secretly hoped that the
bus ride on this initiatory trip would never end. We were standing as
usual in our favorite place on the open rear platform, which, at every
stop and start, bounced up and down. In those prewar days, the green
Renault buses in Paris all had a rear platform on which some eight or
nine people could stand and from where the *contrôleur* signaled to the
driver by means of a chain he yanked in an experienced manner that
made the pear-shaped handle fly up and then swing for a while. I still
see the dance of the chain and smell the unmistakable Parisian bus
exhaust that often made me slightly sick—and on this occasion almost
quelled my courage.

We had been talking about 122, rue de Provence for weeks, planning
and postponing, inspired by our disreputable but much admired classmate Pierre Masselli. The problem for me was the money. There simply
was no way I could approach my father. That was unthinkable on such
a subject. I had to find another way, even if it meant searching in our

apartment for some object I could dispose of without it being immediately missed. The appropriation of the silver tea-glass holder that came from Russia and the subsequent transaction at the pawnshop on the rue de la Tour remain foggy, as in a dream. It is the bus ride that is clear on the playback screen of my memory.

So are the lengthy discussions on our walks back from the lycée. And now, relived in a repeated present, apprehension gripped me as I followed Jacques, who kept bantering me, on our way to what the English clients, we had heard, called the "One-Two-Two." But here things get blurred. Was it on my first or my second visit that I noticed the softly lit, carpeted staircase on which one felt far removed from the bustle outside? And the large room with mirrors, where multiform graces in diverse attires and poses expected to be chosen as the one-hour favorites of today's budding two pashas? Or was it a later literary association? Jacques and I, of course, never heard the famous call "*Ces dames au salon!*" which the madam is supposed to utter. But there they were, assembled as on a stage, on display. We made our choice—I did so almost blindly, lifting my hand and pointing in the direction where I had glimpsed a gentle smile. Then another muffled staircase, the pressure of an arm around my waist, tender words no one had ever spoken to me quite in that way.

I see myself in a room all softness and silence. Her name was Maggie, and she looked a little like the sad-eyed singer Edith Piaf when she was still known as "*La Môme Piaf.*" There was nothing threatening in her gestures, her poses, the ritual of ablutions. "Is this the first time?" she asked, astride me. I denied this vehemently. But I took no initiatives, letting things happen. Maggie was impressed by my silk shirt, which I had been reluctant to take off, and which she unbuttoned swiftly, examining the breast pocket on which my initials appeared inside the woven image of a pagoda. The shirt was a recent present from my uncle who lived in Shanghai, where he managed the local branch of my father's business. Maggie wanted to know if I had a girlfriend. She seemed curious about the girls we knew. I told her that my friends and I kissed the girls, and held hands at the movies, sometimes fondling their breasts— but that otherwise we did not touch them much. She shook her head but seemed to understand. What I did not tell her is that we entertained

powerful dreams about their mothers, whom we imagined to have lascivious dispositions and to be experts at dispensing caresses with their
mouths and tongues precisely in the way Maggie did so naturally and
almost innocently.

Tender and solicitous, she wanted to talk. She asked me whether I
would come back. I later wondered what a visit of two adolescents
meant to the women in that shuttered house with the sober façade
standing quietly on the busy street near the district known as the
quartier de l'Europe. The irregularity might have titillated them; we
were, I am sure, legally underage. Their smiles may have betrayed
maternal dispositions, though some of them were probably not much
older than we were. In any case, our appearance in the salon must have
come as a relief between the visits of thick-necked, square-jawed busi-
nessmen and inebriated English or German clients.

Maggie's and her colleagues' amusement I can only guess at retrospectively. I do not remember how or to whom I handed over my ill-
gotten money. When Jacques and I met in the street, he was visibly
annoyed. Upon taking his leave, he discovered that he had forgotten to
bring the money his father had given him. He offered his wristwatch to
the huffy and barely civil madam as a guarantee that he would come
back and redeem it. He did just that the following day, to the surprise of
the much softened matron, who called out to the girls, "Look, he has
come back to pay!"

Over the years, Jacques and I never failed to go over the entire
episode, retelling it to each other in elaborate detail, laughing at the
same junctures, congratulating ourselves on this early exploit, delighted
by this special complicity that kept us close. The invasion of France in
1940 separated us. Jacques served as a bombardier pilot in the American
Air Corps and later became a successful businessman in Belgium. We
lost track of each other for more than thirty years. When we finally met
again, it was near the battlefield of Waterloo, where he had settled in a
bucolic house close to the ravine where Napoleon's cavalry met its
doom. We were both married by then, and had been for quite some
time. But this did not prevent us from once again going over the high
moments of our early teenage adventure, which in the proximity of the
famous battlefield acquired an added mythical dimension. We did not

quite conclude, as do the two friends at the end of Flaubert's *Sentimental Education,* "This is the best we've had." I always liked that ending. There is something at once cynical and touching in that novel's final pages. For in fact nothing much happened during the recalled visit to the establishment known as La Turque. Intimidated by the assembled women, Frédéric took flight, and since Frédéric had the money, his friend Deslauriers had to follow. Our story was different. Yet we also somehow did not lose our innocence on that winter afternoon near the Gare Saint-Lazare. Whenever I teach Flaubert's novel, I feel that I have a special understanding of that last chapter. The lived experience and the literary one now color each other. Perhaps this is the best way to read books.

I COULD NOT speak about such matters with my father. Not because he was cold or distant; I never heard him say a harsh word to me. But he was prudish and afraid of disease. There was nothing of the assertive male or seducer in him. He could tell an off-color joke, such as the one about the wealthy Muslim in his harem with a bon mot at the end about providential potency, but it never sounded right in his mouth. He lectured me with embarrassment about the ravages of syphilis. Noses that crumbled, perforated palates, paralysis and madness. *Tabes* is a word he learned somewhere, and he brought it up as the ultimate horror. He may not have read medical textbooks, but he was familiar with their popularizations, and he also echoed textbook indictments of masturbation. He had read and seen Ibsen's plays and deplored the fates of Baudelaire and Maupassant—writers he somehow placed on the same level. I sometimes wondered what his own sexual initiation had been like. But then, even sex between him and my mother was hard to imagine, despite outward signs of tenderness and physical contact. They would interlock their little fingers impromptu, without any discernible reason. I later learned that this was their signal for reconciliation.

No, an amorist he certainly was not. His nickname was Jascha. He was gentle, almost meek. As a little boy, shy myself, I was not yet offended by his submissiveness, which hid a capacity for carrying grudges. What remains most vivid from my early memories are his soft hands, his myopic, watery eyes looking at me lovingly, the close-up view of the marks near the bridge of his nose when he took off his pince-nez. He later gave up these glasses clipped to the nose by a tight spring and adopted round, dark, horn frames that made him look less like a utopian scholar and a little more like a modern executive. The softness of his hands was due to his use of glycerin every time he washed them, which he did with concentrated energy and always three times in a row, with much splashing of water. He was almost completely bald, yet he used two stiff brushes that he vigorously, and I imagine painfully, applied to his reddening skull in the belief that it would bene-fit his remaining hair.

In the mornings before leaving for his office, he would spread a small rug on top of the Chinese carpet in his study and proceed to exercise in his pajamas. He called it *"ma petite gymnastique"*—doctor's orders. It was nothing like the sweat-producing aerobics of today, but rather a leisurely one-two-three-four movement of the arms, then the torso, then the pivoting head, bending now and then to barely touch the toes, and then concentrating, as though it were particularly strenuous, on opening and closing the hands—all this accompanied by considerable huffing and puffing, and by grunts of effort as well as satisfaction. The exercises were ritually followed by the ingestion of a yogurt that came in a glass jar covered by a tough, parchmentlike, translucent paper that made a special crackling sound when it was pierced with the spoon. My father always offered to share some of the yogurt with me and had another clean spoon ready for that hygienic early morning communion.

The two syllables *hygiène* covered a great many things, above all warding off dreaded infections, a dirty word in our household. On my father's strict injunction, the apartment was always well stocked with bandages, adhesive strips, and of course iodine, which was applied under parental supervision at the slightest scratch. Fear of rusty objects (*rouille* was another dirty word) related to the same dread of infectious disease. One of my father's cautionary anecdotes was the story of a cir-cus strongman called Breitbart, whose Germanic name translated for me the image of an immensely wide beard into a symbol of Herculean strength. This reputedly unbeatable weightlifter was vulnerable after all—like Samson, though in a less poetic way. He neglected to take care of a tiny self-inflicted wound from a rusty nail. He died, so my father told me, within a few days. A simple application of iodine would have saved him! No wonder I could not approach my father about the planned expedition to the rue de Provence.

Jascha, as he was affectionately called, loved to walk briskly, with a strut. "*Gambader*" was my mother's expression for his way of prancing, as he inhaled and exhaled the air audibly and with visible satisfaction. She would make fun of the way he thrust his feet outward, much as she made gentle fun of his large, spread ears. She saw to it, after my birth, that my baby ears were taped to my skull in order to avoid this heredi-tary blemish. Jascha looked forward to summer vacations in Vichy or Karlsbad, where he would parade up and down the promenade near the spring wells that made those places famous. In town I often accompa-nied him to the avenue du Bois or the Bois de Boulogne, admiring the way he held, twirled, and swung his cane. He was himself something of a *frant*—a Russian word he teasingly applied to acquaintances whom he considered dandies. On these walks, he wore spats and a dapper hat, smartly tilted. I don't recall ever seeing him outdoors without a hat. That was the custom: even on the Promenade des Anglais in Nice, where we spent Easter vacations in search of the sun, or on the Croisette in Cannes, where we accompanied my mother when she played in bridge tournaments at the Hôtel Miramar, men and women were never seen without headgear, even on the mildest days. I recently came across a newspaper photograph of the Promenade des Anglais going back to the turn of the century. It was taken at midday, judging by the shadows cast. All the men sported derbies or fedoras, all the women carried open parasols. Even young boys wore the stiff straw hats known as *canotiers*. Looking at that old black-and-white picture, I realize how little the scene had changed between that distant Belle Époque and the 1930s.

My father's way of dressing, much like the seriousness of his dedica-tion to restorative vacations and daily siestas, reflected the values and phobias of his bourgeois world: cult of solvency, aversion to idleness and dissipation, obsession with health (both personal and social), fear of any disorder, addiction to cures and spas, respect for doctors, for law, and for political stability. Vestimentary appearance was a program of correctness. Behind my desk chair, on one of the bookshelves, stands a photo cutout of my father, the kind known as photo statuette. It carries the Czech name of a studio in Karlsbad, and the date 1924—one year after my birth. It shows my father standing very straight, almost stiffly, holding his gloves in one hand, the handle of a cane with the other (the rest of the cane broke off long ago), with a *pochette* neatly tucked into his breast pocket and a pearl pin in his tie. The expression on his face is at the same time dreamy and grave.

Jascha was indeed a dreamer, not really made, I believe, to be a tough businessman. He had a weakness for sentimental poetry and for *opéra-comique*, with which he became familiar during his law school days in Paris. He knew a number of poems by Verlaine, and liked to recite the one about tears and raindrops in the heart: "*Il pleure dans mon coeur . . .* " He also recited poems by Lermontov and Pushkin, as did all those who had had their schooling in Russia. His favorite musical work was Bizet's *Carmen*. For my benefit he would sing, quite off-key, the street urchins' chorus of Act I as they imitate the marching new guard and the sound of the trumpet: "Ta ra ta ta, Ta ra ta ta. . . . " He would treat me to his own imitation of this imitation, as he came to wish me goodnight at bedtime, making sure during these ritualistic visits that the flowers and plants in my room had been taken out to save me from the "bad air" they gave off at night.

He would also sing, not at bedtime, but equally off-key, Carmen's "Habanera," as well as the lively Andalusian seguidilla "*Près des remparts de Séville . . .* "—both of them almost unrecognizable. Yet, strange to tell, I seem to have been able to effect spontaneous mental corrections, so that when I finally heard a real Carmen sing those tunes with a voluptuous mezzo-soprano timber instead of my father's falsetto, I was not at all surprised. They sounded entirely familiar. Stranger still, the paternal humming and singing of snatches of Bizet's opera aroused in me a range of erotic reveries. Maybe that was because he had described to me how the gypsy Carmen, in Lillas Pastia's tavern, dances provocatively to the sound of her castanets for Don José, who quite loses his head and becomes a deserter in order to follow her into the mountains. These sensuous premonitions were confirmed when my father took me to the Opéra-Comique on my twelfth birthday. I still feel the shivers of pleasure I experienced when Carmen sang flirtatiously with her hands tied behind her back, seated in front of the guard house.

But what my father most loved to sing for me were the melancholy songs of Aleksandr Vertinski. In this case, I was able to make the musical corrections quite simply, by putting on the Vertinski records we owned. My father's favorite Vertinski songs had to do with jealousy, betrayal, and thorough Russian despondency. Two songs, or *romansi,* moved him in particular, though at times he also laughed at their excessive rhetoric. The first, on a tone of great intimacy, whispered, more or less, "Do reassure me, say that you are still mine." The other was more Chekhovian in mood, and after the first words, *"Do svidanie"* (Goodbye), went on to increasingly sweeping statements about the worthlessness of life.

Other Vertinski songs sounded a less desperate note. They were in turn witty, surrealistic, and decadent. Vertinski wrote his own words and music, and from all reports he had appeared on cabaret stages in Russia made up and costumed as a Pierrot *lunaire,* all in white. At his own level of entertainment, he showed affinities with the poets Tristan Corbière, Jules Laforgue, and the lesser Russian symbolists. His preposterous rhymes and puns alerted me at an early stage to the poetic potential of incongruity and wordplay. There was the song about Princess Irène, who catches her lover's heart thrown to her like a rubber ball; another weird one about the death of the "gray-eyed king" whose body was found near the ancient oak tree; and, most eccentric of all, a short ballad, "Where are you now?" about a "lilac-colored" black butler in San Francisco helping a supremely elegant lady into her coat in the presence of an imagined admirer who kisses her delicate finger tips. It was all very confusing. Why lilac-colored, and why San Francisco of all places? This song never failed to make my parents' Russian friends chuckle with pleasure, though it also suggested lost hope and hopeless love.

What did these songs mean to my father? After all those years, what do I really know about this soft-spoken man who was devastated by the death of his five-year-old daughter on the operating table, and whose spirit was undermined by various business calamities resulting from political upheavals, by a succession of exiles, and by a peremptory cigar-smoking brother and business partner for whom I have had a visceral dislike as long as I can remember?

My father was not alone in his fondness for Vertinski, who was a favorite with the Russian émigré colony in Paris. His songs were laden for them with nostalgia for pre-revolutionary days. Even now, more than sixty years after I first heard these songs, I bring tears to the eyes of a Russian-born lady who lives in Tuscany when I sing one of them to her after dinner on her terrace overlooking Siena. For I had learned Vertinski's songs on those old records by heart and can still imitate his very special nasal tone and affected diction. They entered my repertoire at the age of thirteen, before I began to have fantasies of becoming an opera singer.

Those daydreams of starring in basso roles coincided with my growing impatience to attain manhood. It was the year of the rue de Provence that I discovered the bass voice of Fyodor Chaliapin on records that my parents treated with special reverence. His name was pronounced with awe, and my mother would describe to me how, in recital, he stood majestically in front of the piano, mesmerizing his public into total silence before he began his first song or aria. Chaliapin. The three syllables meant the death scene of *Boris Godunov* (the record had a crack), Mussorgsky's "Song of the Flea," Glinka's "Midnight Review," together with another song about the Napoleonic myth, Schumann's "Two Grenadiers," which Chaliapin sang in Russian, and even a resounding "*Marseillaise*" that he projected with unexpected Mephistophelian intonations. My interest in the French Revolution and the Napoleonic saga thus had a distinctly Russian accent. It was colored by Chaliapin's occasionally sardonic voice, which I also learned to imitate, and which in my memory is associated with the pungent smell of cabbage that at certain hours wafted upward to our second-floor apartment from the concierge's tiny quarters below.

Chaliapin, like Vertinski, had left Russia a few years after the Revolution and resided in Paris at the time I was a student at the Lycée Janson de Sailly. His tall frame could be seen walking in the vicinity of the Trocadéro, not far from my lycée. There was talk of his being sick, for he now rarely appeared on the opera stage, though he still made a film,

Don Quichotte, with music by Jacques Ibert, which my mother took me to see in a movie house at the other end of Paris. Images of windmills mistaken for giants and charged by the melancholy knight in his ludicrous armor, on his emaciated horse, blend with other images of rowdy country taverns, paunchy servants, dusty roads, coarse women transfigured into fair ladies, and Chaliapin's towering presence, his heavily made-up sculptured face, and his voice filled with noble lamentation. These images colored forever my reading of Cervantes' novel and determined my perception of the Spanish landscape when I travelled in La Mancha, Estremadura, and Andalusia many years later. The operatic film was the occasion of another impressive Chaliapin death scene that made my mother cry. My mother's crying at the movies never failed to embarrass me, even though I was at times also quite moved. Between us there was a silent complicity; we pretended not to take notice of each other's moist eyes as we emerged into the light.

Chaliapin himself died soon after, in 1938. There was a much-talked-about funeral service, with the participation of the opera chorus, that was broadcast from the Russian church on the rue Daru. It was at about that time that I heard the story of a distant cousin of ours, a soprano who, while singing with Chaliapin during one of his last performances, heard him mutter "Jewess" under his breath, as he looked straight at her. The Russian word "*zhid*," whether in its masculine or its feminine form, hardly requires an adjective to sound derogatory. How true the story is, I cannot tell. It was told with some amusement, without rancor, as were so many other anecdotes of anti-Semitism, which in my family was simply taken as a fact of life.

My father, I am sure, relished Vertinski's songs more than the dramatic performances of Chaliapin. These songs, playfully sentimental and unheroic, satisfied his need for tenderness and his penchant for self-pity. And marks of tenderness, it would seem, he did not always get. One day, as I skidded around a corner of our corridor, I heard a crackling sound coming through the ajar door of my parents' bedroom and saw in a flash my mother's hand land on my father's cheek. The image and the sound did not seem to coincide. *Gifle*—the French word for "slap"—hissed through my mind. As I reached my own room, I could still see my father's astonished expression, and his red face. I felt vaguely embarrassed and humiliated, as though I had been the recipient of the blow, standing beside the parental bed. Why have I never mentioned this moment to Bettina? And what could have provoked my mother's ire? Perhaps it was Jascha's voiced jealousy, some offensive suspicion. I later learned that Monsieur Émile, our obese concierge, had felt it his duty to denounce my mother for having gone out every night during my father's business trip to London.

But perhaps it wasn't that at all. Jascha knew perfectly well that his Vera's bridge tournaments kept her until late hours at the Golfers' Club near the place de la Concorde, and he knew the people she played with. Perhaps the slap simply expressed her accumulated exasperation at what she perceived as his general ineptitude: the way he constantly checked the stove in the kitchen, never trusted his eyes or his memory that he had really signed the document, really dropped the letter in the mailbox, really closed and locked the door, left nothing behind in the taxicab. On exiting the apartment, he used to pull the door handle so hard and so repeatedly that it came off one day with a jerk and he lost his balance, finding himself with the torn-off brass handle in his hand as he fell backward a few steps down the staircase.

I probably found my father's mishap in his battle with the door funnier than did my mother. But I myself was only too aware of his foibles. He was hardly an inspiring model for a young adolescent who spent hours reading about dashing musketeers, cloak-and-dagger intrigues, and the cool exploits of romantic bandits and master spies. I loved the rough soccer games after school, and developing my forehand at tennis soon became a passion. True, my father encouraged me to become a tennis player; he paid for coaches, enlisted me in the rather snobbish Racing Club, from which Jews were later expelled during the German occupation, and never failed to refer to Henri Cochet, Jacques Brugnon, Jean Borotra, and René Lacoste—the five-time winning team of the Davis Cup between 1927 and 1932—as the "four musketeers." But though he used the word "sport" in at least three languages as a magic word standing for clean morals, good manners, and guaranteed good health, he was hardly what could be called a sportsman. His prudent calisthenics and his hygienic walks failed to impress me as athletic exercises. Could he even swim? I am not sure. I recall seeing him waist-high in the sea, in Cabourg and Deauville, and only when the waves were behaving.

But then, how many European gentlemen of his generation were swimmers? And not only gentlemen. Were there not countless stories of sailors in times past who drowned in shipwrecks simply because they did not know how to swim? I did, however, see my father skate, but always with decorum and in proper attire, in what was essentially a social activity, couples gliding forward arm in arm, the ladies with their hands in a fur muff, one-two, one-two, while the loudspeaker blared hoarsely a familiar Viennese waltz. I don't believe he ever held a tennis racket in his hand. He was not even a dancer, if dancing means more than swaying from one leg to another, or shuffling one's feet with no more than an approximate respect for the beat. These were perhaps all reasons why my mother, talking to me about music or literature, often mentioned, with a mixture of disapproval and ill-disguised admiration, the figure of the elegant seducer Don Juan, a name she always pro-nounced à l'espagnole, whether she referred to Richard Strauss, to Mozart, or to the character of Eugene Onegin in Pushkin's poem and in Tchaikovsky's opera. These were some of the same reasons why I could not confide in my father about the visit to the rue de Provence.

It was about the time of this visit and of my great friendship with Jacques Blum, whose father was for me a paragon of parental enlighten-ment, that I began constructing fictions about passionate affairs my mother might have had at the time I was born. Had she not herself given me to understand that while attending finishing school in Vienna, where she was sent to perfect her German, she had fallen in love with a medical student? But this happened before she met Jascha, my father. Had she married him on the rebound? And what about later, after the honeymoon in Copenhagen and the picture-taking along the canal, when they settled for a while in the vast apartment in Leipzig, near the Gewandhaus? My mother always seemed moved at the mere mention of Tristan und Isolde, Richard Wagner's celebration of tragic adultery and love-death. I chose to see this as a sign. Perhaps there had been more dramatic, more exotic liaisons than the early infatuation with the med-ical student. Perhaps I was the offspring of some truly exciting person-age. My father was perhaps not my real father. Even though I indiscriminately opened all sorts of drawers, I never did come across, say, a fifteen-year-old love letter that would prove that I was what they call *un enfant naturel*, not the fruit of a tired bed. Such discoveries do, after all, occur in novels. I was thinking of the opening pages of André Gide's *The Counterfeiters*, which my older cousin Shura, dismissed by my parents as an ineffectual bookworm, had read to me. I failed to make a distinction between what one might find in fiction and day-dreams about my own romantic origins. I tried to imagine my mother's lover. I saw him in turn as a Russian artist who wooed her with his bal-alaika, a passionate Hungarian socialist who later converted to Zionism and settled in a kibbutz, or even as a monocled French baron of suave charm and dubious pedigree with whom I saw her consuming oysters while watching the greyhound races at Courbevoie. Mama did occa-sionally spend evenings with friends at Courbevoie, though I do not recall that she liked oysters. I soon gave up imagining this lover, per-haps struck by Gide's flippant observation that not to know who one's father is cures one of the fear of resembling him.

Yet my resemblance to my father has become more pronounced over the years. The ears, thanks to good fortune or my mother's vigilance, do not stand out. But I cannot deny that my chin and my hands are his. There is more. I, too, check the stove repeatedly, not trusting my eyes. Have I really slipped the letter into the right slot? Did I take the pills? My physical traits, it pleases me to think, come from my mother's side. I have, however, often caught myself playing distressingly my father's role, rehearsing my father's cautionary monologues, especially as I set about admonishing my son—same urgent tone, same unbearable seri-ousness, same warnings about improbable catastrophes. And there is the worried expression I sometimes catch in a public place when I unex-pectedly meet my face in some mirror. Worry was indeed my father's great occupation. One morning he seemed particularly troubled. He could not remember what he should worry about. He himself laughed. But his own laughter did not reassure him.

It is difficult to escape from resemblance and repetition. More and more often I hear myself muttering my father's fatalistic "What can I do?" which so used to bother me, and against which I felt the need to rebel. My early eagerness for train travel, even when my father was seated in the same compartment, may already have signified a taste for freedom, for the liberating sense that I was meant to be a stranger in our own home. The fun of boat travel came later. The first transatlantic experiences were not exactly hedonistic. The zigzag crossing to avoid German submarines when, late in 1941, we escaped from the clutches of Hitler by way of Spain on a banana freighter overloaded with human cargo. Then, soon after, the American naval convoy in the opposite direction, after my assignment to the armored unit that was to land in Normandy. But later still, especially during those precious sabbaticals, how I looked forward to the leisurely crossings on liners with Bettina, who chatted in Italian with the officers and then repeated their flirtatious compliments to me as we lay snugly together in the lower bunk of our cabin. Those crossings on the *Saturnia*, the *Italia*, or the *Cristoforo Colombo*, which now seem to belong to another age, filled me with dreamy drowsiness as I leaned over the railing and watched the endlessly same foaming dark waters speed by. Today plane travel provides the less poetic numbing sameness of international airports, but is then followed by the elating sense of a fragile victory over space and time.

The crassest travel advertisements suggest yearnings for an elsewhere—for adventure, discovery, revelation. But mobility and change of scenery can also bring one closer to one's center. My trains of thought most often carry me home again. Writing and travelling have much in common for me. When I sit at my desk, I escape into reverie while believing that I am in charge. As I write, or think about writing, I am still little Vitia—looking up words in the large Larousse dictionary, getting distracted by the illustrations, forgetting what it is I looked for, opening guide books, checking old travel pictures and diaries, just as I did when, instead of doing my homework, I read snatches of Edgar Wallace's detective novels that I kept hidden in the top drawer of my writing table. As I dream, I get lost; as I write, I discover. The old train stations inhabit me because they were all at once places of departure, of transit, and of arrival.

In those Paris days, only train travel was a concrete reality. The car was for the city, occasionally for excursions to the surrounding countryside—Chantilly or the forest of Saint-Germain. My parents did not like long automobile trips. Planes were hardly ever considered for travel, not even in the movies. As for ocean liners, they were in my childhood associated exclusively with my Shanghai uncle, my mother's adventurous brother, whose tall, thin silhouette seemed to step right out of the well-tailored world of British diplomats as I imagined it from films I had seen. Every few years, he would appear on the European scene, disembarking in Genoa or Trieste, and announce his arrival by calling us long distance from the ship, which at the time my father judged an extravagant mode of communication.

Of the half-dozen or more railway stations in different parts of Paris, only three or four were familiar to me. They were all on the right bank of the Seine. The Gare de Lyon, very close to the river, with its top-heavy clock tower, still evokes my uncle Lola's arrivals from the Orient—but also our yearly pilgrimages to the Mediterranean sun. The Gare Saint-Lazare meant summer departures for Normandy—but also, as of a drizzly winter day, a very private memory of a carpeted staircase and heavily scented rooms. The Gare de l'Est, with its immense arched window and aristocratic arcade, stood for travel to Alsace, a region my parents still linked to Germany. The most oppressive was the Gare du Nord. What made it so oppressive in my eyes was not its heavily sculptured façade with its huge pilasters, but my father's departures. My mother and I usually accompanied him to the station. The *salle des pas perdus*: I was struck by the image. The hall of "lost footsteps." It all made me immensely sad—the vast concourse, the sheds, the pale light filtering through the glass roof. It wasn't that my father was leaving for distant Troy; he was only crossing the Channel, on his way to auction sales in London. But I would cry as the train slowly pulled out of the station. To console me, my mother usually treated me at once to a cinema on the Grands Boulevards. Those were the days of *cinéma permanent*. One made one's way into the dark theater in the middle of a film, guided as though into a mysterious underground sanctuary by a woman usher carrying a flashlight and expecting a ceremonial obol.

I had cried, though I knew that my father would soon return to tell me about the heavy sea, the passengers who were sick, the enormous Cumberland Hotel near Marble Arch, the orators on their boxes in Hyde Park, the double-decker buses, the kippered herring for breakfast, and those huge posters advertising ale or beer. My goodness, my Guinness.

Papa always gave me extra pocket money before boarding the train, and I knew that more was coming my way upon his return to our apartment on the rue Eugène Manuel. It was never very much. You must not be extravagant—a favorite expression of his. I was not to talk about our circumstances, our money, especially in school. I was never to make anyone feel bad or inferior. Always be discreet, considerate. Luxury hotels were for nouveaux riches and *Hochstapler*—a German term he dragged out, meaning "swindler" or "con man." He said that I should always tell him of my needs. Anyhow, all that was his was also mine. I knew of course that almost everything I might say I needed was going to be too much. He kept telling me that between a father and his son there should be a real friendship. That he was my friend. He told me about his own father, the well-to-do bearded *koopets* in Moscow, who pointed to the large cupboard in his room, saying that if he needed money he should feel free to open it at any time and serve himself. That's how he loved and trusted his son. My own father did not have a large cupboard, and I doubt that he kept much money at home. At any rate, he never extended a similar offer. All I received was the weekly allowance, and the extras before and after the business trips to London.

I never got to know my father's father, except on formal old photographs with a stiff cardboard back. He died, I believe, not long before my birth. I cannot even call him my grandfather. How true was the story of the large cupboard? He must have been broad-minded at any rate, for he sent his son, my father, to Paris to study the law, providing him with several years of freedom on the place du Panthéon in a hotel that still stands today, the Hôtel des Grands Hommes, facing the law school. He did not have far to go in order to take notes at Professor May's lectures. What do I really know about those student days of his? Papa was not very talkative on this subject, or the past in general. He did speak admiringly of this Professor May, who apparently had taken an interest in him. He explained to me that, unlike his classmates, he never worried on exam days because—as he also told them—he was well prepared and knew the answers. This must have endeared him to the other students. He seems to have had a special friendship with one Joseph Millner, who enjoyed something of a reputation as a blade, and who some thirty years later played a courageous role saving Jewish children during the Occupation.

What to make of the one personal anecdote? My father had borrowed a friend's wedding ring, which then slipped off his finger in the hotel shower, going down the drain. Why would my father, even as a lark, wear someone's wedding ring? He did not explain. He did tell me, however, about his idols at the time. In 1910, he heard Jean Jaurès, the powerful socialist orator and militant pacifist who was murdered for his beliefs just a few weeks before the outbreak of the Great War. Papa spoke at length about Jaurès, evoking his splendid voice, his fervent rhetoric, his humanism, urging me to read his history of socialism. Papa's other idols were Anatole France and Émile Zola, who had been great champions of justice at the time of the Dreyfus case. And above them all, in posthumous glory in my father's personal pantheon, towered the figure of Victor Hugo, whose national funeral attended by millions was still talked about, and who in my father's student days had assumed the mythical role of patriarch of the Third Republic. All I knew were some long extracts from *Les Misérables*, and a few sentimental and patriotic poems our teachers required us to learn by heart. The heavy leather-bound volumes of his collected works in my father's oak bookcase seemed formidable and almost inaccessible to me. It took me years to approach them.

Papa's law school days remain largely unknown to me. I would have wished to learn from him what Paris was like before the First World War, a time my imagination endowed with the poetry of horse-drawn omnibuses, gaslit streets, and bohemian groups. But my father was reticent. He did not confide past experiences and emotions. Perhaps he did not care to remember. Perhaps he was not skilled at describing anything. But what was the use, I asked myself, of talking about friendship, if we did not share memories? The famous friendship between a father and a son failed to convince me.

Yet I felt dejected when he left for London. I must have loved him. We often held hands. He carried me on his shoulders when I was a child. He made me laugh impersonating various monsters. He tried to amuse me, and later to encourage and console me. But could he begin to understand my needs? And is it fair to ask that much? As I think and write about my father, I recall our Latin teacher, who explained to us the meaning of the word *pietas*. It wasn't piety in a strictly religious sense, but reverent love, dutifulness, compassion, devotion, an act of kindness. My *pietas* toward my father is tinged with shame. The worst is not the sale of the silver tea-glass holder that gained me access to the rites of the rue de Provence. There was the theft of the money belonging to the maid—which, it is true, I replaced soon after. My father never found out. But what must have hurt, what he must have received as a deep offense was when I greeted him so rudely the day he came to the club to watch me play tennis with my friends. What are you doing here? Even as I pronounced these words, I knew they were terrible, and that my father did not deserve them. There was even worse later. The shame of being ashamed of his mannerisms and foreign accent, which he must have felt.

He had always treated me as a dauphin—a little king. My birthday was a special event, made even more special because it fell on the day of a national celebration in France. November 11 is Armistice Day, marking the end of the war in 1918 and victory over Germany. *Le jour de la victoire*. Victoire, Victor. My father gave me to understand—I may have been ten or eleven—that it was a combined celebration. He would on this occasion take me to the great parade on the Champs-Elysées. Units of the French army, banners flying, trumpets blaring, sabers exposed, marched briskly toward the Arc de Triomphe and the Tomb of the Unknown Soldier beneath it. The crowds cheered, waving small flags. Exuberant children were being carried on their fathers' shoulders. I was amused by the peculiar pace of the *chasseurs alpins*, the elite mountain troops, with their small, swift, almost comical steps. The French open-palmed military salute expressed a theatrical dignity. Everything was festive and martial. The familiar "Sambre et Meuse" march, carrying the names of rivers near France's northern border, was a reminder of heroic resistance to the invader. Military and republican fervor blended in the music. The revolutionary "Marseillaise," launched by the words *"patrie"* and *"gloire,"* is a call to arms filled with images of ferocious soldiers and blood soaking the soil. "Le Chant du départ," perhaps an even more stirring song, similarly extols war, threatens revenge against all tyrants, and proclaims the obligation to live and to die for the

Republic. On those birthdays, I learned how closely French militarism was wedded to the national consciousness and the myth of the Revolution. Inebriated by the fanfares, the crowd's enthusiasm, the sight of the marching units, I chose to believe that the national holiday was also a celebration of my special day. On our way back to the place Victor Hugo, where we lived at that time, Papa would suddenly cross the street in order to drop a coin into the extended hat of some beggar. He was in fact looking for beggars to spread his largesse as an offering of joy and thanks for having me as his son. I was the best, I could do no wrong.

My shame and guilt are the greater for this inflated self-image. Yet Papa also irritated me. On ordinary days, like an upper middle-class Polonius, he uttered sententious precepts. Always to reserve one's judgment, never to enter into a quarrel, not to borrow money, not to gamble. I resented his code of prudence. He had a horror of debts and an almost superstitious fear of the law. Perhaps this explains a recurrent nightmare of mine. In this nightmare I discover with extreme anguish that I have incurred a huge debt, the origin of which remains hopelessly shrouded—a debt that has accumulated an even more enormous interest that I am simply unable to pay. The discovery of this calamity, which is somehow always made in a dimly lit cellar where my mother's corpse lies hidden, makes me aware that I am living on borrowed time. The judgment and the sentencing are not far off. The acute realism of the nasty dream lingers for hours. It can easily affect me for an entire day. Only recently, as I read Kafka, did I realize that it was not the judgment, but my transparency that I feared most. A father doesn't need to be taught to see through his son. That may be the one thought in Kafka's story "The Judgment" that most struck home. From that thought there is only one short step to the penal colony's credo that guilt is never to be doubted.

Chapter 2

EROTIC FANTASIES

L
ong before that late afternoon on the rue de Provence, I was inhabited by images of women and reveries of a specific nature. The *mundus muliebris*, the attributes of feminine ambience, intrigued and preoccupied me. This was different from those spontaneous arousals, the nocturnal flow of images that so often led to sensations blurring the boundaries between the imagined and the real, when images almost literally turned into flesh. My reveries changed with time. The erotic and the sexual gradually became differentiated. At the beginning, together with the sensations and memories of the night train, I recognize my mother's fur muff, her gloves, her fur hat. There was her ample fur coat, and the cut crystal cologne flask on her dresser from which I decided one day to take a swallow, crying out almost at the same time: fire! (I recall the soothing effect as Elsa, our cook, gently rubbed my chest and belly with soap in the lukewarm water of the portable tub on the kitchen table, next to the jar in which she kept her pet frog.)

In family conversations, frequent mention was made of fur, for reasons of business as well as fashion. Astrakhan, chinchilla, beaver, sable, mink were familiar words overheard in sentences in which the Russian word *shooba* (fur) came up together with occasional references to the exotic-sounding Hudson Bay Company, a chartered London-based trading company going back, I was told, to the days of English adventurers in Canada, Indian trappers, and rival fur traders from various nations. When I was a boy, I loved to touch Mama's fur coats, especially once my father had shown me how one goes about judging the quality of a fur by gently stroking my mother's coat in both directions. I stroked and smelled her furs and relished the names of the small bottles of perfume displayed in her bedroom: Lanvin, Chanel, Patou. I took whiffs and kept repeating these names I had heard my mother pronounce in a casual manner. Their sound alone—especially the two syllables "Pa-tou," which brought my lips forward as for a kiss—titillated me.

Mama was not the only woman who appealed to my senses. There was my grown-up cousin Yula. That I was in love with her—I was all of eight years old—became clear to me on her wedding day, together with my resentment of her soft-spoken Romanian bridegroom, who looked a little like Gary Cooper. The wedding took place just around the corner from the Leipzig Gewandhaus, and I came to associate Yula's sensuous face with the temporary baldachin in the large living room, the ritualistic shattering of the glass, and the names of Haydn and other composers gracing the streets of that musical quarter. I had fallen in love with Yula's immense dark eyes, her contralto voice, the faint Russian singsong of her speech, and the pale down above her upper lip.

Though smell and touch affected me, the sound of the human voice carried an even stronger erotic charge, especially in the lower registers. I was ready to be stirred by Carmen and Cherubino long before I heard these roles performed. Gender disguises appealed to me. Mozart's young page Cherubino, sung by a mezzo-soprano, appears at some point in the opera dressed as a young woman. And Beethoven's intrepid Leonore in *Fidelio* saves her enchained husband in the tyrant's dungeon by disguising herself as a young man. Such situations aroused me as much as the dark timbre of the voice. I am of course skipping a number of years, for I did not discover *Le nozze di Figaro* and that hymn to love and freedom that is *Fidelio* until after we escaped from France during the Occupation, at the close of my adolescence. But the eight-year-old boy at the Leipzig wedding and the prurient teenager in Paris, filled with cravings, were quite the same as the budding opera fan who stood in line at the old Metropolitan Opera in New York, impatient to be once again enveloped by the mellifluous voices of Bidú Sayão and Ezio Pinza.

I have kept a picture of my mother as a volunteer Red Cross nurse in Russia during the war. The photographer had her pose in her white uniform, her eyes lifted toward an invisible azure, bringing out the oval contour of the face to make her look like a Renaissance figure. The madonna-like quality of the expression is both inviting and strangely remote. There exist less iconic representations of my mother, such as that other snapshot revealing her dreamy face half-hidden by a broad-rimmed hat tilted à la Greta Garbo. In the live images sheltered by memory, I see her tender, at times ironic smile. I admired her movements, her composed gestures, the way she held the slightly flattened Turkish cigarette between her long fingers, allowing the smoke to veil the features of her face. I observed the imprint of her lipstick on the cardboard tip. She allowed me to keep her empty cigarette boxes, which for months continued to carry the faint odor of Oriental tobacco blended with her perfume. Mama was a habitual smoker, especially after meals and at the card table, and I was eager to imitate the self-possessed way she had of drawing on her cigarette, including the delicate tappings of her forefinger, with which she flicked the ashes.

Mama was far from a chain smoker. For that kind of greedy inhalation I had the less appealing example of her steady bridge partner, Madame Solal, whose yellow arthritic fingers held a perennial Gitane cigarette tremblingly, and who always came accompanied by her lover, Monsieur Baudry, a lanky man, mostly silent in his black suit, who looked a little like the actor Louis Jouvet. It was from Mama, I believe, that I first learned the word "*amant*," the French word for "lover," which I somehow came to associate with low divans, opaque lamp-shades, and the Chinese game of mah jongg, which in those years occasionally diverted my parents and their friends in the evening.

My own friends at school, when we were about fifteen, exchanged or invented secrets about mothers in general, and more specifically about the mothers of girls we knew. These were secrets of a mythical nature—sex fantasies about older women. We did not know the word "fellatio," nor today's aseptic expression "oral sex," but we were excited by the verb "*sucer*" and the vulgar locution "*faire un pompier*." We lived at the same time with the decorous familiar image of *maman*, and that other image of an unknown figure, her disquieting and alluring other incarnation, as she undressed and revealed herself in the intimacy of a man. These were mysteries. And the stories we told one another, in what amounted to confabulatory contests, more often than not described the taste of certain mature women for young boys and adolescents. In other words, we all had a chance.

These fantasies were embroidered, some of them given as the truth or half-truth of what had been experienced by one of us, or more likely by someone we claimed to know. It didn't matter. We all pretended to believe what was reported, telling and retelling details of amorous successes as we walked each other home after school on those gray winter days, reluctant to separate (I walk you home, you walk me home), until it was almost dark and there was no further way of delaying the return to the late afternoon snack and the hated homework in physics, chemistry, and solid geometry.

Occasionally, as in the case of our classmate Pierre Masselli, good fortune seemed to take a more concrete shape. Masselli, with his handsome Corsican profile and alabaster skin (most of us exhibited the usual teenage acne), was more mature than the rest of the class, having had to repeat two entire years. He was what was known as a *cancre*—a hopelessly lazy student. He taught us to play poker, cheated regularly, figured out countless ways of conning the more gullible in our group, and regaled us with detailed, though unverified, accounts of trysts with an opulent blond widow who owned the bakery around the corner from our school. Masselli was in fact expelled from the lycée when he jumped out of the first-floor window of the study room on his way to an appointment at the bakery and landed in front of the *censeur*, the chief administrative officer in charge of school discipline.

My private dreams of commerce with women fluctuated between sensations of indolence and images of pleasurable pain. I had heard that it could be a savage sport, with no holds barred. These shifting moods, in which I saw myself alternately as the aggressed and the aggressor, led me to incongruous mental associations. As I sat fondling Nitscha's small breasts in a movie theater in the far-off working-class district of Barbès-Rochechouart—a theater owned by her Levantine entrepreneurial father—I kept thinking of the professional wrestler who was said to be her mother's lover. I imagined this wrestler-paramour wearing the defiantly tilted cap of the Parisian pimps as one sees them in the movies, dancing a sexy *java* with Nitscha's heavily made-up mother. I myself had never danced the *java,* nor even come close to any of the dance halls, or *bals-musettes,* where promiscuous proletarian couples unhinged their joints to the sound of an accordion. But in the films of the period, the kind in which a young Jean Gabin might have been featured, one could often watch some ruffian and his woman dance with quick small steps in bumpily syncopated three-quarter time.

Certain words, if I came across them in print, aroused me. They aroused me even more when I repeated them to myself aloud. One such was the word *"sein,"* for the female breast, which I first glimpsed in a novel my mother was reading. Other words, learned in the schoolyard, had a still more powerful effect: *"bander,"* for the stiffening of the male organ, *"branler"* for a pull-and-thrust manual caress, *"jouir"* for orgasm. These words did not strike me as crude. Their metaphorical nature gave them special potency, for *"bander,"* related to archery, suggests a bow stretched to the utmost; the verb *"jouir,"* from the Latin *"gaudere,"* points to the essence of pleasure; and *"branler,"* the energetic word for masturbation, was centuries ago associated, no doubt because of the brisk to-and-fro movement, with a regional folk dance known as *le branle.* I was certainly far from suspecting at the time that the efficacy of metaphors was central to the nature of my lascivious thoughts. Though we learned about metaphors and similes at school, I did not really understand how they functioned. Retrospectively, I like to think that an early taste for poetic figures of speech was closely related to my lasting aversion for crude terms, especially of the four-letter Anglo-Saxon variety. These words, with their explosive onomatopoeic sounds, I later came to associate with the heavy drinking and violence I so often witnessed in the army.

Sounds were in fact inseparable from voluptuary sensations. In a novel by Colette that lay on my mother's night table and which I leafed through stealthily, I found a transcription of a woman's moans as she is overcome by mounting pleasure. I returned again and again to the same page, seeking to fathom its secret. I kept imitating those moans as I walked in the street and could feel my own excitement rising. I also kept repeating the word *"maîtresse,"* which I looked up impatiently in various dictionaries in my father's study. But the dictionary definitions—a woman who grants her favors to a man who is not her husband—failed

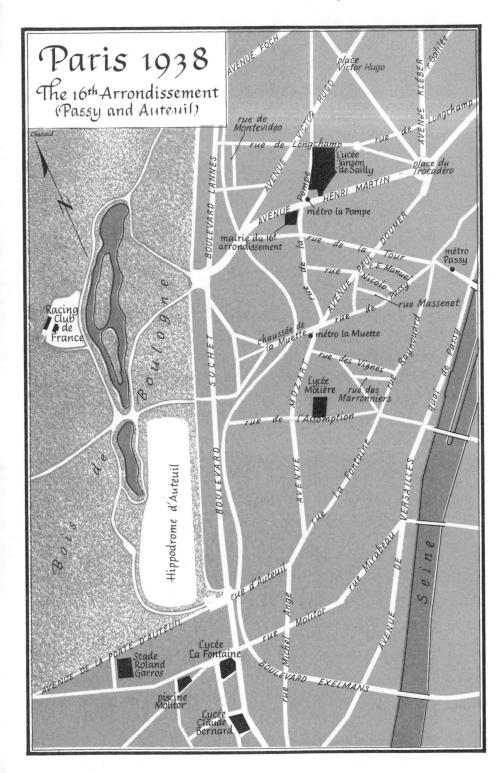

Paris 1938
The 16th Arrondissement
(Passy and Auteuil)

to satisfy me. They seemed so much colder than the two magical syllables. The word "favors" was especially disappointing. It had no color
and no smell to it. "*Maîtresse,*" on the other hand, suggested domina-
tion, enslavement, perhaps even cruelty—and it stirred me.

Yet as I look back at my behavior with girls my own age, I do not
find myself very enterprising. Mia, the tomboyish daughter of our dentist, had returned from her summer vacation making fun of my inexperience. I didn't even know the meaning of the word "*flirter,*" which she
pronounced with an affected British accent. As for Dany Wolf, my central occupation during the summer of 1939 in Deauville on the brink of
war, she gave me a most memorable thrill—I was then almost sixteen—
when on a rainy day, coming up behind me as the rest of us were playing a game of Monopoly, she simply placed her hand on my shoulder
and then moved it to my neck, where I could feel the warmth of it. This
unsolicited affectionate gesture moved me more deeply than the kisses
we exchanged at night on the beach. Yet this was a year or more after
the visit to the rue de Provence.

My bolder fantasies were played out in imaginary situations, in nocturnal scenarios that brought me to the verge of a release from a drawn-
out tension, when semiconscious movements would complete in a
half-awake state what the dream had begun. For hours I was unable to
forget what had seemed so real, including the shape and features of the
woman in my dream. Years later, in my classes, when commenting on
the opening pages of Proust's novel, where he describes how, in his
sleep, a woman was born from an awkward position of his thigh, like
Eve from Adam's rib, I glossed this transparent and symbolic evocation
of what is vulgarly known as a wet dream, trying myself to remain delicate and decently allusive. But I knew only too well what young Marcel
had experienced, including the keen longing for the dream-woman who
had vanished, and whom I was determined to find somewhere.

I never liked the term "*se masturber.*" The very sound of it conjured
up images of twisting and torturing, of movements distressingly
mechanical and lifeless. It also suggested a blemish, a shameful surrender to a harmful habit. My parents, without dotting the i's, without ever
referring directly to me, talked in oblique and ominous fashion about
self-abuse, solitary vice, the dangers of mental debility, even downright

insanity. Dark rings around the eyes (I immediately checked in the mirror) were supposed to be tell-tale signs. These were commonplace notions fostered, it would seem, by old-fashioned medical textbooks and imparted to families by stern family doctors of the kind I knew and feared as a child. Views have evolved. Best-selling surveys and studies now advocate self-caressing. Sex counselors apparently insist that solitary exercises are not at all reprehensible or harmful, but sound training, that they develop the sensitivity for good love-making and skills in self-control. If such counselors had a poetic fiber, they might add that solo practices activate the imaginative process and fantasy in general. Between the literary imagination and solitary erotic activity there exists a bond by no means limited to the enjoyment of the type of amatory books that, as the saying goes, one reads with one hand. Flaubert somewhat crudely likened the act of writing to an onanistic performance. It may well be that all solitary pleasures involve the invention of a scene, even the invention of the other. Such inventions can turn out to be invasive when it later comes to a real partner in love.

MAGGIE'S QUESTIONS ABOUT the girls I knew may well have betrayed a genuine curiosity. In that softly lit room on the rue de Provence, she was hearing about the mores of a distant country. My friends and I did not much more than kiss the girls we went out with— and even that seemed quite daring. The upper-middle-class world of the 16th arrondissement was far removed from the promiscuities evoked in the songs of Maurice Chevalier and Mistinguett, or in the films with Jean Gabin and Arletty. In our district, which included Passy and Auteuil, girls and boys not only studied separately, they played apart. The boys went to the Lycée Janson de Sailly or to the Lycée Claude Bernard; the girls to the Lycée Molière (where Simone de Beauvoir taught in those years) or to the Lycée La Fontaine near the Molitor swimming pool and skating rink, where we often lingered. The Lycée Molière stood across the street from Jacques's modern apartment building, which featured the innovation of an underground garage. One of the attractions of the building was going down to the garage at night and starting his father's car. But the real attraction was to wait in the street for the exit of the girls when we got out of our own classes earlier. We stood on the sidewalk, exchanging jokes, hiding our pleasure and embarrassment behind a blasé expression, pointing out this or that girl, comparing the ones we found attractive, or those with whom we thought we might have a chance, as though we were worldly connoisseurs. The girls themselves chattered away, at best acknowledging our presence with a sneaky side glance. Then they dispersed. It was all so close, yet so distant.

Some of us occasionally gathered at my friend Leo Lamont's apartment from where, with the help of binoculars, we could peer into the gym of the Lycée La Fontaine. We were five or six, fighting to take turns, for we had only one pair of binoculars. In all truth, we did not see very much—only what the narrow windows and their deceptive reflections allowed. And what we did make out was not very revealing. In those days, students did not really undress or change clothes for gym class. We just shed our jackets and our ties. The girls took off their outer garments. The gym room, with its hanging ropes, parallel bars, and wall ladders, remained permanently odorous. The real redolence, however, filled our imagination, as we watched, or thought we watched, those girls from a great distance.

Scant contact made for feverish fantasies. School decorum affected even the awareness of our own bodies. Did I ever see the naked body, or even the bare torso, of any of my schoolmates? I remember faces, some last names. (The use of the first name, a sign of some intimacy beyond the school grounds, was strictly reserved for close friends.) It was different, of course, at the sports club, the swimming pool, or during the summer at the seashore. There we consorted with friends known to our parents, congregating in groups, or *bandes,* that included girls. But even at the beach, there was a certain discretion or modesty. Bikinis were unknown, and even boys still wore bathing suits, some of which did not fit too well. Thighs were not on display. In the 1930s, tennis champions like Fred Perry and Gottfried von Cramm still wore white flannel trousers during the tournaments we watched at the Roland Garros Stadium. And when we boys played ball in the inner courtyard at school, we kept our long trousers on, which did not prevent us from scraping our knees painfully. The memory of the hard falls on the cement is mixed with that of the acrid smell wafting across from the urinals in the *préau*, the covered part of the courtyard.

Boys who had sisters found it easier to meet girls, provided these sisters were neither too young nor too old. Jacques's sister Denise, some three or four years younger, was to her great chagrin excluded from our colloquies. We simply did not pay attention to her. I myself did not have a sister, for she lay buried in another country. But I had a cousin approximately my own age, Irène, who lived two streets away from us, on the rue Massenet, where I spent many hours playing fierce ping-pong with her brother, Sascha, who became one of my steady companions. One day when Sascha was out for a while, Irène and I, in a playful mood, began to wrestle. Soon we found ourselves on the floor. I felt her strong legs clasping me around the waist, and she could feel my arousal. We both jumped up, our faces flushed. We never wrestled quite like that again.

Irène later served as my confidante and well-intentioned, though not always successful, go-between when, during the summer of 1939, I became seriously infatuated with Dany Wolf, whose nipples I could make out through her wet bathing suit—a fact I refrained from mentioning in the love poems, plagiarized from Alfred de Musset, that Irène, my trusted emissary, kept bringing to Dany's room so as not to awaken the suspicions of her parents, who might have wondered about the deluge of these missives had they arrived by mail. To be an assiduous plagiarist at the age of sixteen did not help me uncover the coveted treasures of Dany's body, but it taught me more about metrics and metaphors than all my Latin and French classes combined. Eventually I came to understand that the pastiche was not merely a device for satirizing the style of different writers, but a salutary exercise for finding a voice of one's own.

In 1937, when we were between fourteen and fifteen, our only mixed social gatherings, except at the seashore close to our vacationing families, were the fairly stiff tea and dance parties planned by our parents, when tea and lemonade were served, and chairs were lined up along the walls of the salon and the dining room—hardly the right atmosphere for unrestrained romance. But by 1938 and 1939, as we moved closer to war, we discovered the excitement of more spontaneous occasions initiated by one of us, known as *surprises-parties,* pronounced the French way. These *surprises-parties,* which were no surprise at all, still required parental approval for the boisterous event to take place in some apartment from late in the afternoon until well into the evening. The parents in question would discreetly leave the apartment during these hours, doubtless with some misgivings, hoping there would be no disaster, but also relieved not to have to witness the din and the confusion. We tried our best not to be too wild for fear of compromising our chances for future use of the premises.

I don't recall a *surprise-partie* ever taking place in my parents' apartment. Maybe I never asked, knowing that they would be reluctant. They were much too afraid for their Meissen, Rosenthal, and Limoges porcelain on display. This concern of theirs may well be at the origin of my aversion to porcelain figurines in general, and to figurines of ballerinas in particular. Even the presence of a single friend could be disastrous. When Ernest Lash, whom I had befriended in England, came to stay with us, we quickly succeeded in maiming the figurine of the famous ballerina Anna Pavlova dancing "Swan Lake"—a special favorite of my mother's—by throwing tennis balls in the living room. *Surprises-parties* represented a far greater threat to the integrity of porcelain ballerinas.

Our noisy social occasions required the indispensable *pick-up*—another English word we misused. All it meant was a portable electric phonograph that one of us provided, since not all our friends' apartments came with a phonograph. We all brought records, mostly of the swing and jitterbug variety. We were fond not of the big bands, but of what we considered real jazz. We revered the names of Coleman Hawkins, Louis Armstrong, Benny Goodman, Duke Ellington, Fats Waller, Count Basie. We had our local heroes on the French scene—Django Reinhardt, a guitar virtuoso of gypsy origin; Stéphane Grapelli, a masterful jazz violinist; and those who later joined them to form the Hot Club de France. English, or rather the American idiom, was decidedly the fashion. France had its own crooners like Jean Sablon, and jazz bands like those of Jo Bouillon and Ray Ventura. And there was the whimsical chansonnier Charles Trenet, known as *le fou chantant.* But we responded with greater enthusiasm to foreign imports like Lionel Hampton and Teddy Wilson. I myself was especially fond of saxophone improvisations.

For our parties, we bought cheap imitation champagne known as *mousseux* at the Prisunic, a French version of Woolworth's. We perspired abundantly dancing the hectic "Tiger Rag" and the not much more temperate "Honeysuckle Rose." But we also liked the slower tunes that allowed us to hold each other tightly and dance "cheek to cheek," an expression we had learned from a Fred Astaire film. Some tunes became the recurrent accompaniment of a specific romance. Nitscha and I would melt to the languorous rhythm of "Music, Maestro, Please," the full lyrics of which only recently came back to me, prompted by a retired American scholar I met in the Chianti. I can recapture the sentimental mood as Nitscha and I swayed in each other's arms: "Tonight, tonight I must forget . . . " It amazes me how much English we heard and repeated, without really knowing or understanding it. But we were learning from the crooners, much as I later got my first snatches of Italian from the opera buffa recitatives I learned by heart.

The *mousseux*, needless to say, went to our heads. Some of us became sick and were soon sprawling on the floor. At one of these events, on or near the avenue Mozart, I remember finding myself on top of a parental bed next to a girl with whom I had been dancing and drinking until she began feeling dizzy. She was out, and I kept kissing her though she was completely unaware of it. She was pale and unconscious. We lay there fully dressed—even I was mostly motionless—until we were discovered by the parents, who had decided to return earlier than expected. I am not sure any *surprise-partie* took place in that apartment soon again.

Anita was the name of the dark-haired girl who had been so vivacious until she became ill and passed out. We both acquired something of a bad reputation with my friend's parents. I was not altogether proud of having kissed her inanimate lips. I hoped to redeem myself in my own eyes. I succeeded in making an appointment with her in a newly created Pam-Pam bar on the Champs-Elysées ("pam" for *pamplemousse,* or grapefruit), the latest rage, where young people—the kind that the extreme right was denouncing as decadent—congregated to sip exotic fruit juices. But I never managed to get to the appointment. All of a sudden, I developed a fever and a disfiguring rash, which turned out to be a belated case of chickenpox, an ironic reminder that I had not really outgrown my childhood. It felt like a regression, as I lay in the dark, with my mother again assuming full control over me. I consoled myself listening to Radio Luxembourg, a station that for some reason played a great deal of jazz in those days. The other consolation was that for a couple of weeks I was out of school with a valid excuse that made me feel almost virtuous. But by the time I was in circulation again, Anita was no longer available. She had taken up with a supercilious fellow by the name of Guy, who somehow always managed to look suntanned and whom I detested. Anita disappeared from my horizon. It was a lesson in the impermanence and mutability of things.

Another mishap in timing occurred soon after I met Suzy, a very tall girl who was an extraordinary dancer, who taught me to jitterbug, and who consoled me after the loss of Anita. I soon became proficient at spasmodic dancing. It was difficult to separate Suzy's physical attributes (she not only was lanky but had a long nose) from the seductiveness of her dancing movements and the fun of the lessons. My infatuation, at any rate, was real while it lasted, and her entire person, including the way she pushed back her hair and laughed when I made a clumsy step, was an indissoluble part of it. Just as I was making progress in various ways, my parents announced that we were leaving for "winter sports" in Megève. "Winter sports" struck me as quite funny, since my parents did not ski and were hardly what one would call sportspeople. I was not thrilled, to say the least, to spend that vacation time in their constant presence. The worst was the timing. I was sure to lose Suzy, as I had lost Anita. I did not wish to leave, gave all sorts of reasons, claimed to abhor the Alps, created scenes. My mother was not fooled. She saw right through my reluctance. It seemed to amuse her. Her ironic smile irked me. But there was no escape. I left with my parents by the night train, in a foul mood. For once I did not enjoy the train ride.

Megève, a ski resort not far from the chain of Mont Blanc, was a disaster. I disliked it from the moment our taxi made its way through the street covered with dirty snow and fresh horse manure. Not only was I relentlessly in my parents' company when I was not with the ski group (where I made no friends), but my mother and father insisted that I wear those infamous itchy woolen undergarments known as winter *combinaisons*. My durable distaste for skiing is surely related to those endless days of epidermic discomfort. The discomfort was compounded by the political mood during that winter of 1937–1938. Many of the clients in the small chalet-hotel could be overheard angrily referring to "that Jew," Léon Blum, who had a year or so earlier become prime minister. The Front Populaire, a coalition of leftist parties, had come to power and launched a program of highly controversial social reforms, such as the forty-hour week, salary raises, and a system of workers' representations giving increased power to labor unions. The forty-hour week, in particular, seemed to provoke intense anger, as did the sit-down strikes, any talk of intervention in the Spanish Civil War, or the most casual recall of the Stavisky fraud case—a financial scandal that had led to the famous riots of 1934 that rocked the foundations of the Third Republic. My father, aware of the guests' comments, explained to me what I had not already gathered from the newsreels. Behind it all one perceived mounting chauvinism and anti-Semitism to which even a fourteen-year-old boy was sensitive. French Jews themselves could be heard making anti-Semitic remarks, referring to the influx of unwanted German Jews, and even worse, of East European Jews, especially since Hitler's National Socialist Party had taken over in Germany.

"*Juif*" (one did not even have to say "*sale juif*" or "*youpin*") was for many an offensive word. If one wanted to be delicate, one called the Jews *israélites,* which is how assimilated French Jews liked to refer to themselves. It did not help that Léon Blum was by his background and inclination an intellectual, and that other prominent names in his cabinet were those of Blumlein and Georges Mandel, who was later murdered by the Vichy militia. Before launching on a political career, Blum had been trained as a scholar at the prestigious École Normale Supérieure, had served as theater critic for an important avant-garde literary journal, had taken part in the Dreyfus case, and had written one book on Stendhal and another advocating sexual experience for women before marriage. None of this endeared him with the arch-conservatives. As for my mother, she greatly praised his book on women and marriage, which seems to have made more of an impression on her than his socialist theories.

Daily exposure to the other French families in the hotel made me aware of a malaise deeper than the itch produced by the long woolen underwear. France had developed its own brand of fascism. There was much talk of a certain Colonel de La Roque who had been president of the Croix-de-Feu, a rightist, ultranationalist confederation of war veterans. This same Colonel de La Roque had recently created the fascist-inspired Parti Social Français, a forerunner of the party led today by Jean-Marie Le Pen. And there was the even more sinister ex-Communist, Jacques Doriot, leader of the P.P.F., the Parti Populaire Français. Doriot was soon to become a venomous collaborator of the Nazis during the Occupation and a model for the Vichy *milice* that specialized in hunting down and torturing Jews as well as members of the French Resistance.

Much as I was preoccupied with thoughts of Suzy, of jazz, and of my Parisian friends, I was experiencing a sense of estrangement, even a rift, during that brief winter vacation in Megève. I became aware of an anomaly. Socially and economically, my parents belonged to the well-heeled world of the mostly non-Jewish families in the hotel. Politically, however, my parents were moderate liberals with vague sympathies for the non-extreme left, linking the values of culture, freedom, and tolerance to the notion of an *intelligentsia*—a word that was always pronounced with respect and with a Russian accent. The Communist Party they despised out of bitter experience, even though it now posed as the great champion of liberty and as the only valid anti-fascist force. As for the ultranationalism and xenophobia of the French variety, they had every reason to fear it. My parents were suspicious of both extremes. No wonder I felt that they were out of tune with the other hotel guests.

What ruined that ski vacation almost more than the combined effect of my separation from Suzy, my parents' oppressive presence, the itchy underwear, and the climate of political hostility, was the fear of the imminent arrival of the school report, the *bulletin trimestriel*, which was bound to be calamitous. Even though I had bribed our concierge, Monsieur Émile, into promising to intercept that report, my apprehension throughout the stay in Megève spoiled what little fun I might have had.

How right I was to suspect that something would go amiss. The cries of indignation I could hear coming from another room shortly after we returned to our Paris apartment left no doubt in my mind as to Monsieur Émile's betrayal. Obviously my father was a more generous and more reliable client.

SOON I WAS dancing again cheek to cheek with Suzy to Fred Astaire's tune "Heaven, I'm in heaven . . . " We enjoyed repeating and appropriating fragments of lyrics, making foreign expressions, which we frequently misused, part of our daily vocabulary. English words were the fashion, even for those who, in those ideologically charged years, deplored the weaknesses of British parliamentary democracy or looked askance at the American cult of the dollar and the complacent faith of Americans in their never-never land of endless success and happy progress. English words and English-sounding verbal appendages were common usage, long before there were outcries about the bane of *franglais*. My friends insisted on calling me Vicky, imagining that it had an English flavor. Victor, with its sonorous accent on the second syllable, sounded too pompous. There was the bearded, patriarchal figure of Victor Hugo, who seemed to be remembered exclusively for his bombast and oracular pieties. And there was the laughable figure of the Italian king, Victor Emmanuel III, with his diminutive body and underslung jaw. Vicky sounded less antiquated to our ears than Victor—a name that, pronounced the French way, lent itself to puns and stale jokes about cuckolded stationmasters.

We were affected by an Anglo-Saxon fad. It mattered little whether we understood all the words of the songs. We repeated the titles and the refrains without bothering to probe for their meaning. I believe I understood from beginning to end "You must have been a beautiful baby . . . " which I learned from a record by the Andrews sisters. I soon knew it by heart and sang it expressively to various girls, always stressing "'cause baby look at you now." I still sing the song, with nostalgic repetitions of the words: "'cause baby, 'cause baby, 'cause baby."

English had invaded many domains in the 1930s—not only popular

music and the world of movies, but politics and sports as well. *Le swing,
le jazz hot, le jitterbug,* le Hot Club de France, were common terms.
American films had familiarized us not only with the faces of James
Cagney, William Powell, Myrna Loy, Clark Gable, Loretta Young,
Tyrone Power, and Gary Cooper, but with what we took to be the
everyday amenities of American life, such as plush nightclubs where
guests revealed themselves as accomplished performers and were
launched overnight on phenomenal careers, fancy golf clubs where
clever impresarios met hard-drinking tycoons, well-stocked bars in the
basements of suburban homes, and resplendent station wagons such as
the one driven with panache by Katharine Hepburn. English expressions were prescribed on the tennis court, and we always said "ready"
as we were about to receive our opponent's serve, "deuce" to indicate
the tie (the French "*égalité*" seemed too prosaic), and we referred to a
game as a "match." Tennis was, of course, not a proletarian pastime in
those days. But anglophilia contaminated even less elitist sports. Soccer
was called "*le football*" (or more succinctly "*le foot*"), "*dribbler*" was an
accepted verb, and "corner" as well as "goal" and "penalty" entered
accredited dictionaries, though they were pronounced with a stubborn
French accent. Even the world of politics was touched. One referred to
"*un meeting*" where "*le leader*" of a party was to give "*un speech.*" The
terms, I discovered, are all perfectly at home in the *Petit Larousse Illus-
tré*. Taken for granted, naturalized French, they made it possible, even
without schooling in English, to acquire a sizable vocabulary.

My own schooling at the lycée had very little to do with the English
tongue as it is spoken. It was as abstract, as academic, as obsolete a language as Latin or Greek. It came indeed to be officially recognized as a
substitution for one of the "dead" languages. When I entered the upper
classes, both Greek and Latin were required subjects for at least four
years. But then the option of replacing Greek with one of the modern
languages was offered by government decree, and my parents insisted
that English would be of greater use to me in life than the language of
Homer and Hesiod. I did, however, continue with Latin, though my
translations from Virgil remained, to put it mildly, whimsical.

In our English classes, conversation or any idiomatic usage was out of
the question. Grammar and stylistic exercises led to arduous renderings

of prose texts from English into French and from French into English. These were the typical class exercises and home assignments, known as *version* and *thème*—translations from and into a foreign language. In addition, we were required to learn a great deal of poetry by heart, and to recite it in class, though our erratic pronunciation was hardly ever corrected. There would not have been much point to that; our teachers' declamation of the language of Shakespeare would surely have puzzled British ears.

Before assigning a poem to be memorized, our teachers would first read it to us aloud, often bombastically, and with patently fake British intonations. The very idea of American English was frowned upon. Lycée teachers of English (the poet Mallarmé had been one of them) were often eccentric individuals. Our most memorable *prof d'anglais*, Monsieur Labé, appeared to me as uncanny as Coleridge's ancient mariner, whom he seemed determined to reincarnate. He, too, had a long gray beard and a glittering eye. The expression "gray-beard loon" at the beginning of the poem was as though conceived with him in mind. With a visionary look, Monsieur Labé would raise himself full height from his desk chair, book in hand, one arm outstretched, and declaim the opening lines in solemn fashion. He became a seer, and no longer saw us. Yet he was not ridiculous. His vatic manner amused but also impressed us. I was titillated by the sound effects of his nasal chant and the marked scanning.

> *The fair breeze blew, the white foam flew,*
> *The furrow followed free . . .*

It was then and there, and not in my French classes, that I first tasted the delights of alliteration and assonance.

Monsieur Labé could become quite oracular, and then his forked beard would respond by flowing in separate directions, as though agitated by the conflictual winds of inspiration. He initiated us to Wordsworth's sonnet:

> *The world is too much with us; late and soon,*
> *Getting and spending, we lay waste our powers:*

Little we see in Nature that is ours;
We have given our hearts away, a sordid boon!

I did not quite understand what a "sordid boon" could possibly be, nor why it deserved an exclamation mark. Nor did I have a clear idea of how and to whom we had given our hearts away. The words "spending" and "powers" also remained somewhat foggy in the context. But no matter. Something did click. And I enjoyed reciting the poem. As Monsieur Labé chided us for our mistakes, filling in the gaps in our memory with reproachful emphasis (we were not allowed to glance at the textbook when we recited), he began to look more and more like the wraiths of Proteus and old Triton at the end of the sonnet, as I imagined them rising from the sea and blowing a contorted horn.

Another sonnet by Wordsworth that Monsieur Labé revealed to us with contagious enthusiasm added significantly to my notion of the London cityscape. The poet's view from Westminster Bridge extended well beyond my father's descriptions of Hyde Park and the Cumberland Hotel. I loved the rhythm and the breadth of the opening line,

Earth has not anything to show more fair . . . ,

and I was very taken with the visual survey:

. . . silent, bare,
Ships, towers, domes, theaters, and temples lie
Open unto the fields, and to the sky . . .

I was good at learning these assigned poems by heart. I enjoyed reciting them to myself as I walked to the lycée in the pale morning light, hoping to be called upon to stand up and recite them to the class. I was especially fond of some of the songs from Shakespeare's plays, partly I suspect because they were short and easy to learn, but also because their surface simplicity allowed me to imagine things as mysterious as the underwater sea changes that transform the bones and the eyes of the drowned father into coral and precious pearls:

Full fathom five thy father lies . . .

I could not imagine my own father at the bottom of the sea. He was neither a sailor nor a swimmer, and I hardly saw him in the company of sea
nymphs. The great moment in the song came with "Hark! now I hear
them . . . ," announcing what was really the silence of a revelation.

There was also the more domestic Shakespeare poem about winter,
"When icicles hang by the wall . . . ," describing everyday scenes and
gestures associated with the cold: Dick who "blows his nail," Marian's
nose looking red and raw, and milk found frozen in the pail. What I
liked best in this song was the nonsense refrain "Tu-whit, tu-who,"
merrily imitating the sound of the owl. Monsieur Labé looked his most
vatic when he read to us with elegiac languor and Gallic stresses Keats's
autumnal ode:

> *Where are the songs of Spring? Ay, where are they?*
> *Think not of them, thou hast thy music too . . .*

We recited obediently, but remained mystified. We did not discuss
the poems. Literary analysis, or *explication de texte*, as it was called, was
reserved for classes in French literature, where we rehashed platitudes
about Racine's biblical play *Athalie* or the heroic Spain of Corneille's
Le Cid, whose grandiloquent couplets we were tempted to parody
rather than admire. But it was my English classes in the Parisian school
that illustrated, well before I came across it in another life and on distant shores, T. S. Eliot's assertion that great poetry can communicate
before it is understood. As for my familiarity with the English language, it was in those days limited to a strange blend of the crooners'
idiom and that of nineteenth-century British poets. Years later, American army talk would add to it another dimension. That army language,
as I found out, was hardly romantic or sensuous. Nor did it induce complex erotic reveries. It was far removed from the world of my mother's
fur muff and her subtle perfumes.

Chapter 3

TENDERNESS WITHOUT WORDS

My father indulged me (Vitienka can do no wrong) and acted as if he were always about to reach out and pinch my cheek lovingly. He carried me on his back, bumping my rear gently against the bedroom wall in rhythm to a nursery song. My mother, on the other hand, seemed eager to treat me as a grown-up and impart lessons in self-discipline. Her distaste for self-indulgence was perhaps part of her own mother's legacy. Anna Vassilievna, my grandmother, was a legendary figure in our family and among their friends. She was respected and feared for her imperiousness and polyglot wit. During our late-afternoon sofa sessions in Leipzig, where she and my grandfather lived in a wing of our apartment before we moved to Paris, she insisted that I lie perfectly still and repeat lines of Russian poetry by Lermontov and Pushkin that she slowly whispered to me, carefully separating the words so that I had no excuse for making mistakes.

Earlier still—I must have been five or six—when Nora was still alive and our parents were vacationing without us, my grandmother was put in charge of my sister and me. At such times, she felt free to implement her educational and hygienic theories. I still remember my father's dismay when, upon returning with my mother from Venice and the photo-recorded feeding of pigeons on the piazza San Marco, they found my head closely cropped, maybe even shaved, because my grandmother held to the unshakable opinion that my hair would grow sturdier as a result. This capillary prophylaxis, radical and perverse in my parents' view, did not prevent me from developing, at first, what is called a "high forehead," then a receding hairline, and ultimately an undeniable baldness—like all the men on both sides of my family.

When my grandparents moved to an apartment of their own a few streets away, I would visit once a week and have lunch alone with Babushka. First she served his daily omelet to my grandfather, who, some thirty years older than she, was then in his nineties, quite frail, but endowed with an impressive appetite. After the daily omelet came the daily question—"How was it?"—followed by the daily answer, "It was good, but it was better yesterday." It took me years to understand that this was more than a trivial and predictable answer to an equally predictable question. It was a statement about marriage and life in general.

Dyedushka, my grandfather, walked slowly but without a cane. When, as a child, I accompanied him to the park, I recall how he stopped now and then, turning around with his hands clasped behind his back, to appraise a feminine figure that had just passed us. He looked carefully and made no comments. He was rather taciturn, and I do not recall conversing with him in any language. I was told that he had all his teeth, and that he did not wear glasses. He used to sit for hours in his armchair, scrutinizing through his magnifying glass the financial page of the newspaper that listed the latest quotations of the stock exchange—the *birja*, as my grandmother explained—though he had lost everything he owned at the time of the Revolution: his sugar refinery, his properties, and his investments in the Russian railroad, which, as an engineer, he had helped develop. I heard it said that he was the first Jew admitted to the Polytechnic Institute under the tsars—some time in the mid-nineteenth century. He had amassed a not inconsiderable fortune, but that was now all in the past. A ruined émigré in Germany, he was supported entirely by his son-in-law, my father.

After my grandfather's omelet came my turn to have lunch tête-à-tête with my grandmother, while my grandfather returned to his armchair and to the scrutiny of the newspaper. This was the time for a lesson in good manners. I would reach out for the food, if necessary by stretching my arm across the table. My grandmother would slap my wrist with her napkin, adding the inevitable "You must always ask." One day I replied, perversely, "Yes, but what if I'm alone?" The answer came without hesitation: "Especially when you are alone." I remained speechless. This surprising reply to my provocative question was not lost on me. I could not have explained its deeper meaning then and there. I have often wondered whether my grandmother was aware of it. As I think about her person and character, the answer must be yes. She was giving me a lesson in dignity and self-respect. It applied to any and all so-called private activities—washing, dressing, thinking. It is undoubtedly the same lesson that, many years later and against all logic, made me stubbornly polish my army boots in the muddy fields of Normandy after we landed in June of 1944.

"Especially when you are alone." Babushka's lesson, I know, also prepared me to appreciate that passage in Primo Levi's *Survival in Auschwitz* in which the Jew Steinlauf (who had earned an Iron Cross in the former Austro-Hungarian army) sums up survival wisdom, exhorting the newly arrived contingent of death camp inmates to wash their faces daily, if need be in dirty water, to polish their shoes regularly, and to walk erect—not in order to please the SS guards, but so as not to become beasts and "begin to die."

Babushka thought that my parents thoroughly spoiled me. She was scandalized that they agreed to rescue me from my first summer camp, at the age of seven or eight, when I complained that the counselors made fun of me because I could not tie my shoelaces. I had pleaded to be allowed to come home, declaring that I was "unhappy." Later, there was the record of her voice on the small, cheaply made plastic disk that she sent us in Paris (lost, alas, during the 1940 debacle) with a list of admonitions for my benefit. My parents and I played it over and over again with considerable amusement, until it developed a crack and the voice almost faded. The recorded message was in Russian, which my grandmother insisted I continue speaking daily. It concluded with the sentence "*Chtobi tiebja ne tak kutaly*" (Tell your parents that they should not pamper you so much). And it ended, to our lasting entertainment, with a firm German "*So*," to indicate, we assumed, to the attendant in the Leipzig department store Kaufhaus Brühl, where the disk had been incised, that she had come to the end of her recording. The Germanic "*So*" became a family joke.

My mother had an unswerving sense of duty toward her parents. Her perseverance and ingenuity enabled her, through relatives in the consular service, to get them out of Samara on the Volga, in the heart of

Russia, where, after the Revolution, they had been virtual prisoners in a single room of their large house, occupied by coarse Soviet officials. And it was again her perseverance, after my grandfather died in Leipzig in 1937, that brought my grandmother to Paris, out of Nazi Germany. Just as she later managed—almost a miracle in 1942—to rescue my grandmother out of Occupied France and have her join us, via Spain and Portugal, in New York, where we ourselves had only recently found refuge.

Mama's sense of filial duty was related, I guess, to her oft-repeated recommendation, rooted in who knows what emotional experience or intuition, never to take leave of a dear one on a cross note, never to postpone saying the kind word or doing the kind thing. The impressive dread of having to face a forever "too late" placed a supreme value on human relations but also made one vulnerable to the dictates of sentimentalism. It could lead to viewing life from a posthumous perspective.

Mama behaved toward her mother with a mixture of affection, irony, and reverence, even though Babushka was domineering and often peremptory and did not hesitate to state in a most categorical manner whom my parents should or should not frequent or what dress my mother should wear on a given occasion, not to mention her views on correct toilet training—just as, later on, she did not hesitate to express her firm opinions on what would or would not be a proper profession for me. Correctness in one form or another was a major concern. "Noblesse oblige" was a favorite expression of hers, suggesting that achievement and rank impose obligations. She considered her family more distinguished than the one her daughter comfortably married into, and she reminded me, so that I might view them as models, that among her relatives were respected professionals, several scholars, and even an orchestra conductor. She did so without ostentation, as though high attainments were something to be taken for granted.

It is chiefly to Babushka that I owe my ability to speak Russian, for she set aside time to instruct me. I did not always make language teaching easy for her. I can still see the massive oak tree, in the Rosenthal Park in Leipzig, next to which she stopped, somewhat out of breath, to make me repeat in Russian the supposedly useful adjectives "southeastern" and "northwestern," and I quickly proceeded to exasperate her by concocting incongruous adverbial combinations like "northsoutherly" and "eastwesterly." It is she who found the Russian tutor, a jobless émigré journalist and putative poet, whose airless attic room I visited twice a week at the age of six or seven, staring listlessly at the table ventilator and the decapitated flies that littered papers and notebooks, while he droned on about the intricacies of Russian declensions, conjugations, and inflections of irregular verbs.

I have often pondered that I do not have a "mother tongue," if by that is meant that one's first or true language is the language that was also native to one's mother, and in which she spoke and sang to her infant. Mama's native language was Russian, which I heard, or rather overheard, from early childhood but was not encouraged to speak until some years later. With my nanny Lotte, and then with Fräulein Marianne, who accompanied us to Paris, where she remained for a couple of years, I spoke German. And although my mother, who was fluent in several languages, spoke German to me on occasion, she made a point of addressing me in French as early as our stays in Nice and Montreux, but especially after we settled in Paris. French became my language. It was the language of my playmates, of school, of the street and the soccer field, of my discovery of books and ideas. Other languages—English and Italian—I learned later, and I established very special relations with them. But it is French that defined my way of perceiving the world.

Some time ago, I came across a passage in Marguerite Yourcenar's *Hadrian's Memoirs* in which the Spanish-born Roman emperor, who was learned in Greek and most at home in Hellenic culture, explains that the true place of birth, the real fatherland, is where one awakens to intelligent consciousness of others and of self. I reflected that this may point to the distance between the concrete, blood- and family-rooted mother tongue and the more abstract word "fatherland." The French are fond of the word *"patrie,"* derived from the Latin *"pater,"* for "father." But it is a metaphor that may have less to do with real paternity than with an ideological weaning process. The *"enfants de la patrie"* of the "Marseillaise" are no longer enfolded in the maternal bosom; they no longer have their roots in the soil of a given province. They will even be expected to lose their regional accent.

MAMA INHERITED HER mother's aversion to self-humoring and indolence. One simply could not, must not, let oneself go. One Russian word, "*raspushchinast'*," summed up the absence of self-control and discipline. It was the equivalent of moral anarchy. One had to be vigilant against it during all waking hours. After savoring her cup of hot chocolate and her morning croissant, Mama would have me come to her bedroom on days when there was no school. I was twelve or thirteen, and still in the lower forms, studying fastidiously, at times winning prizes— on one occasion even the coveted *prix d'excellence*. This diligence did not last.

Mama was in her dressing gown, her oval face and loose, dark hair set off against the white pillow. We would go over some fables of La Fontaine that had been assigned. Those were the French poet's short, early fables, still close to their classical source, the Greek fabulist Aesop. I could not begin to guess how elegantly subversive these and especially some of the later fables were of the monarch's authority, what sort of political critique of Louis XIV's regime was embedded in these charming and ironic mini-dramas. All my mother and I derived from La Fontaine's fables were picturesque, amusing story-lessons of animals behaving exactly like human beings, displaying common failings and vices: selfishness, greed, grandiose illusions, cowardice, cruelty, violence, pride, self-importance—like the parasitic fly that imagines its buzzing is what impels the horses to pull the heavy coach up the steep slope. Mama asked questions, then made her own comments about human foibles and people's behavior in general—comments quite different from the formal and linguistic observations provided by our teacher, who was bent on explicating archaic expressions, points of versification, and rules of grammar.

Later, when I began to suffer from year-round spring fever, I began to skip school. Listless, I was dreaming of what lay beyond the classroom walls, beyond the confines of our apartment. I became refractory and inattentive to my teachers, reluctant to make even a minimal effort, especially in geometry and algebra. The result was predictable, as the report that so shocked my parents upon our return from Megève made clear. A year or two later, when I was sixteen, my entire summer vacation would be spoiled because I needed to prepare for the make-up exam in the fall if I wanted to avoid having to repeat the entire year, even in those subjects in which I had done adequately. That was the rule.

This crisis put my mother's disciplinarian virtues to the test. In Deauville, where we were vacationing in 1939, she planned my daily schedule, set a timetable, and engaged a tutor in nearby Blonville who was to coach me specifically in mathematics. Only after I had sat at my desk and prepared for the lessons was I allowed to join friends at the beach and play volleyball. Three times a week I was to pedal a few miles to Blonville to meet my tutor, carrying with me the money to pay him. After a while, finding that I had better things to do, I no longer showed up. When my mother discovered that my tutor had not seen me for over a week, and that I had pocketed his fee (but what else, in fairness, was I to do with it?), she grabbed the nearest object in sight, which happened to be an umbrella, and proceeded to strike me. The umbrella, so useful in Normandy, was damaged in the process, I believe, and so were, for a while at least, my relations with my mother.

In Paris my piano lessons with maestro Lieberman, though they ended less dramatically, also proved to be a disappointment to my mother. I relied on my ear and my memory, did not read the music carefully, and practiced in a slovenly manner the Beethoven sonatina, the relatively easy Chopin waltz, the even easier "Happy Peasant" piece by Schumann. Yet I loved to hear them played for me by my piano teacher during the lesson, and I encouraged him, partly as a delaying tactic, to play for me yet another time the pieces I was supposed to have learned. Mama was outraged, but also amused, I believe, when she heard that I had succeeded in flattering the maestro with the aquiline profile and elongated fingers into playing the Chopin waltz once more for me because I claimed to admire so much the way he played, and to be so moved.

As time went on, my poor performance at the lycée, my wiles, my secretiveness, the friends I frequented (even when they were more responsible than I), my interest in girls, even my passion for tennis, all began seriously to worry my parents. Part of their worry was justified and had to do with the French school system, which was strictly competitive and intellectually elitist in spirit, eliminating the less-qualified along the way. In contrast to young Americans, who are given a second and third chance, and then still another one, French students had to choose their direction in their mid-teens (the choice was between letters or science), and then they had no way, really, of changing their minds. Competitive entrance examinations determined whether or not one was admitted to the prestigious École Normale Supérieure, the École Polytechnique, or similar institutions. Only a certain percentage, established in advance on a national basis, could even expect to pass successfully the all-important *baccalauréat* (or *bac*, as it was commonly called), which marked the completion of the secondary education and was the gateway to a serious career. French democratic principles were rooted in the notion of free and compulsory public schooling, yet the entire educational system, pyramidal, centralized, and state controlled, was essentially geared to training cadres and forming a meritocracy—a distant legacy of the Napoleonic regime.

My parents' worries proved well grounded. My mother—for it was she who carried on the serious discussions with me—kept reminding me that in the modern world, replete with instabilities, it was indispensable to have a *remeslo,* a Russian word that I understood to mean a trade, a craft, a professional occupation, a skill. But it was even better to enter one of the respected liberal professions in which one could become a luminary. It was not enough simply to inherit a father's good name and wealth. My mother did not tire of bringing up the cases of émigré aristocrats who were now taxicab drivers in Paris because they had no real profession and could do nothing else. Did I want to be a *chauffeur de taxi?* Was that my aim in life?

Mama had a competitive spirit. It came out even in her bridge playing. By all reports, she was an aggressive bidder, whatever that meant, and enjoyed taking chances. As a form of relaxation, she also played poker—in fact, any card game. At heart she was something of a gambler, welcoming any opportunity to confront the roulette wheel in various casinos. For her there was nothing frivolous about these activities. Watching her at the bridge table, at home or during tournaments, I was

repeatedly struck by the fixity of her fine features, her air of serene concentration, the speed of her moves. No emotion could be read on her
face, which at other times was so mobile and expressive—in conversation, when she desired my affection, or when she was angry with me.

Mama's sense of discipline extended to matters of health and
hygiene. I was to take care of my body as though it had been given me
in trust. I had no right to neglect it, to abuse it. Any damage to it was
my responsibility. If I bothered a pimple, stayed too long in the sun,
there came the inevitable reproof and the warning that I would do
myself some harm. How could I have avoided feeling a special kind of
guilt, together with the fear of falling ill, of not being ready (for school,
for a departure), or worse, of inflicting on myself some irreversible
damage? The long-lasting effects of this delegated overprotectiveness
escaped me at the time, but my fear of medical tests became indistin-
guishable from my fear of school exams. In either case, I knew that I
could be poorly prepared. The outcome was my doing; I was responsible. Ultimately, I perceived sickness itself as a form of guilt.

When a friend of my mother's told her that she found evidence that
her son and I had been smoking in the toilet, my mother took me to Dr.
Binkin, our family physician, under the pretext of a routine check-up.
Since she herself had to consult him about her gallbladder, it would be
convenient for us to go together. Dr. Binkin lived only a few streets
away. He was stocky and had a childlike, slightly Mongolian face. He
had practiced in St. Petersburg, and later in Berlin, where he had previously attended medical school, and he had acquired a reputation among
émigré circles as a fine diagnostician. I was not to mention him to my
schoolmates, for he did not have a license to practice in France. He
nonetheless had a fully equipped office in his apartment, including an
X-ray machine operated by his wife, who was dressed as a nurse, with
her hair pulled straight back. The comings and goings of his patients
could not possibly have escaped the notice of his concierge, and
concierges notoriously informed the police about the activities of ten-
ants, especially if they were foreigners, *étrangers*—a category of people
deemed suspect by definition. I can only imagine the sizable bribes that
over the years kept the concierge's otherwise communicative tongue
under control.

Dr. Binkin, after examining my mother in another room, came out carrying my chest X-rays and showed me the way to his study. "You smoke. No use denying it." He looked straight at me through his thick lenses. He then proceeded to show me two sets of X-rays, which he held against a lit glass screen. He pointed with his pencil. "Here are those of a nonsmoker, all clean. And here are yours. Dark spots." I was intimidated. But I began to suspect that the entire visit had been staged, that my mother had alerted him and asked him to talk to me, that the gallbladder was just a pretext, and either the X-rays were fake or there were no shadows at all. Mama's good intentions and Dr. Binkin's dubious method might have proven disturbing to a fourteen-year-old boy with less of a disposition to become a hypochondriac. We walked home in silence. I felt humiliated and impressed at the same time. But Mama's stratagem and the Binkin method did work, at least for several years. I did not light another cigarette until the time of the German occupation, when the difficulty of procuring English-taste cigarettes and black-market prices made the pleasure of smoking irresistible.

The care of my skin was also under my mother's close supervision. Every so often, to my keen displeasure, I was obliged to come along to Madame Miletski, her beautician on the Champs-Elysées. There, in a brightly lit room, vulnerably seated as in a dentist's chair, I was subjected to the indignity of hot facial compresses, a cleansing lotion whose acetone smell sickened me, and then a special small metal instrument with a tiny hole in its head by means of which Madame Miletski proceeded insistently to extract whiteheads, blackheads, and other so-called impurities while I stared at the mole on her cheek. I really hated the whole process and even more the spotty redness of my face after it was all over. My mother's visible satisfaction with the result as we walked out of the building only contributed to my embarrassment. I never said a word about these visits, even to my close friends Jacques Blum and Maurice Lécuyer.

There was another indignity, but this one, at least, took place at home. Mama insisted on shampooing my hair. This torment occurred regularly once a week, usually in the evening. (More frequent washings of the hair were considered unsalutary at that time.) There was no escape, no reprieve from the hated ritual; Mama would always remember. She must have derived some deep satisfaction from soaping and rinsing my hair, proclaiming that she was getting all the brilliantine out. Her pleasure was in no way shared by me. I loathed being manipulated, rubbed, flooded by the water that was always too hot at the beginning, feeling the sting of the soap in my eyes. I resented my mother's stern commands not to squirm, to hold my head still over the washbasin while she hosed it energetically, and, finally, not to interfere with her rubbing my hair briskly with the rough towel until it was all dry and my scalp felt raw. To this day I dislike having my hair washed by hands other than my own. When hairdressers, especially in Europe, insist on administering a shampoo before cutting my hair, I try to resist, usually with little success. At times, I have left the shop without a haircut.

Mama's weekly designs on my scalp lasted until the first year of the war—I was by then sixteen—when we had settled in Deauville for the winter. I vividly recall that the cleansing and flushing ceremony had just taken place a few minutes before an air-raid alarm sent us all, wobbling grandmother included, scurrying with our gas masks to the nearby beach, from where, sitting on the sand, we watched in the far distance across the bay the pyrotechnic spectacle of the huge oil tanks near the port of Le Havre being blown up by German bombers on a mild May evening in 1940. That act of war put an end, I believe, to my mother's shampooing tyranny.

In the days before the war, while we were still ensconced in Paris, my mother did not neglect what she considered my intellectual hygiene. On many a Sunday, she announced that I was not to go roller-skating with my friends in the little park of La Muette, that instead she and I were going to the Louvre. On those occasions, we never seem to have gotten beyond the Egyptian rooms, either because we tired on our way to other collections, or perhaps because of a secret devotion of my mother's to Isis and Osiris, or simply because of her fondness for Verdi's opera *Aida*. These supervised ambulations through endless rooms filled with outsized and repetitive statuary made me quite dizzy and probably account for an aversion to Egyptian artifacts that lasted until many years later, when Bettina finally persuaded me to travel to Luxor, Karnak, and Abu Simbel. Mama, who insisted on giving me advance instruction before we reached the Louvre, talked to me—also repetitively—about Memphis, Thebes (which for a long time I failed to distinguish from the Thebes in Greece), the proximity of the Canaeens, the pyramids, the cataracts, and the ubiquitous River Nile.

As we entered the Louvre on those dreaded Sundays, Mama led me, I don't recall in what order, past mummies, representations of riverboats destined to carry the dead to their burial place, stone slabs covered with hieroglyphs. Mama maintained that all spoke of an advanced culture (although I tended to associate advanced culture with radio sets, elevators, and sleek locomotives), that even some commoners and some women were able to decipher those strange-looking engraved characters. The latter accomplishment somehow seemed particularly admirable to her, because in modern, enlightened France she was chafing under various restrictions, she explained; she could not, for instance, without my father's authorization, open a bank account of her own.

Mama's great moment came after we had proceeded past endless quantities of spatulas, alabaster vases, miniature bronze cats, and even a monkey playing a lyre. We entered a vast room crowded with huge figures of sphinxes with human faces and lions' bodies, the ibis-headed god That, goddesses with the heads of various animals, and statues of other gods that went by the fierce names of Hathor, Amon, and Horus. We never saw anything else in the Louvre, finding ourselves quite exhausted by this assemblage of hieratic shapes. Only years later did I overcome the memory of the tedium and of aching feet, when on a leisurely and sensuous trip up the Nile, Bettina and I followed the traces of the journey that had carried Flaubert toward Assuan, past Esna and Edfu, at a time in his life when, in his slow-moving riverboat, he was beginning to dream of Emma Bovary's insatiable yearnings amid her drab life in Normandy. It amused me to think that Flaubert visited Egypt in part to escape from his mother.

THOUGH I RESENTED it when Mama breached my privacy and attempted to structure my activities, I took pride in her appearance and in the admiration of her friends. She never embarrassed me, unlike my father, who, in spite of his repeated admonitions to watch out for bones and not talk while we ate fish or rabbit, would regularly choke on his food, especially in public places. His sneezes and coughs were also attention-getters. What irked me perhaps most in my father was his excessive caution, his lack of impulsiveness, his seeming incapacity to indulge in even a momentary act of impetuousness. "Be reasonable," was his refrain. No madness whatsoever. Mama delicately repressed her sneezes, as though she carried an implosive silencer in her air passages. But she was given to improvised, delightfully unpredictable actions. She often surprised me, particularly in my father's absence, as when, having just exited from the movie theater on the Grands Boulevards after my father's departure for London, she asked me, impromptu, whether I would like to see another movie right then and there. The expression on my face made any answer superfluous. We immediately entered another movie theater, again in the middle of a film. I still remember that it featured Louis Jouvet and the comedian Larquey. But what remains memorable is not their performance, nor the plot—which I have totally forgotten—but the sense of freedom and fun my mother communicated to me.

Her bridge-playing memory never failed to astonish me as I overheard morning telephone conversations from which I gathered that she had total recall of all the hands dealt the previous evening. My mother's ability to concentrate, remember, and plan enabled me to appreciate feats of "blind" chess playing, or the perhaps even greater feat of the blind scholar Pierre Villey, who edited all of Montaigne's essays, which so thrilled me when I discovered them in graduate school.

As a fledgling bridge player, I certainly did not impress my mother, who had recently won the French championship. She watched me once or twice, then decreed that I was *un idiot des cartes*. It is true that I preferred to converse, often forgetting what the trump suit was. Mama and her tournament partners played in complete silence. It was not, however, for the spectacle of her playing that I looked forward to the days when bridge tables were set up in two large, adjoining rooms. The real reason was that Mama would order delectable canapés and petits fours of various colors from Coquelin, the pastry shop on the rue de Passy. I swallowed them whole, several at a time, then took some more to the writing desk in my room, disposing of them at greater leisure as I turned the pages of the latest detective novel with the characteristic yellow cover featuring the emblem of a black mask.

Social events at home were not limited to bridge parties. Every so often my parents received friends for buffet suppers, for which five or six smaller tables were set up for dining, before they were converted for other purposes—gin rummy and poker. But before the games and the gambling began, lanky Zinaïda Sameievna, the wife of a deaf fur merchant, would get up with a shy look, one shoulder thrown back, curtsying in an ungainly fashion, and read in her shrill voice a poem, in Russian or French, written by her especially for the occasion, and then complain in even shriller tones about the intolerable smell of ashes in the ashtrays. And there was humming and singing of Russian folk tunes. On those festive evenings, the typical Russian hors d'oeuvres, *zakuski,* were served with ice-cold vodka, and there was much loud conversation and laughter. I had for some time been pillaging the contents of the vodka bottles, and while I was relishing various herrings, lovely cold pink salmon, and *kulibyaka,* I kept worrying that someone would notice how much weaker the vodka had gotten as a result of my having added some water to make up for the amounts consumed with the help of a friend or two. But no one ever seemed to notice, which made me somewhat skeptical of their connoisseurship as they smacked their lips and grunted with satisfaction. I loved those events, for which my mother always produced a cool, smooth, aromatically seasoned, crunchy fish salad, the recipe for which went back to old places that I would never know, but that I came to associate with the plays of Chekhov.

Occasionally—but this only for family or a few close friends—my mother would treat us to fluffy, golden-hued *blini* that she herself prepared (the recipe called for beer), and for which red caviar, smoked salmon, and inordinate amounts of *smetana,* or sour cream, were obtained from the Russian delicatessen on the nearby rue Nicolo. I have never again had *blini* like that, certainly not in St. Petersburg, where we were recently served, under that name, what looked and tasted more like crêpes, unrecognizably folded and sweetish in taste. In the Paris of the 1920s and 1930s, Russian specialties were still available and had retained their pre-Revolutionary flavor—and this not only in the fancy restaurants like Moskva and Korniloff that were sometimes mentioned at home.

Parts of my parents' social life, when I was asked to join, seemed unremittingly dull to me. On certain Sundays in the spring, but also in early fall, starting when I was twelve or thirteen years old, I was expected to drive out with them to the surrounding countryside—to Bougival by the Seine, to the forest of Fontainebleau, to Montfort l'Amaury, or the valley of Chevreuse—to meet friends of theirs in a garden café or restaurant for interminable lunches followed by hours of just sitting around drowsily until the waiters began setting tables for the evening meal. I was often the only young person. I tried to distract myself by walking to the nearby pond or by reading a few pages of a book I had brought with me (a precaution I still take on all outings). But I, too, had grown drowsy, and it felt as though the slow, lazy hours would never come to an end.

Those drawn-out, sun-speckled afternoons, in sight of a curtain-row of poplars reflected in the river, or under some opulent chestnut tree, afternoons heavy with dreamy boredom now seem graced by a special glow. The well-known song "*Les enfants s'ennuient le dimanche*" (Children are bored on Sundays) sums up the particular sadness that came over me on those dominical excursions, which accounts in part for my continuing aversion to Sundays. Yet the wariness that invaded me is now associated with certain canvases of which I came to be fond. It does not matter that the sequence is out of order, that I had probably not yet seen a Renoir or a Sisley painting, nor heard of Impressionism at that time. What counts is the reality of the shuttle, between past and present, between images and sensations derived from the artists' vision and those provided by what is called "daily life." With the years I have become increasingly unable (and unwilling) to separate the two.

The Russian émigrés enjoyed, or tried to enjoy, the best of French life. They were aware, when the Hitlerian hysteria began to be heard from across the German border, that the French were reluctant to fight another war, that they preferred the *douceur de vivre,* the pleasures of the table and the daily amenities of life, even when the plumbing was deficient. The Russians in exile had their own newspapers (*Poslednie Novosty,* or "Latest News," was the most commonly quoted), their literary and intellectual circles. Many of them had known French since childhood, and some of them, including my father, held degrees from French universities. Their children, the younger ones born in France, felt totally assimilated in French school life, held French citizenship, were expected to do their *service militaire*, and engaged in French professional life—as was the case of my cousin Tovy Millner, who became an outstanding young lung surgeon, by all accounts destined to have a brilliant career.

I was told to look up to Tovy as a model, especially every time my school report came in, casting a gloomy spell. I did not mind, because I admired Tovy's intestinal jokes (some of them, I later discovered, came directly from Rabelais), his taste for garlicky snails and mustard-flavored sautéed kidneys, and in general his rare appetite for living. He died quite suddenly in his late thirties from a stroke it would seem, coming out of his apartment building on rue Monsieur-le-Prince, the very building in which the religious philosopher Pascal had lived and which, long after the writer's death, was classified as a *monument historique*.

DEATH HAD BEEN an early reality, yet I never came to live on familiar terms with it. I resented its intrusion into my childhood, its way of denying what ought to be reliable and repeatable. Perhaps what I resented above all was my mother's inconsolable grief after Nora died. That grief itself became a steady presence. Mama never got over it, not even after twice moving to other countries and putting more than four thousand miles between her new existence and Nora's tomb. I have a picture of that tomb carrying the dates 1925–1930. It was taken shortly before the Nazis desecrated the cemetery. Unlike the tombless death of anonymous millions who soon after went up in smoke, Nora's is at least recorded on that faded and creased print of a vanished tomb.

I resented my mother's suffering, to which I seemed to have no access. I have since discovered that, alas, the suffering of others excludes oneself. Despite the reassuring etymology of the words "compassion" and "sympathy," both of which declare shared suffering, can we really ever feel someone else's pain, even a simple toothache?

Perhaps we can, through the intercession of images and metaphors, in art. My mother's occasionally pensive and sorrowful face remained impenetrable. Her large, dark eyes then signaled that inward glance—not for long, but I could tell. In repose, her otherwise smooth face was lined by a bitter crease or two around the mouth. She suffered from spasms of the esophagus that must have had a nervous origin. I sensed, without having to reason it out, what fears impelled her to overprotect me. The slightest indisposition, the passing complaint of a numbness or tingle in my fingers upon awakening sent her and my father into a panic. Instantly, I was taken to our doctor for a check-up and consultation. And it was again impressed on me that my body was precious, and that I was to be its responsible guardian. I chafed under this responsibility, which I translated into a permanent guilt.

Mama displayed several faces. There was the cheerful, outgoing being, much sought after, surrounded by friends. She valued warmth and affection and the presence of joyful company. She knew many ways of giving pleasure. Her quick wit and unassuming elegance of bearing were pleasing—even though my father's family, critical of anyone who did not resemble them, found her a little "too proud." But then they could not imagine anyone worthy different from themselves, anyone who did not share their views or did not live according to the norms of their clan. (Simon Millner, who married into their family, and who spent much of his time in luxury hotels, where he insisted on being addressed as "Dr. Millner," was according to them just a bluffer with a distinguished-looking mustache. When it turned out that he had famous friends and was president of a learned society devoted to the seventeenth-century Dutch philosopher Spinoza, that only confirmed their negative view.) My father, up to a point, took after them. He tended to be skeptical, even misanthropic. After my mother died, he shied away from old friends, living an increasingly lonely existence.

Mama's other face seemed to disclaim her zest for company and good cheer. It spoke of the gravity of life, which she was perhaps afraid to love too much. Aware of the deceptiveness of beauty, the fleetingness and evanescence of all things, she appears to me in retrospect not unlike Mrs. Ramsay in Virginia Woolf's *To the Lighthouse*, who brandished a metaphorical sword at her antagonist, life.

My sense of remorse, as I think of my mother, is altogether different from the guilt I felt toward my father. It is more like a betrayal, for I failed to respond adequately to her affection. The caressing hand on my head (perhaps there lingered the memory of too many shampoos) caused me to bristle. I withdrew. Mama called me a *cachottier*, a secretive fellow. I would conceal my activities, even the books I was reading. I was reluctant to tell her about my fallings in and out of love, even more reluctant to have her meet any of the girls I was going out with. Years later, I sometimes failed to inform her of public lectures I was to give for fear that she might show up.

My guilt is reflected in a recent dream that I recorded upon awakening. I am called to the phone in a clubhouse cabin. A voice tells me that Mama died in the hospital. I am disconsolate, but resigned. Her son, I understand from her brothers (my uncles), gave her grief, but she had learned to accept it. I felt great pangs for not having called her from abroad for a long, long time. I had, in fact, forgotten about her. The truth, as I woke up from my dream, was only partially comforting. I realized that Mama had been dead since 1959—more than forty years.

It has taken all this time to begin to guess what worries attended bringing up a boy in the prewar years. It was difficult enough to deal with the mischief and vexations of the rebellious *âge ingrat*, the awkward adolescent years; to suspect that one's son will forever be taken up with frivolities, has no real ambition (perhaps no real gifts), that he is missing out on all the opportunities that call for work and a sense of direction. Then came worse, after the invasion of France: the threat of labor camps, the even greater threat of deportation. And later, once we had reached our haven over which loomed, as an emblem of hope and fortitude, the optimistic smile of a president with a cigarette holder, my mother had to accept my departure for the army and for what she knew was a "just war." After the invasion of Normandy, her worst fears turned into reality: the horror of a newsreel of prisoners taken in the Ardennes, among whom I sit dejected, with my tilted helmet half covering one eye. The newsreel was shown over and over again in New York. The helmet hiding part of the face may explain the confusion. Yet my cousin Sascha and others who were consulted (including an ex-FBI expert who compared the newsreel print with available photographs of me) all concurred: it was me. When I was later shown the picture, I myself was fooled. How can I ever grasp my parents' distress at seeing that newsreel? I make a vain effort, retrospectively, to experience it with them, day by day, week by week, until they finally receive a letter from me. I was safe—somewhere, for we were not allowed to tell where. The prisoner in the newsreel had been someone else.

After settling in New York in 1941, Vera Salomonovna still had a restricted number of close friends, those who had also succeeded in escaping from France and who had settled, for the most part, on the Upper West Side, between Riverside Drive and Central Park West. Life had resumed, on a modest scale. But Mama's gambling instincts, this time on the stock market, bore disastrous results. And an ill-starred investment in a resort hotel, in partnership with an unsavory character who looked and behaved as though he had stepped straight out of a novel by Dostoevsky and who took perverse delight in insulting the hotel guests, ended in failure. The hotel had to be sold, at a great loss. To help out my father, who was ailing and had never really adjusted to American business mores, Mama for a while took a job as a saleswoman in a fashionable department store on Fifth Avenue. The long hours on her feet, selling ties and gloves, did not improve her varicose veins. This was not the first time she had shown courage in adversity, and in the circle of her friends, used to political and economic vicissitudes, she suffered no loss of social standing.

One day I realized to my surprise that she was well over sixty. I also learned that the gallbladder problems had not been just a pretext for having Dr. Binkin lecture me about my teenage smoking. Her esophageal spasms required regular visits to Philadelphia for uncomfortable dilating sessions. Then her ulcers began to bleed. She was hospitalized, administered coagulants, and developed phlebitis. A blood clot began its occult work. She died from a pulmonary embolism, in the hospital, at night, alone, not heard by the nurse she may have called in vain.

In Paris, my parents had a recording of a melodramatic Russian ballad sung by one Viktor Henkin. I remember the name because the ballad made such an impression on me. It is about a fellow in love with an evil woman who demands that he kill his mother and feed her heart to the swine. I learned the song and still recall most of the words. What moved me so was that the mother's heart, as the son was carrying it to the pigsty and stumbled, spoke out softly, asking with great concern whether he had hurt himself: *Moy malchik moy* (Oh, son of mine). The song was insufferably sentimental, but it struck a chord.

There was also a parable, or tale, that perturbed me. It probably carried some political undertones, but what agitated me, upon hearing it, was its almost unbearable pathos. A tyrant informs a mother that her son has been condemned to death, but that he could be pardoned if she succeeds in mowing a large field all by herself before sunset. The feat seems beyond the capabilities of even a vigorous young peasant. Yet the mother in the tale accomplishes the impossible—only to collapse and die when she reaches the end of the field. I shed tears every time I heard the story of a mother's sacrifice beyond the limits of human endurance.

When I reached the funeral parlor on Amsterdam Avenue, I was taken straight to the room where Mama lay, her face exposed. (By a frivolous coincidence, I had just acquired a black fedora, which I thought particularly smart and planned to display at the upcoming professional meeting in Chicago.) There Mama lay, in marblelike immobility in her casket, and I thought of the tombs and sarcophagi we had seen on our Sunday visits to the Louvre. I broke down, sobbing wildly. I did not know I had it in me. Where did those sobs that shook me come from? I cannot even remember speaking to my father, who sat all crumpled in a corner armchair, being consoled. All I remember distinctly are the words spoken by my meek Aunt Helena, whose mouth was more twisted than ever, as she hugged me. (*"Eto syudba"*—that's fate.) It was with her that I had stayed years earlier during the final days of my sister's illness, and she had endlessly, patiently, played with the little boy I was then a silly card game called War and Peace to keep me occupied. And as I stood in the funeral parlor on Amsterdam Avenue, I remembered sobbing together with Mama in her bed as she told me about Nora's death. And then I also remembered her advice never to leave unspoken the tender words one wanted to say to a dear one. And I knew how right she was. Only now it was indeed too late.

Chapter 4

INITIATIONS

The Lycée Janson and Marienbad

he massive façade of the Lycée Janson de Sailly follows the
curve of the rue de la Pompe. Gloomily, it dominates the
street, stretching out for an entire block. On a map, the school
appears even larger, covering an impressive surface all the way from the
tree-lined avenue Henri Martin, with its luxury apartment buildings, to
the rue de Longchamp, which runs straight to the Bois de Boulogne.
The austere official look of the lycée relates it to the bureaucratic world
of French government buildings. This school architecture hardly con-
veys the joy of studies. Nor does it suggest that childhood and adolescence are meant to be a sunny preparation for the delights of life. The
pursuit of happiness is an alien concept here.

By contrast, the *mairie* (town hall) of the 16th arrondissement, standing on the other side of the broad avenue Henri Martin, seemed positively cheerful. In late spring, when the dreaded exams created a yearning
for the elsewhere, the white blossoms falling from the lush chestnut trees
brought the illusion of snow flakes, and for a brief moment played havoc
with the seasons. Little has changed since the years before the war, except
that part of the avenue Henri Martin has been renamed for Georges Mandel, the Popular Front cabinet minister who was murdered by the Vichy
militia. Within a brief walking distance from the lycée stood the towering
Hispano-Moresque Palais du Trocadéro, which in the mid-1930s gave
way to the ultramodern and very "French" Palais de Chaillot in anticipation of the triumphal year 1937, when Paris was to host the Exposition
Internationale. The triumph was short-lived. Only three years later, in
the spring of 1940, shortly after Paris fell to the Germans, Hitler posed

for a memorable picture on the esplanade of the Palais de Chaillot, in full view of the Seine and the Eiffel Tower.

When I returned to Paris in my U.S. army jeep during the heady days of the liberation, in the summer of 1944, I immediately paid a visit to our apartment building near the rue de Passy and then to my old school, only a few minutes away by car. All the distances seemed so close now that I was sitting behind a wheel and there were hardly any other vehicles about. I realized that the *métro* station at the corner of the rue de la Pompe was right next to the lycée, much closer than I remembered, in fact just a few steps from the more intimate entrance of the Petit Lycée, which had in front of it an almost coquettish little garden that I had never noticed before.

This brought me even further back in time, to my ninth or tenth year, when I entered the Petit Lycée. Less severe and oppressive than the school for older boys, it was attached to the unsmiling Lycée Janson de Sailly. We had recently settled in Paris. Fearful that I had some catching up to do, that I might not immediately feel comfortable in the Parisian school ambiance, perhaps aware of French schoolboys' verbal deftness even in exchanging insults, my mother decided that I was in need of some private tutoring to prepare me for battle.

I do not know how she discovered Monsieur Magny, a retired teacher who lived alone in two small attic rooms of the Petit Lycée. She resolutely took me up the flights to his airless abode. Monsieur Magny, a figure all in black, shuffled across the narrow space in his slippers, with a shawl wrapped around his shoulders, and showed my mother to an unadorned chair with a stiff back. Either his quarters were poorly heated, or else he was extra-sensitive to cold, for in the months that followed I never saw him without his dark shawl covering his stooped shoulders, and several layers of ill-fitting clothes. He wore a black, shiny skull-cap. On his chair, I noticed a strange-looking, doughnut-shaped leather cushion, a so-called *rond-de-cuir*, whose purpose is to protect desk-job people against the discomforts of hemorrhoids.

Monsieur Magny received us kindly. He spoke respectfully to my mother, whose broad-rimmed hat, touched by a pale ray of sunlight coming through the high window, lent a contrasting note to the stark surroundings. In retrospect, I like to think that Monsieur Magny was an old-fashioned socialist, perhaps the son of an *instituteur*, a village schoolteacher. With a benign nod in my direction, he kept saying to my mother that I was evidently a "*bon sujet*," meaning, I suppose, that I was a promising student. I did not exactly think of myself as a subject, good or bad. In time, I became aware that these were common expressions in pedagogical and even academic phraseology: a "*bon sujet*" was a studious, respectful pupil; a "*mauvais sujet*," one who was habitually guilty of bad conduct or worse; a "*brillant sujet*" or "*sujet d'élite*," an outstanding, even exceptional one. There was something patronizing about being appraised in front of one's mother as a "*sujet*." But how much better than what was to follow in the regular lycée, where irony and sarcasm were most often the tone of our teachers. And how much less threatening than the massive German teachers from my elementary school days in Leipzig: Herr Oberlehrer Prager, or Herr Lehrer Brenner with his green huntsman jacket, who one day punished me (I was all of six years old) because I had dared walk in the circle of girls in the schoolyard during the break. I tried to hide behind the broad back of a classmate when he came to look for me—but to no avail. I learned then and there to recognize German efficiency in meting out punishment.

Gentle Monsieur Magny never had a harsh word for me. To be sure, I was a private pupil and a source of income. Patiently, he dictated paragraphs from Hugo's *Les Misérables*, which I had to write down as he spoke, and initiated me into the intricacies of the subjunctive and the pluperfect. We went over the basics of French geography. I had to outline the frontiers of France, learn the names of the rivers and draw their courses, recite the names of mountain ranges and of the country's ten largest cities in order of importance. We also went over elementary textbooks with pictures of flora and fauna, as well as classifications of minerals, in anticipation of the regular classwork I was to begin, and in particular the oddly named *leçon de choses* (object lesson) designed to familiarize nine-or ten-year-old children with technical devices and working tools, as well as with natural products and the rudiments of the physical sciences.

At the Petit Lycée, which I entered a few months later, more dictations lay in wait for me, involving the spelling of tricky words. And there was something new: lessons in drawing, for which I displayed an

incredible lack of ability. I tried my best to measure relations and proportions visually by holding up my pencil, vertically and horizontally,
using my thumb to gauge distances while squinting with my left eye. It
was useless. I was clearly even less gifted in the graphic arts than I was
to prove later in the demands of bridge. But I did do more than honor-
ably in penmanship lessons, and in general enjoyed holding and manip-
ulating writing instruments. I still remember discovering the physical
satisfaction of pressing on the pen to fatten portions of the letters on the
downward stroke. I loved the scratchy sound of the nib against the
finely cross-ruled paper in our school notebooks.

At home, in my father's study, furnished with massive leather arm-
chairs, I was fascinated with the inkwells, the fountain pens of diverse
shapes and colors, the dull marble balls in the morocco leather container
for planting pencils and other writing tools, the multicolored pads of
paper, the rocker blotter. I tried out various pens, under my father's
supervision, and sometimes without. It has often occurred to me that
these early sensuous experiences associated with pen and paper are the
real reason I like to sit at my desk and scribble away, eager to *"empir le
carte,"* to fill paper, as the poet Ariosto put it. So far, I have resisted
using a word processor. When I enter a stationery store, I still feel a
child's delight in surveying the articles on display. But perhaps my real
delight is in the child I was, at whom I sometimes look lovingly as
though he were the grandchild I do not have.

THE LYCÉE ITSELF, which I began to attend a year or so later, left
less cheerful memories than my lessons with Monsieur Magny and the
protected world of the Petit Lycée. I continue to see the interminable
façade of Janson de Sailly through the drizzle of dreary winter days.
Except for Sundays and Thursdays, when we were "free," every other
day seemed to be the same. Seven subjects year in year out, thirty hours
of classroom routine every week—not to mention the endless homework in the late afternoons and again after dinner, the Latin compositions, the days of cramming before the various exams during and at the
end of each semester.

There were compensations. The discovery of loneliness in the midst of alternately boisterous and sullen fellow students, each one locked up in himself, led to unexpected friendships that served as a shield against cruelty or downright persecution. There was the excitement of shared dreams and of precious complicities in the face of the Olympian arbitrariness of our teachers. Sadness swelled like nausea at the sight and smell of the long school corridors. But there were also the irrepressible giggles, the *fou rire,* that greeted the deliberately silly answer or rebellious gesture of a fellow student whose boldness reaffirmed our common dignity. There was a prize for such boldness and for such laughter: the *retenue,* the punishment of having to return to school on a free Thursday to sit and work for hours in the study hall under the supervision of an ill-tempered proctor.

On the way to the lycée, half awake as I hurried in the gloomy morning hours with my heavy satchel, I followed the same streets, crossed at the same corners. I had long ago ceased noticing the familiar landmarks. Faintly aware of the smells coming from the bakery, I briefly thought of the *pain au chocolat* I would purchase after school, on my way home. Deep inside my pocket, I fondled the bag filled with clay and glass marbles that I would later throw into action on the moist, uneven pavement in the schoolyard. Still later, after school was out, there would be much noisy confusion, much kicking, running, tripping, horseplay, twisting of arms; many wild screams, snatchings of satchels and caps, and scrapings of elbows and knees on the concrete pavement.

We did not really know our teachers; we never got close to them. They addressed us by our last names and seemed to live in another sphere. Did they have families, private lives? Did they have hobbies? Did they go to the movies, and did they know about jazz and about Fred Astaire? Perhaps we did not even ask ourselves these questions. The teacher simply taught, reprimanded, punished, praised (rarely), and filled the margins of our compositions with corrections in red ink, aggressive exclamation points, and disparaging adjectives such as "inept" and "nonsensical." *Le prof,* as we called him, was an abstract though threatening presence immanently installed on a podium from which he rarely descended. He was often preceded at the beginning of the school year by a legend of ferociousness. But even the less mean-spirited among our teachers (perhaps they were secretly afraid of the unruly "subjects" they felt powerless to tame), seemed to us rather unreal.

Reality, real life, was elsewhere, outside their reach. It took place in the thick of the students' turmoil and preoccupations. This was a world with its own demands and rigors, filled with daily clashes, invasive pesterings, and cruelty that pride prevented us from even mentioning at home. Victims and tormentors alike were involved in the persecution of the weak by the strong, of the isolated and ostracized by the many, until constantly shifting defensive alliances re-established a fragile political equilibrium. Scholarly success at times irritated the group, unleashing hostility. The star pupil, the *fort en thème*, who excelled in translating from and into Latin, had to be strong in other ways too, or else have good legs!

It was not always easy to run or slip away after class when one expected to be waylaid, and woe to him who got caught: exquisite torments lay in store for him. Occasionally a passerby, most often some lady trotting along, intervened by admonishing the tormentors who were ganging up on their victim. It was pointless. The group dispersed for a while, laughing, running, kicking, but at the next corner, beside a newspaper kiosk or in front of the *métro* entrance, the same scene was brazenly re-enacted, only this time no one intervened.

Such persecution did not break one's spirit, however. Persecution, unless radically dehumanizing, rarely does. If anything, it stiffens one's will. And it must be admitted that our violence remained mostly civilized, quite tame, even playful when measured by today's school mores. The damages never amounted to much more than bleeding kneecaps and ears smarting from having been twisted, pulled, and vigorously rubbed.

None of this prevented us from discovering the thrill of friendships, of mutual confidences, of shared daydreams. Some of us, during class, exchanged surreptitious notes making fun of the teacher or of other students. At times, we addressed and received reproaches out of simple irritation or perhaps jealousy. Affection, if that is what we felt, was not expressed—at least not openly. But we did relish composing epigrammatic couplets of the vulgar, punning variety and quoting well-known scatological verse. One song, reputed to have been invented by students in the medical school, was a particular favorite. It was about a pubic louse on a motorcycle, sliding in an anatomic curve and getting bogged down in excrement:

> *Un morpion motocycliste,*
> *Prenant mon cul pour une piste . . .*

This monotone singsong had for generations filtered down from the Faculté de Médecine to the classes of the lycée. It delighted us, giving us the illusion of a precocious promotion to adulthood as we repeated it ad nauseam, in various keys, and often at the top of our lungs.

Some of us shared better than epigrammatic and obscene verse. We discovered and plagiarized the sentimental, vaguely erotic poetry of Musset, some of whose works had school credentials and were taught. Baudelaire, on the other hand, had not entered the school canon. He was considered "decadent," and when we were fourteen or fifteen did not yet loom on our horizon. Later, some more adventurous teachers on their own recommended we read *Les fleurs du mal* (The flowers of evil)—a haunting discovery that made us look down on the mildly ironic and self-indulgent sentimentality of Musset.

We did not feel hostile toward all our teachers, nor did they all treat us with superior indifference. Some we admired, and they did leave their mark. I still remember a fairly young, balding, gaunt teacher by the name of Huguet, probably with a recent degree, who in French class recited to us Pierre de Ronsard's famous carpe diem sonnet—"*Quand vous serez bien vieille, au soir, à la chandelle . . .* "—in which the Renaissance poet warns the woman he loves that she should requite his love here and now, for when she is old and bent over it will be too late. Monsieur Huguet descended from the podium and walked up and down the aisle past forty or so students, his forefinger up in the air scanning the verse. He was visibly inspired by the poem, or by the act of reading it to us. This perhaps was the first example I had of the fervor of teaching, of the thrill when the current passes, directly or indirectly, from page to mind. He mouthed the words caressingly. He did not have to comment or explicate; his way of reciting gave the poem meaning. The rhythm and the intonation were the commentary. I believe that on that day, when Ronsard's sonnet was revealed to me, I understood for the first time what it means to "interpret."

Every fall, when classes began, we awaited our new teachers with some trepidation, ready to test the reputation that preceded them. Some of us feared being disillusioned. There was a special excitement in expecting a teacher whom previous classes had admired. Some of our teachers—this I discovered much later—were respected scholars, even though they taught at the lycée level rather than at the university. In those years, many stimulating, productive scholars were obliged to teach at the secondary level, and in some cases preferred to do so.

But next to the occasional *prof* who came shrouded in a myth of classroom glory, there were the others who knew full well that from year to year their nicknames (usually referring to some anatomical function) and stories of past ridicule clung to them remorselessly. To be known as "*Pète-sec*" (dry fart) or "*Serre-les-fesses*" (tight ass) hardly promoted respect. These alone were open invitations to mutiny and classroom chaos. Over the years, these persecuted types had developed mannerisms and tics that only added to our fun. Every beginning teacher must have felt anguish before facing his first class: would he be *chahuté,* persecuted by class uproars, rowdiness, disruptive noises, disorderly conduct? Would the hour go by in an untroubled manner, or would it be interrupted by paper airplanes, stinkbombs, or the choral humming that could drown out his own voice?

Every so often, after exam periods, the *censeur,* or dean of studies, would suddenly appear, flinging the door open, accompanied by an acolyte carrying a large notebook with a dark cover, and call out our names in order of ranking by our grades. Sometimes, for variety's sake or as a refinement of cruelty, the *censeur* would begin at the bottom of the list: Delvaux, 42nd; Masselli, 41st; Joël, 40th, and so on, creating suspense in either direction, downward or upward, according to whim.

Occasionally we had the visit of an *inspecteur-général* with the red rosette of the Légion d'Honneur in his buttonhole. This was an hour feared by all. We did not quite understand that *monsieur l'inspecteur's* report might affect matters of promotion or transfer for our teacher. But we did know that some of our teachers rehearsed us for the event.

And for once, a bond, not of sympathy but of common awe of official-dom, linked us to the man on the podium who would later take out on us any failings noticed during the inspector's visit.

Classroom *chahut* (the word comes from the hooting cry of the owl, associated with a wild, indecent dance) ranged from clatter and general tumult to more insidious forms of provocation and insubordination. To exasperate our teachers, driving them to the red heat of anger, was a rel-ished pastime. The thick, red neck of Monsieur Parent, our math teacher, would swell and turn a paroxysmal purple as we hurled paper arrows at him while he was writing on the blackboard with his back to the class. Our skill with these paper projectiles propelled by rubber bands was impressive. We rarely missed the mark.

Some teachers, it is true, never lost their composure, and they kept the upper hand. Perhaps it was the quality of their voices or their com-mand of colorful language. Monsieur Pontoux, our diminutive physics teacher, regularly singled out three of us (Masselli and Blum were inevitably my partners), identifying us to the snickering class as "*fumistes*" and "*flibustiers*" (jokers, pirates, rogues), and exiled us to the top row of the small amphitheater to "dominate the situation" from a distance, as he put it—in fact, I suspect, to neutralize us and prevent us from disrupting the class. We admired his verbal agility and his noncha-lant way of disposing of us with a twinkle in his eye, as though he were a secret accomplice or felt nostalgia for his own past mischief in school. The malicious twinkle did not, however, make us any more attentive to his physics demonstrations, and whenever we had failed to prepare our homework, we simply skipped his class instead of disrupting it. Instead, we went about exploring parts of Paris, especially during that long-her-alded year of the Exposition Internationale, when so much was going on near the Seine and the Eiffel Tower.

My personal nemesis at school was a teacher named Rat. For two con-secutive years, it was my fate to have Maurice Rat for both my Latin and my French classes. I still hear his piping, flutelike voice and suave into-nations as he scrutinized the class list, lifting the page close to his myopic eyes. He pretended to search for a name. "Let's see, let's see . . . ," but unfailingly he saw only one name, and it was always mine. Perhaps he wanted to confirm once again what he justly suspected: that I was again poorly prepared, that I would be guilty of barbaric solecisms and worse, that I would make horrendous mistakes translating aloud from the elementary *De Viris Illustribus,* from Caesar's *Gallic Wars,* and later from Tacitus's *Annals,* or that I would misconstrue rather obvious turns in Racine's biblical tragedy *Athalie.* Monsieur Rat visibly enjoyed having me make a fool of myself. For a while I chose to believe that I was being persecuted because I had failed to pay dues to the lending library he had organized, or because I did not enroll in his so-called *petit cours* of supplementary (also paying) remedial lessons. But I was clearly in bad faith and, even then, felt a little ashamed of my suspicion. Years later, I discovered that Maurice Rat was the editor of Montaigne's *Essais* in the well-known Garnier edition, that he was a rather prolific literary historian and biographer who had also penned some lighter works about famous seventeenth- and eighteenth-century women and their lovers, about *héroïnes d'amour* and libertine ladies of bygone days. I eventually read some of these with surprise and amusement, remembering the old days at the Lycée Janson de Sailly. With time, I also recognized that the ire and irony he aimed at me were not undeserved.

IN ALL FAIRNESS, even when I felt harassed by my teachers and sorry for myself, I never detected the slightest indication of xenophobia or anti-Semitism on their part. I do not recall a single instance of a disparaging comment or even a mere innuendo that might have betrayed a bias of this sort. But then, by the mid-1930s, there were too many solidly established, well-to-do Jews living in the conservative 16th arrondissement for anyone to be singled out. Some had settled there long ago; others more recently, as a result of persecution in Nazi Germany. Many were Russian émigrés who, after the Bolsheviks took over, had first moved to Germany, most of them to Berlin, and then to Paris, their favorite city. These Russian Jews, who twice before had escaped in the nick of time, were perhaps the quickest to read the signs of another impending upheaval as Hitler's power expanded across Europe.

The *16ème arrondissment,* which comprises Passy and Auteuil, was too cosmopolitan and bourgeois for any anti-Semitism to be manifested openly or crudely. That does not mean it did not exist. The denunciations that later occurred during the Occupation, and the plundering of abandoned apartments, are proof that the privileged arrondissement was not immune to some of the worst sins of that grim period. The seeds were surely there well before the arrival of the German troops. But anti-Semitism took on a special hue in the region between the Bois de Boulogne and the place du Trocadéro. It was unspoken, veiled, snobbish rather than racist, and altogether different from the bigoted, narrow-minded, religious hostility toward Jews, or the obtuse and coarse brand of anti-Semitism prevalent among the working class.

Anti-Jewish sentiment was more a matter of latent animosity than of outright discrimination. It did not affect our daily activities, our studies, or prospects for future careers. Nor did it affect our flirtations and our friendships with non-Jewish girls and boys. If I was aware of it at all, it was largely because my parents kept warning me that it existed, that I should not be fooled by appearances and overtly friendly behavior. Such talk annoyed me. In the Racing Club de France, my tennis club in the Bois de Boulogne, close by the artificial lake, Jews and anti-Semites played together and exchanged jokes about inflammatory political issues that everyone chose to take lightly.

We were of course aware of the ultrarightist Croix-de-Feu movement and of Charles Maurras's royalist and overtly anti-Semitic Action Française. His *camelots du roi* (the king's peddlers), largely recruited from among the student population, distributed the paper that went by the name of *Action Française,* as well as provocative leaflets, often coming to blows with leftist students. All this was part of the political scene between the wars. And we had heard, of course, about the Dreyfus case, from the end of the preceding century. But we had also been told—and my parents repeatedly made the point—that large numbers of decent Frenchmen, not only Émile Zola and a few intellectuals, had risen to defend the cause of justice at the time of the Dreyfus affair, and that they had prevailed. My father made the additional point that there could not even have been a Jewish officer like Alfred Dreyfus in the German or the Russian armies, that a military career, not to mention a career in the intelligence service of the army, was altogether unthinkable for a Jew in those countries. Whereas in the country of Voltaire,

Victor Hugo, and Jean Jaurès . . . And did not the French Revolution stand for the emancipation of the Jews, the breaking down of all ghetto walls—not only in France, but in every country that was touched by the spirit of the French Revolution, and later by the presence of Napoleon's army? To be sure, France was xenophobic; that was a given. But if you were French, or about to become French, then Jewish or not, did you not have all the opportunities? Were not all careers open? Another good reason for going back to my homework. Thus spake my father.

There was much in the history of the nineteenth century to justify such rosy views. I later found out that, in his private notes, the aristo-cratic writer Alfred de Vigny, a one-time friend of Hugo and himself a stellar light in the Romantic movement, referred admiringly to the role of Jews in contemporary French society. He observed that their "supe-rior gifts" allowed them to win school prizes in disproportionate num-bers, to rise to the top in all fields, particularly in the arts, the liberal professions, and the world of the university. What struck me was the apparent lack of resentment or animosity in Vigny's remarks. True, the French way of almost excessively admiring the so-called intelligence of the Jews could be seen as another manifestation of racism. One way or another, there was no escape.

Mutterings of "sale juif" could now and then be overheard. The influx of refugees from Central and Eastern Europe did not help. The French Jews themselves, feeling uneasy, resented the presence of these foreign types—these métèques, as they were disparagingly called—and not so secretly wished they would go back to where they came from. "Métèque" was indeed a frequently used term in the 1930s. Derived from a Greek word that meant nothing worse than a resident foreigner, it came to des-ignate in modern France unwelcome, "greasy" aliens, and even the French Jews adopted it, looking down on their co-religionists with a German, Russian, Polish, or, worst of all, Yiddish accent. In that, they were not very different from their counterparts, the German Jews, many of whom were proud of their Great War decorations and felt nothing but contempt for those they called Ostjuden, the eastern Jews who had moved to Germany after the war and whom they liked to blame for the growing anti-Semitism in the years leading up to the Nazi regime.

The mood in France was a strange mixture of irony, political anger, and carefree escapism. Charles Trenet and Maurice Chevalier were both singing "*Y'a d'la joie,*" a song of joy greeting swallows, pretty girls, and the thrill of falling in love; Fernandel was clowning his way from film to film; and Jean Gabin was playing tough guys with a tender heart. The most telling hit song, recorded by Ray Ventura's band and heard everywhere, was "*Tout va très bien, Madame la marquise,*" characteristically insisting in its refrain that all was well, while in reality, as the other words of the song made vividly clear, everything was going from bad to worse. Behind this Maginot line of deceptive optimism, the stage was set for defeatism in the late 1930s, defeat in 1940, and then Maréchal Pétain's Vichy regime, which in all haste dismantled French parliamentary and democratic institutions, cultivating an atmosphere of collective mea culpa about the sin of democracy. The militant parties on the right had for some time denounced the presence and excessive influence of Jews and free-thinkers as a moral poison in French society. In this broader effort to discredit democracy, Jews were associated with the long-standing odium for the consequences of the French Revolution. For the political right, they became the living symbol of everything that was not truly French, if by "French" was meant the almost mystical cult of soil and ancestors rather than belief in abstract principles of justice, equality, and social programs. But in the years immediately preceding the disaster of 1940, even those aware of the drift of events remained largely detached and passive, although the tragedy of the Spanish Civil War, the annexation of Austria, the betrayal of Czechoslovakia and annexation of the Sudetenland, and finally the crisis over the Danzig corridor in Poland should have given clear warning. "*Mourir pour Dantzig?*" became the negative, defeatist slogan. Why die for Danzig? No wonder we teenagers did not take things any more seriously.

Even if I search my memories of these prewar years in France, I recall only one rather trivial circumstance when an anti-Semitic insult was hurled directly at me. It was also the occasion of my first and only fistfight. One morning in the school corridor, as we lined up to file into class, boisterously shoving and pushing, I was violently pushed back by a tall fellow named Roussot, who then uttered audibly, as though hissing at me, the two oft-coupled words: "*sale juif.*" Roussot was lanky, lymphatic, and pale-faced, with watery eyes and a large, ugly mouth that became contorted and even uglier as he blurted out the formulaic affront, "dirty Jew." It was immediately decreed by all those who over-heard it that the insult required a duel that very day after school, and that the entire class was to be present, with the exception of the blind welfare student, always dressed in black, who had been raised in a Catholic orphanage where he was still living and where he had appar-ently not been taught to wash, for his feet smelled almost worse than the stinkbombs we occasionally set off during the class hour.

That entire day I could think of nothing else during class. The word "duel" brought to mind the heroic couplets of Corneille's play *Le Cid*, all about honor and courage. In truth, I did not feel very heroic, and not at all like a medieval Spanish knight in a seventeenth-century French tragedy. I also kept thinking of the exploits of D'Artagnan and his mus-keteer friends. But Alexandre Dumas's sword-playing heroes were of little assistance to me. More apt was the recent boxing practice with my cousin Sascha and Jacques Calse in the brightly lit garage of Calse's apartment house, where we tried out the boxing gloves he had received as a birthday present. But the encounter with Roussot was to be with bare fists. I was paying even less attention than usual to the teacher's words and to his demonstrations on the blackboard. I was not even really upset by *"sale juif."* It all came down to a sense of duty, an oblig-ation to the group and to the rules of the game. By agreeing to fight, I faced only one opponent. If I lost heart, all forty classmates would turn against me.

During the last class that afternoon, I kept staring at the long neck of Roussot, who was seated two rows in front of me. When school was out, I was swept along to the open space behind the school. I felt numb, aware of neither courage nor fear, driven forward by a collective move-ment. It was a sensation I was to experience again, a few years later, in Normandy and during the Battle of the Bulge, when fear gripped me and everything I did felt as though I was re-enacting, without willing it, a motion that had been well rehearsed. We were surrounded by a circle of classmates. Roussot stood there with his watery eyes, his hanging lip, his pallid face. Did I take off my jacket? All I recall is that I swung wildly, aiming at his face, and missed. Did I swing again, or did he throw himself against my moving arm and fist? I cannot account for exactly what happened. But suddenly he was standing there with a surprised look and a bleeding lip. There were screams that it was over, that I had won. Won? I did not know quite how, nor was I convinced. A proctor arrived. Our names were taken, questions asked. Students spoke up: "He called him '*sale juif.*'" The proctor was unimpressed. Roussot, his cut lip still bleeding, his eyes more watery than ever, stood dejected—and I somehow felt sorry for him.

The immediate result of the encounter was that we were both punished with a *retenue* and spent long hours alone together in the dreary study hall on the following Thursday, when everyone else was free. I have often wondered what happened to Roussot four or five years later, during the German Occupation, when Jews were rounded up and deported to camps. Did he perhaps save Jewish children? Did he, remembering that afternoon's humiliation, find special satisfaction in denouncing Jews who had gone into hiding? Did he join the sadistic Vichy militia? Most likely, he remained a passive bystander who saw nothing wrong with forcing Jews to wear a yellow star, a moral amoeba fit at best for limbo—one of the many who later claimed that their sympathies had from the start been with de Gaulle's Free French, that they loved America, that they had even worked for the underground, though it would never be known what they had done in the underground except to seek refuge in cellars during air-raid alarms.

After the landing in Normandy, I met many such self-styled patriots and freedom lovers who were now drinking toasts to the victory of the Allies. Some of them were now denouncing one another for acts of so-called collaboration with the Germans. Denunciations took on epidemic proportions in 1944. Often they turned out to be related to professional animosities: one butcher denouncing another butcher, a photographer denouncing another photographer. It was altogether astonishing how many claimed to have been in the Resistance. Much of France, one would think, had been actively opposing Vichy or resisting the Germans. The French themselves were greatly skeptical. They knew the score and called these self-declared heroes "*résistants de la dernière heure,*" last-minute resisters. Most of them were at least a few hours late. One such individual hitched a ride in our jeep as my team and I drove toward Paris. He looked a little like Roussot. The rifle he carried had probably been acquired only a few days before and, judging by the way he handled it, had never been used by him.

THE TWENTY-YEAR-OLD member of the military intelligence team assigned to the armored division that landed on Omaha Beach on June 8, 1944, was in many ways a different person from the Parisian teenager, and not only because he wore the uniform of a new country. Transplantation to another continent, army training, maneuvers on England's Salisbury plain in anticipation of D-Day, had been a more radical initiation to adulthood than the expedition to the rue de Provence and other more traditional initiatory ceremonies.

My bar mitzvah, the first significant ceremony of my adolescence, took place in 1936. It was largely a formality, though a joyful one. For my parents, it meant giving an especially lavish party at home, though it turned out to be not so different from many other of their parties. There was champagne this time, in addition to vodka. And Zinaïda Sameievna's poem, written for the occasion and recited with a voice shriller than ever, was just a trifle more sentimental than usual. In the whole affair, religion played a minimal role. As a child, one day when I had visited a synagogue with my father, I had heard a rabbi or a cantor sing and declared that I, too, wanted to grow a beard. But I was quick to realize even then that my rabbinical or cantorial vocation was exclusively vocal, that religious fervor had no part in it. Even that very limited cantorial aspiration was short-lived. It was soon replaced by admiration for Vertinski and Chaliapin.

I grew up with no religious instruction, so that later I had much catching up to do in order to familiarize myself with the Old and the New Testaments. My parents, especially my father, who often lectured me on the subject at bedtime, warned me against the harm done by doctrines and dogmas (the latter a dirty word in our family), and this was one of the few subjects on which I lent them a believing ear. To make up for their lack of any creed, they were incorrigibly superstitious. They would not begin a trip without first sitting down ritualistically in the living room to pronounce in unison a consecrated Russian formula ending with: "*V dobryi chas*" (In a happy hour). They never passed a salt shaker from hand to hand; that was a bad omen announcing a quarrel. They would never undertake anything new on a Monday, if they could help it. According to my father, hands had to be soaped three times in quick succession. I inherited all these beliefs or habits—small wonder I suffer from chapped hands and cracked skin on my fingertips during the winter. I even improved on this inheritance of superstitious observances. Much like the ancient Romans who welcomed foreign deities, I have eclectically incorporated the most diverse practices. I not only avoid walking under a ladder and immediately retrace my steps should a black cat cross my path from left to right, but I cross my fingers every time I drive past a cemetery, anytime I think of the next medical checkup, anytime I entertain an evil thought or a harmful wish concerning people I don't like. I shudder at the thought of placing a hat on a bed. I will not kiss or shake hands across a threshold. And I will not get out of bed in the morning until I have held my breath for a prescribed number of seconds and then taken in another breath deep enough to carry an extended musical phrase.

My father, in particular, was irreligious. It was he who taught me the word "agnostic." He was not hostile to believers; he merely smiled, gently, as he would at my pranks. After all, he was an admirer of Voltaire, of Anatole France, of Jaurès. As for his Jewishness, he supported the idea of Zionism, especially in its socialist-inspired ideals; he had visited Palestine long before it became a Jewish state, and in the days when the early settlers needed help he invested in an orange plantation to encourage agricultural development. Crates of oranges would arrive in our apartment at certain times every year. Later, when Israel came into being, he sold the plantation to the state, at no profit. I also remember—these are fleeting images from early childhood—blue and white Keren Kayemet money boxes that, in ways I did not quite understand, related to the notion of a homeland.

When my father began to have serious conversations with me, he explained that he had never been a believer, but that out of respect and "*solidarité*" (a word he always used in French), he went to synagogue once or twice a year, during high holidays, without fasting. He admired such solidarity in others, too. I still hear the tone of reverence with which he pronounced the name of the benefactor—Eitingon, I believe it was—who had provided the money to build the old-age home that my father never failed to point out during our walks along that street. I know from others that he himself always gave to charities. But he never mentioned that. He preferred to praise others.

My mother, who had been born and raised deep inside Russia, in a town on the River Volga, knew very little about Jewish life and understood hardly more than two or three words of Yiddish, the sound of which she disliked—she called it, somewhat disparagingly, a *jargón* (with the accent on the second syllable). Her linguistic horizon, in addition to her native Russian, was defined by French and German. She was always taken aback by the sight of Orthodox Jews in their traditional black caftans, and the Talmudic students, with their twirled hairlocks hanging beside their ears. She met my father when she was a law student in Moscow. For a Jewish woman to attend university in Russia before the Revolution was perhaps not a common occurrence, but it was not unusual in families that, because of their economic circumstances or professional status, had permission to reside in Moscow or St. Petersburg. Or so my mother explained to me. But emancipation from *shtetl* existence did not signify denial. Nor did it cancel a specific pride, one that focused on cultural achievements that reached far beyond the Jewish condition. All through my early years, I heard of the illuminating examples of Sigmund Freud, Karl Marx, and Albert Einstein. Ranking even higher in the firmament of prestigious names were those of Spinoza, Heinrich Heine, and Felix Mendelssohn. Even Proust and Montaigne were occasionally cited. It would seem that my parents kept a mental record of luminaries who were only partially or minimally Jewish. How much of Spinoza, Henri Bergson, or Montaigne they had actually read I never bothered to find out.

It was in Marienbad, during the summer of 1936, that I prepared for my bar mitzvah. Marienbad, or Mariánské Lázně, as it was called in Czech, was then a much-frequented watering place in Bohemia, in the western part of Czechoslovakia, surrounded by hills thick with pine forests and crossed by well-groomed paths that most often led to a *Kaffeehaus* where an orchestra played at all hours of the day and summer guests sipped coffee and ingested inordinate quantities of pastries covered with whipped cream. Ironically, it was to relieve their dysfunctional livers, their gout, their obesity that visitors came to imbibe the waters of Marienbad. There were in fact many very fat people in Marienbad, and little indication that they lost weight during their stay.

The hotel room adjacent to my mother's was where I received instruction in the rudiments of Hebrew. A young, local rabbi tutored me for the event. We sat not far from the washbasin, where I kept a fat frog with a broken leg, close by the night table on which stood my portable gramophone. A jazz record that had been playing when the rabbi arrived was sitting on the turntable. That summer when I learned to decipher Hebrew characters was altogether different from the summers we spent in Deauville or Cabourg, where beach activities or indoor games on rainy days imposed a set routine. In Marienbad the days were taken up by movement. One was constantly walking somewhere. "*Spazieren*" was a favorite word, whether it referred to idly strolling or to a more purposeful walk. All grownups carried a *Spazierstock*—a walking stick.

Even breakfast was had at some distance from the center of the resort, at least half an hour's slowly paced climb along well-marked paths. Quite often we ambled to Café Panorama, which, as its name implied, offered an extensive view. There, on the garden terrace, a lavish breakfast was served. I especially enjoyed the two soft-boiled eggs, neatly taken out of their shells, that came in a tall glass, together with the *café mélange*, featuring heaps of whipped cream. There was dancing on the terrace as of ten in the morning. My mother always invited me to dance the foxtrot. Then she and her friends—summer visitors from different countries—began to play cards under an umbrella, while I met my own friends at the ping-pong tables near the tall trees. With the few kronen of my allowance, I sometimes tried my luck at the slot machines, which required a certain skill. Occasionally, a small treasure of kronen fell with a metallic sound into the receptacle. Most often, however, all my coins disappeared, and I went back to ping-pong feeling sorry for myself.

That was only the beginning of the day's activities. Soon, there was the quicker walk back down the hill, amid the smell of pine trees and the sound of birds, along paths covered with pine needles, and then the promenade beside the arcaded colonnade where people kept walking back and forth, holding their glasses of spring water filled directly at the well, to the accompaniment of the band inside the kiosk playing Strauss waltzes and Rossini overtures. Photographers standing behind their tripods handed out tickets to the passersby. All over Marienbad funny postcards were displayed, with rather obvious jokes about the diuretic or laxative effects of the waters, depicting caricatural figures rushing to the nearest comfort station.

In the afternoon, after the prescribed siesta, my mother would ask me to accompany her in a hackney cab, or *Droschke*, to a more distant *Kaffeehaus*. I liked the rhythmic sound of the horse's hoofs and the smell of fresh horse manure as it dropped on the road, immediately attracting a bevy of small birds. But I was impatient with the slow progress of the carriage and the prolonged tête-à-tête with my mother, who would insistently question me about the young girl with whom I had been seen walking in the main street after dinner (why was I so rarely seen with boys my own age?) or warn me against spending too many hours on the tennis court. I was much happier when I could be alone and take the asthmatic old bus with its noisy gear shifts or, better still, walk up through the pine forest that had inspired Goethe's Marienbad poem *"Über allen Gipfeln ist Ruh"*, which I learned by heart that summer.

The goal of my walk or bus ride was Café Rübezahl (so named after a fairy tale character), where stand-up comedians of the Viennese variety delivered satirical punch lines that I only half understood but that kept me spellbound precisely because of the gap between the loud laughter of the crowd and my own puzzlement. At Rübezahl there were also afternoon variety shows with gags and slapstick comedy that required less linguistic maturity on my part. More typically, however, my afternoons were spent on the red clay tennis courts of Café Bellevue, which did not have a view at all but where I lived in a special world of fantasy as I returned difficult shots to my trainer, imagining that I was preparing for the Davis Cup and that I would soon be a worthy successor to Cochet and Borotra, both of whom I had admired at the Roland Garros Stadium in Paris.

Although my mother was concerned about my evening walks with this or that girl, I spent many hours alone. Often I ate by myself. On many evenings, Mama was off to dinner with friends, then to some spectacle or bridge tournament. I did not feel neglected, for she was attentive to my needs and supervised many of my activities. But she knew I enjoyed my hours of freedom. I welcomed the illusion of a separate life, of a mysterious private existence. I welcomed the freedom of ordering my meals in the small garden of the hotel. My culinary curiosity was limited. The food I chose was almost always the same: Viennese-style schnitzel or calf's liver, either of them accompanied by beloved roast potatoes and followed by a typical Austro-Hungarian dessert, *Palatschinken*—a rolled pancake filled with apricot jam and covered with sprinkled sugar. I did not tire of this menu. Later in the evening I would treat myself to *Karlsbader Oblaten*, sweet-tasting, thin, crunchy wafers that, in spite of the reference to religious offerings and oblates living in monasteries, had nothing ascetic about them. If consumed regularly over the years they were by themselves cause enough to need a cure in either Karlsbad or Marienbad. These wafers were also a reminder of my father's proximity in nearby Karlsbad, where he was enjoying a parallel vacation in the plush Hotel Pupp, while my mother and I were residing in a somewhat more modest family hotel on the main street of Marienbad.

That summer of 1936 when I was preparing for my bar mitzvah, learning how to chant the words to which I pointed on the scroll with the silver hand, we did not realize that in Marienbad, at the heart of the Sudetenland, we were all sitting on a powder keg. Just a couple of years later, Hitler brutally annexed this German-speaking Czech border region, which seemed so friendly to the international spa clientele but was in reality already mesmerized by the ideology of Hitler's Third Reich. Yet there were threatening signals for those of us who, in order to return home, had to cross through the nearby frontier town of Cheb, or Eger, where the express train, the *Schnellzug*, stopped for an inordinately long time. Stern-looking German customs officials and uniformed men with swastika armbands communicated, even to a thirteen-year-old boy, the frontier anxiety that I associate, somewhat nostalgically, with railway travel in the 1930s.

⌒〰

OF THE BAR mitzvah itself, for which I prepared in Marienbad, I have preserved only flashes of memory. The service was held in the intimate synagogue on the rue de Montevideo, a discreet modern structure on a peaceful street in our peaceful quarter, just minutes away from my school. Years later, well after the war, a terrorist bomb exploded on another peaceful street in front of another synagogue near the place Victor Hugo. But in the 1930s, such violence was unheard of in the quiet and very proper 16th arrondissement.

On the day of the ceremony I was nervous but not especially moved. I looked forward to the occasion as to a singing performance. My voice was steady and strong for my age, and my recent fascination with Chaliapin is probably what induced me to give operatic intonations to the prayer chanting. I was, it would seem, blissfully unconcerned about making a fool of myself. What spoiled the occasion for me to some extent was that I felt upstaged by my cousin's husband, Shura, whose virile figure as he made his entrance limping down the aisle on crutches, with a bandage across his brow, shifted everyone's attention away from where I was sitting. "To steal the show" is an expression I did not know at the time, but it corresponds exactly to the sudden frustration I experienced while waiting for the service to begin. Details about driving at night in Burgundy, the heavy rain, the fog, the skidding Citroën, the crash—given in a voice loud enough to be overheard several rows away—were embellished as they were repeated. He was the hero, with his defiant look, his broad shoulders, his strong chin. I became even more determined to sing with an expressive and dramatic voice. I simply hated him. Why did beautiful Moussia, his wife, not understand that I had an infinitely greater capacity for love? Far better than he, I would know how to praise her profile, her elegant aquiline nose, the way she crossed her legs as she sipped tea, the surprising agility of her speech as she moved from one language to another in the same sentence. But a thirteen-year-old boy could hardly compete with Shura, in full manhood and on whom all the women's glances converged.

And so my bar mitzvah mingled jealousy and wounded pride with the urge to compete and perform. My vanity was soothed later that day, in our apartment, when I inflicted on the assembled guests a piece of shamelessly orchestrated self-praise. It was Babushka who had given me the idea by showing me a typewritten mock-epithalamium, an amusing wedding poem set to lilting operetta music that, she told me, had entertained the guests at a recent banquet. I spent weeks composing couplets in my own honor, to be sung to a well-known tune from Franz Lehar's *The Count of Luxemburg*. The couplets were typed by a secretary in my father's office, and I now distributed the sheets to all the guests, interrupting conversations. However embarrassing the memory of this adolescent exhibitionism, I also remember the keen pleasure of feeling that I was all at once poet, composer, singer, impresario, conductor, and public. I marvel that my parents, who so valued discretion and good taste, tolerated this self-indulgent display. They must have been especially well disposed and even proud that day, and so I got away with it and basked in the applause. Even Shura no longer seemed threatening, with his heroic bandage over his right eye. Fortunately, I did not take myself quite seriously even then. The champagne, moreover, made me giggle. One of the bottles my father ordered for the occasion somehow survived not only that special day, but the years of the war, the Occupation, and the recovery and move of what remained of our furniture across the ocean after the war was over. When my father died in 1977 that old bottle (having shed its label) found its berth in a Princeton cellar, where it rests, a venerable champagne by now— and I am sure quite undrinkable.

Of the real "Jewish" life in Paris I knew next to nothing. Its world lay far away, in the Marais, or even farther in the proletarian northern arrondissements. The Marais, as its name indicates, was originally a swampy region near the river, just north of the Ile Saint-Louis. Once an aristocratic quarter, it later lost its luster, and with time many of the elegant sixteenth- and seventeenth-century mansions belonging to prestigious noble families became dilapidated and were abandoned or used as warehouses. The Marais, especially in the vicinity of the rue des Rosiers, became a densely populated Jewish quarter, with many kosher delicatessens and kosher restaurants, and at least five synagogues within little more than a quarter of a square mile. In recent years, the Marais has been restored and rehabilitated and has become a major tourist attraction. But in my school days it was run-down and squalid. Neither my parents nor anyone else I knew ever mentioned it. Only years later did I explore it, when Bettina and I discovered its architectural treasures, the *hôtels particuliers* of the rue des Francs-Bourgeois and the harmonious place des Vosges with its uniform brick and stone buildings, where Victor Hugo had once lived.

A Jewish neighborhood I knew a little better was near the place de la République, where my parents sent me for fittings by the Polish tailor Gavronsky. My mother came with me for the initial choice of fabric and pattern. I was usually distressed because Gavronsky had scant imagination, was unaware of British and American fashions, and always made the waists and armholes of the jackets too tight. Though he put on magisterial airs, accompanying his first incision with a grandiose *"Je coupe"* as he used the large scissors on the selected cloth, the results were never what I expected. I had dreams of being dressed like William Powell or Gary Cooper, but the glen-plaid suit or the houndstooth sport jacket inevitably turned out to be an unmistakable Gavronsky creation. As for the repeated fittings, they meant odious and prolonged suffering every time, as I stood in the small tailor shop being pulled, tugged, pinched, and occasionally pricked by the pins. But I did look forward to the *métro* rides, when I traveled alone seeing myself as in a movie traveling to a distant country, and counting the times the amusing advertisement for the Dubonnet aperitif would come up between the Passy and the St.-Martin *métro* stations.

The other distant expedition on which my parents sent me by *métro* was to the family dentist, Docteur Pavlov, in Montparnasse, close by the famous cafés La Coupole and La Rotonde, where international expatriates and artists congregated. I knew I was in for a long wait in Docteur Pavlov's office, and then for the torture of the anesthesia by freezing the tooth, a technique probably acquired in the Moscow dental school and not relinquished even after the introduction of novocaine. His drilling produced exquisite pain, and I was often tempted to bite the hand that poked and bored away, as I had done, so I was told, the first time I was taken to a dentist as a child. Yet even my apprehension of what lay ahead could not spoil the pleasure of the *métro* ride. I simply loved the steamy smell of the Paris subway, a unique smell that still affects me today when it catches me by surprise as I pass a *métro* station or a manhole nearby.

The *métro* ride to the dentist held in store special thrills. At the Passy station the line surfaces and the train crosses the bridge near the Eiffel Tower, offering a sweeping view of the river, a backward glance at the gardens of the Palais de Chaillot, and to the right a glimpse of the Pont de Grenelle, near which stands the smaller version of the Statue of Liberty. For a while the train flew between rows of apartment houses whose windows concealed secrets I could not even imagine, until soon after, like a submarine seen in the newsreel, it again sank below the surface into the darkness of the Parisian nether regions. The Eiffel Tower changed its appearance according to weather and light, sometimes almost graceful, at others massive and threatening. I kept thinking of the song made popular by Charles Trenet and Maurice Chevalier, in which a lighthearted Eiffel Tower, in a moment of spring fever and erotic joy, is seen giddily hopping across the Seine.

The names of the stations on the way to the dentist were laden with history. First came Dupleix, who did much for France's colonial empire, then La Motte-Picquet (I looked him up in my father's encyclopedia), a sea captain who distinguished himself in Martinique against the British and became commander of the French Navy. These two seafarers added a touch of exoticism to my subway journey between the stations of Passy and Vavin, stopping at other stations that evoked the figures of Louis Pasteur, Edgar Quinet, and François Raspail—an onomastic voyage through history, science, and politics that was altogether different from the droning classroom references to the past.

My parents may have thought that my expeditions to the tailor and the dentist were my only *métro* odysseys. What they did not know was that the *métro* became my secret passion, that it was for me the urban substitute for railway journeys and reveries in time and space, that I would skip classes to enter into the vast labyrinth beneath the surface of the city, emerge at random in distant and unknown quarters—worlds that had the distinct character of picturesque provinces or quaint villages—and then, jealous of discoveries I did not wish to share even with my friends, walk in unfamiliar streets, an anonymous adolescent stroller lost in the crowds, seeing but unseen, living to the utmost a brief dream of adulthood and impunity

Chapter 5

THE 1930S AND THE EXPOSITION
INTERNATIONALE

I believe that my curiosity about literature was awakened not by books but by my Parisian walks. Long before I came across Baudelaire's "Spleen" poems or his "Tableaux parisiens," I knew about the delicious loneliness in the crowd as I ambled along rectilinear avenues and explored the labyrinths of crooked streets and blind alleys. When I was finally initiated to Baudelaire's verse and his prose poems, I recognized instantly what he meant by a princely incognito, a river of vitality, a reservoir of magnetic forces, a stone landscape caressed by the fog. Much in the same way, I felt at home on my first encounter with T. S. Eliot's "unreal city" when I read about the yellow fog that rubbed its back in feline fashion against the windowpanes. But unlike the wasteland of Eliot's London, the Paris of my schoolday walks was not a descent into Hades. No ghosts crossed my path, only some eccentric passersby and the many who walked blindly, driven by their daily routine. Here and there I saw a couple locked in a tight embrace. I would slow down to cast envious sideways glances in their direction. The teeming, unreal city that so bewitched Baudelaire—he compared it to a gigantic whore—intensified my erotic reveries.

I find it difficult to tell what takes precedence in the chronologies of bookish and lived experience. Does it really matter? In a sense it does, of course. This undeterminable priority argues against those who would remove art from the activities of living, for whom books are "texts" woven in sublime indifference or even hostile reaction to life, who value literary works as pure constructs of the mind, as games of rhetoric obeying their own rules. Such willful segregation, inviting hermeticism, felt untrue to both the experience of living and that of reading.

Nothing in my early years seemed to destine me for a life of literary studies. If eventually, after many a detour, I came to study and teach what is called literature, it is in large part because I realized at some point that what I had seen, felt, or dreamt was diversely reflected in the books I read, making it in turn possible for me to understand my own experiences; and that, conversely, the books I assimilated allowed me to see the world around me, and perhaps even myself, in a new light. Lived life and literary realities seemed to exchange their resources. Between the two was a shuttle of words and restless trains of thought.

This exchange between life and art, between living and writing, is perhaps what drew me in the first place to Stendhal, my early literary love, whose books and personality gave me some of my keenest joys. It is not easy to forget one's early passions. In Rome, in 1950, I was twenty-seven years old and newly married. I had a Fulbright fellowship and was writing my dissertation on the author of *The Red and the Black* and *The Charterhouse of Parma*, two novels I cherished for having opened my eyes to the bond between irony and tenderness. In Rome, I was discovering Stendhal's *Promenades dans Rome* while Bettina and I visited the streets, the palaces, the ruins he described. I found and bought the entire Divan edition of his collected works in a small book-store near piazza Minerva, where he had stayed. I met some fervent Stendhalians: Professor Pietro Paolo Trompeo, the aging dean of French studies and professor at the University of Rome, and Luigi Magnani, the musicologist and art collector, who became our great friend. But most important, perhaps, I discovered the astonishing open-ing pages of *The Life of Henry Brulard*, those luminous autumnal pages in which Stendhal, atop the Janiculum, embraces all at once the panorama of the eternal city and the panorama of his own life.

I, too, loved to climb to the top of the Janiculum, sit down on a bench in the winter sun, and survey all those sites whose names I still pro-nounce with voluptuous delight: Pincio, San Pietro in Montorio, villa Aldobrandini, Santa Maria Maggiore. I was not yet thirty, and Stendhal had been fifty when he wrote those sunny pages. I had not been at the battle of Bautzen or in Moscow with Napoleon, but I had seen war at close range, and Stendhal gave me a premonition of what it might feel like to be a survivor at the age of fifty and beyond. Only later, much later, did I understand that the beautiful beginning of this very personal text spoke of the fertile tensions between living and telling, that this panoramic overture clearly suggested from the very start that any auto-biography is something of a fictional construct. I first loved these opening pages because they proclaimed in a smiling manner the precious fragility of privileged moments and the beauty of reminiscing. Later I learned to love them in a deeper way. Surveying the historical strata of a city like Rome was obviously for Stendhal the metaphorical analogue of surveying his own life—a form of archaeology.

IN 1937, I was not walking in Rome. I had not even heard of piazza Navona, via Giulia in the papal part of the city, or the popular quarters of Trastevere. The only triumphal arch I knew was the Napoleonic Arc de Triomphe, from which radiated the broad avenues near where we lived. Rome existed for me only in textbooks, where I had read about Remus and Romulus, the she-wolf that nurtured them, and the legendary founding of the city. I had also learned of course that Paris, originally named Lutetia, entered history in Gallo-Roman times, when it was the chief settlement of the tribe known as the Parisii. And I was vaguely aware that somewhere in Paris, beyond the Latin Quarter, there existed the half-hidden Arènes de Lutèce, Gallo-Roman ruins recently excavated and restored—but I was not to visit them for many years.

The closest I came to this arena, which in Roman times was used as a circus and for theatrical presentations, was once or twice a year when I went to sell my textbooks at the Gibert bookstore on boulevard Saint-Michel, close to the Sorbonne. The proceeds were quickly spent on American movies and on English cigarettes—Gold Flakes, I believe— which I lit to give myself a grown-up countenance as I wandered in the streets on afternoons when I cut school in search of adventure. I was vain and terribly self-conscious, repeatedly glancing at my reflection in store windows to check whether my trousers were the right length and broke properly on my shoes. My models were the American movie stars I admired. The French screen actors—Jean Gabin, Pierre Brasseur, Jean-Pierre Aumont—seemed to me sartorially wanting.

Some adventures were inspired by readings. My classmate Alain Topiol, who sat next to me and was expelled because he was caught copying during an exam, shared with me a boundless passion for Arsène Lupin, the dapper, monocled, master burglar who combined the talents of a Houdini with those of an international spy. We had read every novel by Maurice Leblanc in which Lupin appears in his various avatars. One warm spring day, as we were ambling along avenue Henri Martin near our lycée, we conceived an idea on an impulse. We were walking behind a woman who carried a bouquet of flowers and soon entered an apartment building. Without a moment's hesitation, we followed her up to her floor in time to see a maid open and close the door. Our brief adventure had come to an end. But I proposed having some calling cards printed with the name of Arsène Lupin, and bringing her some tulips or roses. We did know, after all, that she liked flowers. On the calling card, once they were ready, I remember writing carefully above the name of Arsène Lupin, "À *Madame* ***, *avec les compliments de* . . ." The asterisks I had seen used in novels to designate a woman of high rank whom the narrator did not wish to compromise. We bought the flowers on rue de la Pompe, though I no longer recall what they were. Entering an apartment building past the concierge's quarters was no problem during the daytime. I could hear my heart pound as we climbed to the second floor of the building and deposited the bouquet with the card on the doormat. We then fled. I have often wondered what went through the mind of the woman when her maid found our offering and brought it to her. Maurice Leblanc, I am sure, would have appreciated the gesture of his two fourteen-year-old readers. It was, however, the last time I offered flowers to anyone under a fictional name.

Less bookish, but equally harmless, were some furtive outings to variety shows and dance halls. Jacques, who was more worldly, took the initiative. On several afternoons when we should have been in class, we made our way in the general direction of Montmartre to performances by Mistinguett and Maurice Chevalier. It was either at the Casino de Paris or at the Folies-Bergères, I am no longer sure. Of Mistinguett I recall little, except that she sang a silly song about having been seen naked. She had a thin, rather high-pitched voice and very long legs, and her costume, covered with feathers, revealed large portions of her body.

She failed to make much of an impression on me. Maurice Chevalier, on the other hand, had me spellbound. I loved the way he moved on stage, with his straw hat rakishly tilted, as he embodied the essence of Parisian lower-class irreverence and wit. What I learned from his slang-riddled songs and proletarian off-color remarks delivered with benign, rascally intonations stayed with me longer than what I might have gotten out of my physics class. One song became a special favorite of mine. It started with the words *"Prosper, youp-la-boum,"* laying special stress on the *"boum."* It was about a much-admired pimp by the name of Prosper, who described himself (after a quick grind and bump following the word *"boum"*) as the charismatic king of the sidewalk. I was simply enchanted and kept practicing Chevalier's *"boum"* and pelvic movements at home—in the privacy of my room, knowing that my efforts at music-hall effects would have bewildered my parents.

Nonetheless, I felt most often clumsy and ill at ease. Jacques had the idea of trying out a *thé dansant* on the Champs-Elysées called Mimi Pinson. It turned out to be rather ordinary, even boring. There were many available young and not-so-young women (obviously not clients), but we never mustered the courage to invite any of them to dance. We sipped our drinks, watching—more intimidated, oddly, than we had been during our visit to the rue de Provence.

Another of our pastimes was more exciting, and potentially more dangerous. Even we were aware that we were pushing our luck. At night, Jacques and I would occasionally make our way to the underground garage in his building and into his father's black Talbot, to which Jacques had somehow obtained a key. He was not old enough to have a driver's license; he had not even taken any driving lessons. He nonetheless made it to the Bois de Boulogne. Along the poorly lit, deserted avenues—in the park and along the lake—we sealed our friendship by speeding along, truly together. Jacques held the wheel while I pressed on the gas pedal. To share the driving even more fairly, we took turns. I would hold the wheel, though not even in the driver's seat, while his foot was on the accelerator. We managed somehow not to have an accident, nor even to scratch or dent the car. But we were both relieved every time the Talbot was safely back in its stall in the garage.

⌒⌒

My MOST MEMORABLE adventures, though, were of a solitary
nature. Most often I took off alone, first by *métro,* the rest on foot. I preferred the *métro* to the bus. The underground network seemed to me
more mysterious, more secretive. Emerging anywhere was always a
surprise. But during the fall of 1937 and into the spring of 1938, the
nearby Exposition Internationale kept me very busy walking. It was
nearby only insofar as its gateway happened to be on the place du Trocadéro. In reality, it extended for miles below the Trocadéro hill—
across the Iéna bridge, past the Eiffel Tower, the parade grounds of the
Champ de Mars, all the way to the École Militaire, and on both sides,
along the banks of the Seine, from the Alma bridge to the bridge of
Grenelle. The exposition, an immensely ambitious World's Fair, occupied a vast area stretched out along the river.

The physical layout and the temporary constructions did not spoil
the perspectives. All along the grounds, often as part of a country's
exhibit, were outdoor cafés with little tables. At night, the illuminations
were spectacular. The pavilions situated along the quais were reflected
in the river. The building materials themselves were a matter of pride—
glass, wood, ceramic, aluminum. The broadly curving Seine was
omnipresent. So was the Eiffel Tower, looming visible, dominant
everywhere, a symbol of modern Paris. It had been built for another
Exposition Internationale, in 1889, to celebrate the centenary of the
French Revolution and the accomplishments of the French Republic.

The only permanent construction of the 1937 exposition was the elegant Palais de Chaillot on the elevation where the towering Palais du
Trocadéro had stood, with its cumbersome and anachronistic moorish
towers. The new edifice retained the elliptical shape of the demolished
building and displayed clean horizontal lines of luminous white stone.
An even more significant innovation: it featured, as a wide opening
between its two wings, a huge terrace or esplanade from which the eye
was unavoidably directed along a north-south axis that passed beyond
the waterworks, beyond the bridge leading to the Eiffel Tower, then
straight behind, to the parade grounds of the Champ de Mars, and at the

far end, to the École Militaire—reminders that the French Revolution was forever wedded to military glory. It was the foreground, however, just below the esplanade, that retained one's attention: the oblong pool (also aimed at the Eiffel Tower), the cascades that were illumined at night, the gilt statues, the gardens *à la française*.

My parents commented ironically on the tall column that had been erected on the place du Trocadéro as part of the Pavillon de la Paix, dedicated to peace among nations. It presided as a monumental overture to the 1937 exposition. The Latin word *"Pax"* was inscribed on the column in large, vertically disposed letters. My father never ceased making fun of the column, pointing out that not only had internal strife in France—labor unrest, a wave of strikes, hostility to the Popular Front—delayed the completion and opening of the exposition, but that on the international scene we had never been further removed from the assurance of peace—and this, merely twenty years after the Great War! Italy had invaded and conquered Ethiopia in 1935 (great heroic feat), the Spanish Civil War had ravaged the peninsula and brutalized the civilian populations, Stalin had set out to purge the Soviet Union ruthlessly of every opponent of his regime, Hitler had occupied the Rhineland and was soon to annex Austria. Within a year after the inauguration of the Exposition Internationale of 1937, the mindless appeasement policies of Chamberlain and Daladier were to lead to the capitulation at Munich and further encourage the expansionist militarism of the Third Reich. The *"Pax"* on the column corresponded at best to wishful thinking. In the meantime, ultranationalist ideologies and the rhetoric of confrontation seemed to carry the day. This rhetoric of confrontation was nowhere better illustrated than by the emblematic and centrally located opposition of the two major pavilions of Germany and the Soviet Union, visible from almost everywhere, and facing each other in dramatic and threatening proximity as though ready for assault on each other.

Other national exhibits were housed less belligerently. My fresh summer memories of Marienbad drew me to the Czechoslovak pavilion. It featured a brasserie (a word that appropriately also means "brewery") with a huge sign advertising the famous Bohemian beer Pilsner Urquell. Large advertising panels were in fact visible all over, sometimes from the top of nearby apartment buildings. Looming above the Italian pavilion there was, for no explicable reason, an illuminated Bayer sign with the familiar circled cross holding out hope for the relief of headaches. The Swiss pavilion advertised its mountain ranges and pine trees in painted outlines that were not altogether convincing. Greece displayed a Zeus (with impressive genitalia) in the act of throwing a thunderbolt. As for Egypt, it exhibited the inevitable crouched Sphinx that reminded me of the Sunday expeditions with my mother to the Louvre. It failed to seduce me. Nor was I drawn to the regional exhibitions of French provinces and their crafts. The reproduction of Arab streets had more of an effect on me. It was a way of traveling to exotic regions. But what really summoned my attention was the pavilion carrying in large letters the hyphenated words *"Photo-Ciné-Phono."* It stood right below the Eiffel Tower and seemed about to be crushed by the tower's huge iron legs. If I remember correctly, there was also somewhere a *Pavillon du Tabac,* glorifying the tobacco that was a state monopoly and therefore an important source of national revenue. Commercial interests were almost as keen as national pride.

Again and again, the mind and the eye returned to the dramatic architectural confrontation of the Soviet and German pavilions. These were impressive, carefully planned ideological structures situated at the heart of the international exhibit, perfectly aligned with the central perspective from the esplanade of the Palais de Chaillot. In their apparent head-on collision they were by far the most memorable buildings of the exposition. Towering and neoclassical in style, the German pavilion carried the word "Deutschland" as though hewn in marble; it appeared as a temple to the glory of Aryan superiority. Cold and willfully sober, it featured stone torches, fluted columns, sculptures of human figures whose athletic "Aryan" musculature had little in common with Hitler's hysterical gestures, Joseph Goebbels's deformed silhouette, or Hermann Goering's bloated beer belly. But there it stood with its Nazi flag, and the immense eagle spreading its wings over the swastika, defiantly glaring at the monumental onrushing Worker and Collective Farm Woman on top of the Soviet pavilion—an emblem of the proletarian couple united in their common grasp of the hammer and sickle, flying forward together with gigantic strides, about to rush at the eagle perched high above the swastika. And above this display of ideological warfare, one could see on one of the nearby rooftops of the 16th arrondissement the reassuring—and in its way also ideological—sign of the well-known French aperitif Byrrh.

There can be no doubt that the entire Exposition Internationale of 1937 was conceived as a manifestation to the greater glory of France—but this at an incongruous historical moment of inner strife and weakness. Paris, city of lights and enlightenment, mirrored itself as the center of the world in the image of all the countries and regions represented. "The Universe in Paris" was one of the journalistic formulas of the year. But the subtext was "Paris as the Universe," Paris as the capital of the world. The survey of human achievements was easily turned into a hymn of self-praise. Paris as the soul of the world is a formula Victor Hugo might have coined. The French really chose to believe it in 1937. But while remembering that they had been taught in school to be proud of the hexagonal shape of their country's frontiers (a supposedly visible proof of the underlying natural harmony of the French nation), and to lay supreme value on a cultural heritage that reconciled Rabelais and Racine, Poussin and the Impressionists, they were dimly aware that somewhere in their country's present condition there was a flaw, a deep weakness that made them look up to the German and Russian pavilions with simultaneous fear and admiration.

WE HAD INDEED been taught in school to admire the hexagonal shape of France and to take pride in its culture and universality, which were now being glorified by the Exposition Internationale. The lycée indoctrinated us. Literature classes in particular extolled the greatness of France's genius. The vaunted method of literary studies known as *explication de texte*, despite its recourse to semantic, grammatical, and rhetorical analyses, hardly encouraged freedom of interpretation. There was an agenda. One turned in circles. We were to examine a given passage from a Racine play, then show that the passage was great because it was typical of Racine. The greatness of Racine was a given—as was the greatness of France's culture, institutions, and historical past.

My father in the Czech
spa in Karlsbad a few
months before my birth.

Myself with monkey, thinking
about trains . . .

Posing with my father.

My mother as I remember her
when I was a child.

Marienbad, summer of 1923. My mother with her brother— the uncle from Shanghai.

With my sister, Nora, shortly before her fatal illness.

Our group in Deauville (summer of 1939). Dany is standing to my right.

Summer of 1939, with Dany on the
boardwalk of Trouville.

With my cousin Sascha in Nice. Part of the Casino de la Jetée is visible.

Nice, 1941. Reading in the sun.

1940. With Parisian friends who also sought refuge in Nice.

1941. With my father in Nice.

My emaciated father on the *Nave-mar*, the banana freighter that brought us to America.

Fall of 1941. On an outing with members of Harrisburg Academy.

Summer of 1943.
During military
intelligence training at
Camp Ritchie.

Normandy, in 1944, with a local farmer, his daughter and son-in-law, and
two Parisian refugees.

Fall of 1944. Our 28th Infantry Division team in a frolicking mood soon after reaching the German border.

Fall of 1944, in liberated Paris. Taken at Yvette's request.

November 1944, before the Battle of the Bulge.

Fall of 1944. Picture of Lieutenant Howe, taken by the author.

Fall of 1944, near the Hürtgen forest. The "bloody bucket" shoulder patch of the 28th Infantry Division is clearly visible.

July, 1945. in Dudweiler (Saarland) with Lieutenant Howe and our requisitioned Mercedes.

July 1945, Saarlautern. Typical destruction during the war, photo taken by the author.

December 1944. The captured German newsreel picture that convinced my family and friends that I was a prisoner of war in the Ardennes.

I was not at all refractory to this cultural doctrine. Because I was not French by birth, I felt perhaps more inclined than others to exalt France. Neither Russia nor Germany could make me feel any pride. The very idea of France stirred me; the sound of the word had a musical resonance. This great love began at the age of seven, in 1931, when my mother and I had temporarily settled in Nice. A recluse in mourning, she was herself sensitive to the luminous beauty of the setting. As I watched the procession of ants in the luxuriant garden of our hotel, it seemed to me that my mother's siesta time would never end. I was eager to walk with her and discover different quarters. I was quite unaware that Nice was hardly a typical French town. Nothing allowed me in those days to recognize the distinctly Italian flavor of a city that had for centuries belonged to the House of Savoy and that had been ceded to France as recently as the second half of the nineteenth century.

The Italian character of Nice, especially of its old part, is now obvious to me. The ochre-colored, arcaded place Masséna has a distinctly Turinese aspect; place Rossetti, dominated by the baroque church of Sainte Réparate, could be the central square of any small Italian town. But in 1931, when in late winter my mother and I came by train all the way from the massive Hauptbahnhof of Leipzig, through snow-covered Switzerland, down to the Mediterranean coast, the revelation of what I took to be the essence of France filled me with a sense of wonder. My infatuation began, deceptively, at Carnival time, with the Battle of the Flowers and the colorful floats along the seafront, the majestic palm trees, the sight of mimosas and cactus plants, and the strangely enticing names of Cap d'Ail, Monte-Carlo, Cap Ferrat, Cap Martin, Roquebrune. I could not of course predict that these impressions were preparing me for the passion I would later develop for Italy. Nor could I know what role Nice was to play in my life—at many an Easter season, and then, after the fall of Paris in 1940, for one entire year of stressful residence, after we had fled Paris, at a time when one part of France was occupied by the Germans and the other ruled by the collaborationist Vichy regime of Pétain.

The real arrival in France took place in 1933, this time in Paris, when I was nine years old. Hitler had come to power. My parents and I, our faithful Saxon maid, Marianne, who was my nanny, and my father's brother and his large family, including a handsome son-in-law of whom I was bitterly jealous, occupied several sleeping compartments on a night train crossing to Switzerland from Leipzig. I remember overhearing ominous-sounding conversations in the train's corridor, at the frontier. The word *"Juden"* was repeated several times. I had been told not to open the door of my compartment under any circumstance, unless specifically ordered to do so. But no one did, and the voices disappeared. The train then moved slowly into Swiss territory, and my mother came to see whether everything was all right in the compartment that I shared with Marianne. Switzerland seemed to be our special gateway to France. Only this time, we first settled for a few months in Montreux, on Lake Geneva, waiting for the necessary visas on our Nansen passports—those special passports issued after the Great War to people who were stateless, or, as the French called them, *apatrides*. We took up a whole row of rooms in the Hôtel des Palmiers, the very name of which enchanted me because of the beloved palm trees of Nice.

There were indeed resemblances to the Riviera: the balmy temperature, the rippling blue waters of the lake—even the palm trees, though they seemed to me somewhat emaciated by comparison. But then there was the impressive snow-covered Dent du Midi towering over the darker, deeper, almost mysterious recesses of the lake. There was also, jutting out into the water, the castle of Chillon, made famous by Lord Byron's poem. I had learned about Byron's prisoner from my older cousin, Ossia, whom I much admired, and who also repeatedly whistled for me Papageno's songs, so that I came to associate once and for all the magic of Mozart's flute, the enviable precision of my cousin's sustained whistle, and the image of the chained prisoner who made friends with spiders and in the end felt uncannily at home in his poetic dungeon. I now see clearly that the idea of the happy prison was planted in my consciousness long before I thought of writing *The Romantic Prison*.

The setting of Montreux, with its swift changes of mood—one moment playful, filled with light and with white sails on the shimmering waters, the next mist-covered and threatening like a dark dream—was to be only a place of transit while we waited for our stateless passports to be regularized. But like Nice, it was to play a role, not always a happy one, in later years. It is in Montreux that our dearest friend James

Gill—the publisher of *2 Plus 2*—lies buried, close to the grave of Vladimir Nabokov, whom he had befriended, the same Nabokov who had given tennis lessons to my cousin Ossia at a German sea resort, and who was mentioned occasionally, not especially as a writer, but because his wife, Vera, was related to my father's family.

When we finally arrived in Paris late that spring and camped for a few days in my Aunt Anya's labyrinthine apartment near the rue du Commerce, I was overwhelmed, this time not by palm trees and sun-speckled bays but by the colorful, noisy, odiferous street market nearby. I had never imagined such a display of fruits, vegetables, and juicy slices of meat. The fish stands made a special impression on me. I discovered huge, pink shrimp and crabs called *tourteaux* that reminded me of still-life paintings hanging in a dark corner of my parents' drawing room. Except that the crabs' tiny legs and antennae were moving. It was Aunt Anya who took me to the market and who also introduced me to artichokes. She had a wrinkled but youthful face and was a widow. About her husband I knew only that he had been a volunteer fireman. Had he died of illness or in a fire? I preferred the more heroic version, but never did find out. It was that same Aunt Anya who, on the board-walk in Cabourg, gave my cousin Sascha and me lessons in human reproduction. She obviously relished pronouncing the word "sperm." I later met her occasionally near my lycée, where she had moved to a more modest apartment. She was then, I gathered, supported in part by my father, but she always seemed cheerful, anointed her face with creams to ward off the invasion of wrinkles, and always praised the virtues of an uncomplicated life, "*une vie facile.*" Aunt Anya was taken in a police roundup in Nice in 1943, deported in one of the cattle cars, and disappeared in Auschwitz. My parents felt guilty for years, reproaching themselves for not having done enough to get her out in time.

We left Anya's apartment after just a few days and settled for a while in the Hôtel Galilée, a small hotel in the affluent quarter near the avenue Kléber. It is strange how I remember the names and peculiarities of the hotels we stayed at when I was a child. At the Hôtel Galilée I recall being fascinated by a type of elevator I had never seen. Small and extra-ordinarily slow, it was pushed upward by a thick, shiny stem that smelled of engine grease. When the button was pressed to call it down, it first gave out a hissing sound, almost an asthmatic sigh of resignation, before agreeing to make its journey back to the ground floor. I also recall another puffing sound coming from my disagreeable Uncle Herman after dinner as he voluptuously smoked one of his enormous cigars in the narrow hotel lounge. He would watch the near-perfect circles of smoke that issued from his pursed mouth, while the grayish ash at the end of the cigar got longer and longer. My uncle explained—when he deigned speak to me—that the length of the uncrumbled ash proved the quality of the cigar. I kept hoping that the ash would crumble and fall, but it never happened. He always made it fall himself by a willful flick of his forefinger, just in time. All the while, he kept sniffing the side of the cigar and watched the increasing length of the incandescent ashes with a mixture of skepticism and self-satisfaction that I found odious.

Marianne, whose role was now largely that of a governess and in whose company I was to keep up and improve my German, took me daily to the tree-shaded square Galilée, where I played with other children while she sat on one of the benches. It was under those trees, while playing with other children, that I distinctly recall feeling for the first time completely at ease in French. I had found my language, a language I could think of as my own.

Soon we moved again, this time to a furnished apartment overlooking place Victor Hugo, at the center of which stood a huge bronze statue of the contemplative poet visible from our living-room windows. The contrast between the delicate eighteenth-century furniture in that room and the massive proportions of the vatic bronze figure made a lasting impression on me. Looking out from that living room, where I was strictly forbidden to play, I had my first encounter with Victor Hugo, whose complete works I later also noticed in their leather-bound patriarchal appearance on my father's shelves.

But that was in our next apartment. A year later, in fact, once most of our own furniture had arrived—it had a distinctly Central European solidity—we settled in the rue Eugène Manuel, a quiet street within walking distance of the gardens of La Muette. I still remember our telephone number—AUTeuil 84-14—as I remember to this day the U.S. army serial number I carried on my dog tag. Much as I used the telephone to call my friends, we were not "on the phone" as young people are nowadays. That would not have been tolerated. As for long-distance calls, they were altogether out of the question. Even our parents made such calls only for exceptional reasons. But my friends and I hardly needed the phone. We knew exactly when we would meet at La Muette. It was there, away from parental ears, that all our transactions, all our planning took place.

It was a short walk from our apartment to La Muette, along the busy commercial rue de Passy. As a boy, I roller-skated on the special concrete alley near the stand where my mother or Marianne bought me cherry-flavored lollipops, and on exceptional occasions treated me to waffles or crêpes filled with jam. In the fall, there was always the same ambulatory vendor of roasted chestnuts. When there were other boys my own age, we played ball, improvising goals. A few years later, La Muette became the rallying point of our adolescent gang. We would gather after school, or on Thursdays and Sundays—that is, when my mother did not drag me to the Louvre. We met across the street from the Art Nouveau entrance to the *métro*, in front of the *bar-café* that sported the sign of PMU (Pari Mutuel Urbain)—a ubiquitous agency that held the monopoly on the very popular off-track horse-race betting. We did not bet and were underage in any case, but the proximity of those excited men arguing and consulting the racing papers and all the talk of "win" and "place" gave us a feeling of independence and maturity. We were a noisy bunch, too, with our chaotic chatter about *surprises-parties*, boxing bouts, Gary Cooper films, and lengthy debates as to whether to go skating at Molitor or at Saint-Didier. All the while, our lanky, heavily bespectacled school buddy Joël insisted on reading aloud some pseudo-epic verse he had committed to paper describing in gory detail Joan of Arc's burning at the stake, with her entrails bursting through the cracked flesh of her belly. But Pierre Masselli's voice was the most strident, as he interrupted everyone, perorating about horses and jockeys with a pretense of inside knowledge, or bragging about his latest sexual exploit. Women or horses, they were all the same to him—an occasion to gamble and win.

My own erotic associations with the park at La Muette are of a much later date and had nothing to do with Masselli's vulgar bragging, or with the betting fever of the crowd at the PMU bar. I met Yvette in 1944 just a few months after the liberation of Paris, when I was briefly recalled from the front lines near Holland to U.S. army intelligence headquarters in Paris, and naively believed that the war was over for me. It was at La Muette that I explained to Yvette the meaning of "*carpe diem*" and why we must not waste one single day. It was there, on one of the park benches, that she told me about her boyfriend, whom she tried to arouse but who was not interested in sex. Before meeting Yvette, I had rented a tiny flat on the rue des Vignes. Our trysts usually began with a glass of greenish-yellow liqueur. She often spent the night with me. Her boyfriend, who lived in another city, apparently did not mind. But I took no chances, and always kept my army pistol within reach.

La Muette. The name itself is like an archaeological site. Childhood, adolescence, early adulthood in military uniform—and now occasional pilgrimages on my way to the Musée Marmottan, the home of some exceptional Monets. The name is also symbolic of a feminine secret, for it means "the mute woman," the silent one. The secret, in this case, has to do with my puzzlement over myself. It is not clear to me which layer holds the truth. Different selves, at different times, haunted this space. I came to understand that Stendhal was surely right in asking himself, as he surveyed in his puzzlement the city of Rome from the top of the Janiculum, Who am I, what have I been? The eye cannot see itself. The panoramic survey of Rome's archaeology was a meaningful emblem. Strata disappear and then emerge again. The very ruins served to build anew.

I was never more keenly aware of the layers of time and memory, of the resurrected presence of the past together with a sense of ironic distance, as when driving by my old lycée during my Guggenheim fellowship year, or more recently, when taking the night train to Nice after dinner in the 1900s décor of the Train Bleu restaurant at the Gare de Lyon. My trains of thought were, in both cases, as happens so often, associated with vehicular movement. Growing up, changing, remaining the same, somehow blended. Elias Canetti wrote that since the age of ten he had felt that he consisted of many characters. Personally, I felt neither duplicity nor contradiction, but something akin to the satisfaction of discovering that although words undergo changes over time, occasionally acquiring a very different meaning, they somehow at their root remain faithful to themselves.

To be attached to the life of words means to take possession or repossession of sounds and signs that are charged with echoes, reminiscences, unexpected alliances, surprising betrayals, yet also carry at their core a permanence that promises an eventual return home.

TO MY LYCÉE education I owe a lot, even though I ceased being an attentive student the year my eyes began undressing women in the street, in 1937—the year of the rue de Provence. What impressed me more than Greek mythology, Napoleon's campaigns and administrative reforms, snatches of Latin poetry, or accounts of theological debates surrounding Pascal and Jansenism was the mystique of France that we were exposed to in daily doses. It is now hard for me to believe how seriously I absorbed this mystique, even though I still keep a tiny tricolor flag on my office desk, between two reference works. My love for France lasted even after we experienced the Vichy regime. It accompanied me during the months of our difficult escape from Europe, feeding my hope that the United States would enter the war and come to the rescue. When Japan attacked Pearl Harbor, I could begin to hope that I would soon be landing in France with the American troops. My adolescent fervor for the notion of France was no doubt heightened by my frustrated longing for French citizenship. For unlike my cousin Tovy, who had been born in Paris, I would not become a citizen until I was called up for military service—and the German invasion of France forestalled this desired event.

I doubt that I was truly interested during those prewar years in political events and in the outside world. My glance was turned largely inward. I am struck by the regularity with which I kept a daily appointment with myself. Not that I listened to myself, that I auscultated myself in the manner of a congenital hypochondriac—though an incipient hypochondria may well have been part of my adolescent self-centeredness. Did I really find myself so endlessly interesting in all my nooks and crannies? The fact is, much as I played hooky in order to escape to distant quarters of Paris, I also gladly stayed alone in my room, a space I liked to consider inviolable. My room, my fortress. Years before I came across the ambivalent image of oppressive and protective walls in Kafka's writings, I felt attached to my cell in such a way that I welcomed any cold, any fever, any minor illness, that would allow me to stay in bed, with my door closed and the curtains drawn. The muted jazz coming from the radio next to my bed somehow harmonized with the silence. The satisfaction of not attending school for a legitimate reason was puny compared to the pleasure derived from long hours of reveries, which my fever seemed to intensify.

If fever produced vivid reveries, my delight in those reveries in turn taught me to produce the fever that would allow me to be confined to my room—or rather, to simulate that fever. I discovered that by delicate flicks of the finger on the bottom of the thermometer I could gradually bring up the mercury reading to the desired level. I had to practice for a while to achieve the proper skill. A single overly vigorous flip and the mercury would separate. A clever friend recently told me that I could have achieved the same result more efficiently by applying the tip of the thermometer to the lit bulb on my night table. My method was primitive by comparison. But the result was what counted: my parents were duly worried, each time, ordered me to stay home and in bed, and had me take my temperature every few hours, most often with a crescendo effect.

Sometimes there was a price to pay for the right to pursue my fantasies while listening to jazz in a horizontal position. On the third day of one of those simulated illnesses, a doctor I had never seen before made a house call. He seemed especially interested in my throat. A good thing he was called, I remember him saying. He could see pus pockets that needed to be emptied. To me he explained that the procedure was not going to be altogether pleasant, but he knew I'd be brave. He spoke of my being brave much in the same patronizing tone as those teachers who, in my early years, had categorized me as a *bon sujet*. Before I knew it, he pulled out a longish tube from his bag and inserted it into my mouth. I was prepared to be stoical, though bravery, even then, was not my forte. The second attempt at vacuuming my laryngeal crypts left him apparently satisfied. He departed, after a brief exchange with my mother in the corridor, though not before pocketing his fee, handed to him discreetly in an envelope. Fake patient, fake doctor, I thought to myself while my throat now ached for good. The episode prepared me to appreciate more fully some of Molière's medical satire. *Purgare, clysterium donare.*

Distaste for school and a penchant for indolence do not adequately account for my attachment to my room. I now believe that if I went to the trouble of disquieting my parents with my mysterious fever and remained stoical in the face of an invasive doctor, it was because I cherished my privacy and the kaleidoscope of my daydreams. I still like to withdraw within the four walls of my study to get lost in my thoughts and pursue my whimsies. One of the reasons I like my profession so much is that it allows me, when at my desk, to escape into reveries between notes I take for lectures, between the beginning and the end of the sentences I write, while intermittently staring through the window at the garden and the flower beds that, at this moment, offer to my roving glance a profusion of lilies, geraniums, and delphiniums. At times I have felt a monastic urge. Within the confines of my study, I evoke cloisters with Romanesque arcades opening onto a garden with a covered well, places of seclusion and peaceful meditation. And I think of poetic prisoners, characters in the novels of Stendhal, or historical figures like Benvenuto Cellini and Silvio Pellico.

Sitting in my room, pen in hand, I occasionally wonder why I write these pages. Maybe it is the spell of the future perfect, the desire to view the past from an ideal, ultimate vantage point, where nothing can change anymore. The fear of nonbeing has on occasion driven me to the mirror in search of reassurance. Perhaps people write memoirs and expose their vulnerabilities in order to exorcise private demons. What they are after is perhaps not so much self-knowledge as self-possession, a way of holding on. I keep telling myself that I almost was not. In order to conceive me, my mother traveled all the way to Berlin for a chancy operation performed by a well-known specialist. Dr. Mumm, I seem to recall, was his name. I can never drink the champagne that goes by the same name without making a mental toast.

There were, of course, real fevers and real illnesses. Up to a point, I enjoyed those, too, because of the enforced passivity, unless I felt truly miserable—as when I suffered from that itchy chicken pox that prevented me from pursuing my courtship of Anita, the dark-eyed girl who had passed out on a bed next to me at one of the *surprises-parties*. I even learned to love—almost as an experience that justified real fever and real discomfort—that period of reawakening sensations called "convalescence." I discovered that convalescence, the regaining of health and strength, could be a poetic experience as well as a metaphor for the intense awareness of being alive. In families such as mine, convalescence was a ritualized return to normalcy regulated by doctors and parents. At first, a half-hour walk at midday, preferably in the sun if it was winter. The walks would gradually be longer, but I was not allowed out without being properly muffled up, even in the spring. I received strict injunctions to walk slowly and avoid perspiring. Frustrated though I was by those admonitions and by the measured-out re-entry, I myself felt inclined to prolong the joy of gradually rediscovering the simple pleasures of a walk in the sun, the tingle of the fresh air, the smell and taste of fruit, even the inebriating sensation of a glass of cool water. This was indeed a return to the world of the living. I came to develop a belief, though I could not have formulated it then, that all of life should be lived out with a convalescent's joy, that convalescence was also a metaphor for renewal and survival.

During such periods of convalescence, sometimes still in my pajamas, I would act out dramatic scenes in front of the mirror. These were usually scenes of inflicted violence or death agony that ultimately brought me down to the floor, where I could no longer watch the expression on my face. There were duels with complicated swordplay and scenes of prisoners tortured slowly by Chinese executioners or savage Indian tribes. One of my favorite dramatic renderings was the death of Boris Godunov. I had listened many times to our old record, the *plastinka,* as my parents called it, of Chaliapin singing the famous death scene. I loved especially the way he projected the words "I am still the czar"—the first time as a desperately proud affirmation, the second time in a more subdued and almost trembling manner. Then Boris collapses. I had never seen the opera, but my mother had described the scene to me in vivid detail. I could visualize it all, including the collapse and fall from the throne, so that when, many years later, I attended a performance in New York at the old Metropolitan Opera, it was quite familiar. And when Ezio Pinza, singing sumptuously the role of Boris, finally fell, I relived the scene I had often played out in front of my mirror—except that Pinza fell far more expertly.

My mirror games may explain why I have never been able to take myself altogether seriously. Bettina says that I need and love mirrors more than windows. That is somewhat unfair, though true in a sense. I do love windows, whether in my room or on the train. But a mirror is for me also a window through which I can move beyond my confines, a threshold that abolishes all lines of demarcation between the inside and the outside. My private little acting stage was probably a way of reaching out. Soon, however, this private theater and sense of privacy were to be threatened by the larger and very real drama of war. The *drôle de guerre*, the phony war, was about to begin.

Chapter 6

PRELUDE TO WAR

The *drôle de guerre*, the "phony war," as it came to be called, refers to the period of wait-and-see between early September 1939 and May 1940. On September 3, 1939, France and Britain declared war on Germany after Hitler attacked Poland. The following May, a lightning German offensive speedily crushed the Dutch and the Belgian armed forces and then outflanked, splintered, and routed the supposedly invincible French army. Within a matter of weeks the French government was forced to flee to Bordeaux and then to ask for an armistice. The chaotic days that followed May 10, 1940, when the German army unleashed its Panzer divisions and dive-bombing Luftwaffe, were not to be forgotten by those who lived through the cataclysm, especially the many—literally millions—who fled on congested roads just ahead of the fast-advancing German army.

But between September and May, during eight long months as the 1930s turned into the 1940s, nothing seemed to happen. A disquieting lull settled in, as the two war machines faced each other with hardly a shot fired—blocked, it would seem, by the collective memory of the trench warfare of two decades earlier, the horror of barbed wires, murderous artillery barrages, and insane bayonet assaults to gain a few hundred yards of terrain. Both sides, this time, seemed intent on a war of attrition. A few skirmishes were reported now and then, otherwise all was quiet. After the early fears of attacks on the civilian population had proved unwarranted, the standoff on the front provided the illusion of stability, almost the assurance that nothing serious would happen.

The feeling of security was enhanced by an unquestioned faith in the Maginot Line, that reputedly impregnable system of fortifications built in the 1920s and early 1930s, which extended all along the frontier with Germany. The only problem was that it did not cover any of the Belgian frontier, and it did not extend all the way to the sea. Nor was it of much use in a modern war of mobile armor and massive air assaults. Such a war, as the young officer Charles de Gaulle had been quick to perceive, could not be merely defensive. But no one listened. When the Germans launched their blitzkrieg, the famous Maginot Line was easily flanked. It turned out to be even less effective than the Great Wall of China.

In a way, the Maginot Line could be considered a metaphor for the many illusions of security with which we lived during the period preceding the May–June 1940 disaster. All through the winter, we saw posters and heard slogans that were to give us the conviction of invincibility. I remember one poster especially: It stated in bold letters, *"Nous vaincrons parce que nous sommes les plus forts"* (We shall win because we are the strongest). The poster displayed a map of the globe with all the French and British colonies and possessions in color. These included French West Africa, Algeria, Morocco, Tunisia, French Equatorial Africa, Madagascar, Syria, Lebanon, Indochina, Canada, some smaller South Sea islands, New Caledonia, Guiana, Martinique and Guadeloupe, and Djibouti. Next to these vast colored areas, Germany, including the annexed regions, seemed puny. To boost this overwhelming self-confidence, there was also the popular song recorded by Ray Ventura and his band, *"On ira pendre notre linge sur la ligne Siegfried"* (We'll hang our wash on the Siegfried line). It was on everyone's lips, and it replaced the bittersweet optimism of an earlier song launched by the same band, *"Tout va très bien, Madame la Marquise"* (Everything's just fine, Madame la marquise), though the song reveals one disaster after another.

We were all dimly aware that this optimism was unwarranted, that it rested on self-deception and simulacra of strength. Daladier, the thick-necked war minister and premier since 1938, became in a sense the symbol of this pretense of strength. He had succeeded Léon Blum, had taken a strong anticommunist stance, and received a mandate to toughen and prepare France for all contingencies. In 1938, Daladier had signed the infamous Munich accord that disposed of Czechoslovakia.

He was nonetheless called the "Bull of Vaucluse" (his electoral district), in part perhaps because of his stocky stature and thick neck. "A bull with snails' horns," Chamberlain is said to have quipped. But Chamberlain himself was no exemplar of heroic decisiveness against the Nazis.

France's weaknesses were manifest. My father talked about them at some length at the dinner table—that is, when he was not watching out for fish bones. Pacifism of every persuasion went together with willful blindness. He made fun of a sentence that came at the end of an official film about the preparedness of the army: "You can sleep peacefully, we are well defended." In point of fact, few slept peacefully. France lived in dread of war, largely because it was afraid of so much else, and most of all of its own inner dissensions. The optimism of its songs was a façade. The country was bitterly divided on almost every issue and lived with the still-recent memory of the Great War that had bled it of two million of its young men. Mutilated middle-aged individuals remained a common sight in the street and on public transportation. Some had horrible facial scars. I remember crossing the street whenever I saw one of those war victims approach. They were known as *gueules cassées* (disfigured mugs).

Ironically, the information minister of the supposedly tough Daladier government was the successful and elegantly poetic playwright Jean Giraudoux, author of *La guerre de Troie n'aura pas lieu* (The Trojan War will not take place). My mother had taken me to see the play, hoping that it would be an edifying experience. One could hardly escape the political undertones and preoccupations of the day; they were ubiquitous, by direct reference or by innuendo. But what was truly difficult, even impossible to decipher—especially for a teenager, no matter how alerted to the political realities—were the many signs of disarray. A declining birthrate, a discredited parliamentary system, pathological fear of social unrest, divisions even within the antifascist left as to how to deal with the foreign threat, a hodgepodge of pacifist theories, anti-Bolshevism, xenophobia, even defeatism of various shades—all of these combined were symptoms of frailty. Only they were not properly interpreted at the time.

What we were vaguely aware of was that ideological stubbornness blinded people to the Hitlerian threat and led to strange paradoxes.

Chauvinistic Germanophobes turned into pacifists, preferring fascism to a war that they feared might unleash social unrest and a Bolshevist revolution in France. Even the antifascist left felt that war was not the best way of fighting fascism, that fascism was not an external but an internal threat. In the meantime, the more aggressive Germany appeared, the more suspicious and "undesirable" became the presence of refugees, the victims of the Nazi regime who had sought asylum in France. Foreign Jews in particular were accused of pushing for war with Germany, and at the same time of undermining France's strength. Never was the scapegoat theory more applicable than in the 1930s, while Germany was rearming itself with vengeance in mind.

I remember in particular the disparaging word "*métèque*," commonly used with regard to conspicuous foreigners who spoke demotic or strangely inflected French. The word was not limited to distinct Levantine types but extended to all undesirable aliens. It carried racist undertones. To my ears it sounded a little like "*macaque*," a kind of monkey, also used to characterize ugly people. I have since learned that the ancient Greek word "*metoikos*," from which "*métèque*" is derived, had no pejorative connotation. It simply meant a foreigner authorized to reside in Athens with certain privileges, but without the voting rights of a citizen. The insulting, hostile misuse of the Greek word seems to me now further proof that the French, in the 1930s, had forgotten their country's proud tradition of offering political asylum.

Xenophobia easily focused on Jews, particularly the recent immigrants. French Jews themselves, feeling superior, and to some extent embarrassed by their non-French co-religionists, deplored the arrival of German and eastern Jews fleeing from Nazi persecution. Bad faith and ideological confusion took many forms. The extreme right accused the Jews of warmongering; they were seeking revenge against Hitler at the cost of French blood. The extreme left denounced international Jewry for urging a war that could benefit only international finance, bringing about the ultimate triumph of ruthless capitalism and plutocracy (a word dear to Hitler). But it was militant communism that deserved the palm of bad faith, pretending in the editorials of the daily *L'Humanité* to stand for the defense of social justice against any form of tyranny, yet theorizing quite openly that military conflict was a necessary evil in order to bring about the Marxist revolution on a grand scale, a revolution that would inevitably triumph in those countries most affected by the calamities of war.

Xenophobia, perhaps endemic in the French, was exacerbated when the influx of refugees from the Spanish Civil War—many of them former fighters in the defeated Republican army—raised the specter of anarchy and violence. Reports of atrocities in Spain—Goya-like images of horrors committed against nuns and priests—circulated widely, feeding the French psychosis about evil forces at work to destroy the nation. There were repeated rumors of an imminent putsch, of terrorist hit lists, of paramilitary forces ready to liquidate their enemies and take over. In the 1930s, the France of Maurice Chevalier and Mistinguett was on the brink of civil war. Street demonstrations by right-wing vigilantes were met by violent leftist counterdemonstrations. In February 1934, six years before Vichy, the radical right almost toppled the Third Republic and its democratic institutions. Four years later, after the strike of 1938, it was the government of that same Third Republic that repressed the workers' movement. Though I knew about most of these events, I did not understand their full significance. But what I retained from my father's impromptu dinner perorations, to which I usually lent only half an ear, was that France was trapped in its own selfish and self-centered isolationism, blind because of ideological obsessions and fears to the realities of Nazi racism and expansionist threats. Shrugging his shoulders as if to indicate that it was hopeless, my father said the French had turned into sleepwalkers—*somnambules*.

EVEN FOR A teenager very taken with himself, it was hard to be unaware of events. Newsreels, radio programs, ubiquitous arguments and discussions, large newspaper headlines—all kept us sensitized to the bitter strife between political parties, the frequent changes of government (though the same political figures kept reappearing in each new cabinet, in what amounted to a national game of musical chairs), the endless debates about intervention or nonintervention in the Spanish Civil War, which the more lucid observers saw as a prelude to a general war. We were aware of the fascination experienced by intellectuals on the right when they reported on the mass Nazi rallies in Nuremberg. We were also aware of how fashionable it had become for intellectuals on the left to praise even the patent flaws and excesses of the Soviet Union. England produced ambivalent reactions but was mostly viewed with diffidence and often referred to as "perfidious Albion." As for the United States, it was hardly a political presence, though the 1929 Wall Street crash had had a disastrous impact worldwide. Meanwhile, Hollywood films conveyed the image of a never-never land where every success was possible, and President Franklin Roosevelt quickly became a familiar, benign-looking figure, with his perennial smile.

In the summer of 1938, when I was sent to summer college in England to learn English as it is really spoken, my sense of the political situation was more developed than that of most of the boys I met there. Rather than send me to stay with the English family in Howe where my cousin Sascha had spent the previous summer, my parents decided on a college in Brighton. Their reasons: I would be closely watched and less likely to get into trouble, and I would also learn English better. As it turned out, they were wrong on both counts. I remember arriving at the school very self-conscious. Just two weeks before leaving home, while playing ping-pong on the porch of the Racing Club, I had stumbled trying to retrieve a smash and fell with my face against the long metal bar of the entrance door of the clubhouse. The gash under my lip required six stitches. I arrived in Brighton with a swollen red lip; the stitches had barely been taken out. To make matters worse, the English barber I ventured to on my second day at school mangled my hair, leaving here and there small, bizarre-looking tonsured areas.

I soon forgot about my hair and my lip and cheerfully joined in the life of the school. But one of my parents' assumptions soon proved utterly mistaken. There were no English boys in the college during the summer session. My companions were French, Romanian, Swiss, Greek; there was even an older Egyptian boy who gave us boxing lessons. They all came from well-heeled families. Soon my Parisian friend Maurice Lécuyer also arrived. I hardly ever spoke or heard a word of English outside of class. Aside from the classroom, the dining room, or school-organized outings, the only English contact some of my schoolmates and I had was an English army corporal whom we somehow befriended. I don't quite remember the circumstances. Perhaps it was on the long and busy pier. But this extramural contact pointed up my parents' other miscalculation. Far from being carefully watched (as my cousin Sascha no doubt had been by his English family), we boys in the college slipped out every night through a dormitory window and then climbed over a wall. The school authorities either did not suspect anything or closed an eye to these expeditions. We went off to town, to the movies, to the amusement park, to the pier with the slot machines, to a pub where we were admitted—often in the company of this corporal, who called himself Raleigh G. H. (that is how I remember his name). As for classes, I recall being tormented by erotic images and physical desire. The return from our nocturnal escapades sometimes posed a problem. On a few occasions, we found the window shut. Reentry then required some ingenuity, though I no longer remember how we made it back into our dorm.

Certain images and impressions from those summer months in 1938 are still vivid: the color and particular odor of British buses; the velvety fruit-flavored milk shakes (a new sensation for me, for France was hardly a milk-drinking country); the enormous cinema theaters with organ music during intermissions (Parisian cinemas were intimate by comparison); the smell of Corporal Raleigh G. H.'s uniform, which I later came to identify with British army units (every army has its own peculiar smell); lessons in cricket, a sport that was incomprehensible to me; the public toilets one unlocked with a coin (the first time I had to use one, the coin I did not possess was charitably offered me by a passerby who sensed my urgent need); a school outing to the shipyards and port of Southampton. I could not possibly imagine that six years later I would slowly roll toward the same port in an American army jeep. The Normandy invasion truly began for me in that congested convoy of jeeps and armored vehicles, when I saw Southampton again, this time with countless antiaircraft blimps hovering almost playfully over the naval installation. But this was no play—and the England that by then had experienced the blitz was an altogether different England from the somewhat bland country I had known during my summer vacation in 1938, a vacation from which I returned to meet my mother's annoyance and reproaches, not because of my unauthorized evenings on the Brighton pier (about which she knew nothing), but because I came back having forgotten to pack most of my underwear as well as a pair of trousers.

My father, on the other hand, unconcerned about the loss of my underwear, was deeply troubled by the turn of political events. I remember that, lying in his foamy bathtub while I shaved with his heavy brass razor I so loved to handle, he pressed on me the seriousness of the situation. In Spain, Generalissimo Francisco Franco, known as "Il Caudillo," had reached the Mediterranean and cut the Republican zone in half. In France, the Socialist party was badly divided. The government of Daladier, himself not long ago a leader of the Popular Front, was now taking a tough stance against the labor unions and reconsidering the sacrosanct forty-hour work week, one of the most controversial achievements of the Blum government. The tune had changed. It was time to put France to work again. The forty-hour week was no longer viable with Germany rearming at full speed. But the more austere outlook was bound to result in social unrest.

Soon there were even more disturbing developments, and the fall of 1938 proved particularly anxious. At the end of September, after Chamberlain and Hitler met in Berchtesgaden, the Munich agreement was signed by Daladier and Chamberlain in the presence of Hitler and Mussolini. This act of appeasement led to the dismemberment of Czechoslovakia and gave Hitler the green light for further claims and aggression. The vast majority in France acclaimed Daladier upon his return from Munich, and the Chamber of Deputies overwhelmingly ratified the accord. "Peace at all cost" was the motto. The Cassandras of the day—the political journalist Geneviève Tabouis being one—were not heard.

To be honest, my father's dire predictions had little impact on me; my mind was on other matters. I preferred to read up on the Tour de France that I had missed while in Brighton, which was won that year by the legendary cyclist Gino Bartoli. I also remember having been obsessed—but perhaps it was a year later—by a film with Jean Gabin and Michèle Morgan called *Quai des brumes*. One of Gabin's terse lines kept echoing in my mind: "*T'as de beaux yeux, tu sais*" (You've got beautiful eyes, you know). This story about a deserter had political overtones, I now realize. At the time I was aware only of its somber erotic elements.

THE FOLLOWING SUMMER—the summer of 1939—was for many of us ominous from the start. Sunny days can be counted in Normandy. That summer in Deauville was no different. Yet in retrospect it seems to me that the sky was overcast more often than usual. Oppressive days, humid and drizzly, were relieved occasionally by radiant hours when everything seemed to shimmer and the sea, beyond the wide stretch of beach, had an almost Mediterranean hue. Never before had I felt so strongly that the summer was bound to be the end of something. It is from that point in time, I believe, that I came to view every vacation, and later every sabbatical leave, indeed every privileged period, as a bittersweet analogue of life itself, pointing up the almost visible inevitability of the end. That summer in Deauville, there was a sense of inescapable loss; and for me, who had to take a special exam in the fall, there was, like a *basso continuo*, the fear of an impending calamity. How I sympathized, years later, with the elegiac lament in Virginia Woolf's *To the Lighthouse*: "It will end." Vacationing in the insular calm and stability on one of the Hebrides islands, Woolf's protagonist recognizes her own finite nature in the ebb and flow of the pulsating sea all around her. Normandy was not an island, but in 1939, all of France was insular, assailed by evil forces preparing havoc.

The return from summer vacation—*la rentrée*, the French call it— was usually fraught with autumnal sadness and a latent feeling of anguish. "*Adieu, vive clarté de nos étés trop courts*"—Baudelaire's line about the brevity of summer, and winter beginning to invade the soul— captures a common childhood frustration. Vacation at any time carries its own distress. The word itself suggests vacuity at the core. The more or less brief period of leisure and freedom is at best a reprieve that cannot cancel the awareness of a terminal date. That summer in Deauville, there was in addition the prospect of the impending exam that would determine whether or not I would have to repeat the previous year. My mother daily reminded me of that inexorable event. I still marvel at the violence of her anger (she was usually self-controlled) when she learned that I had failed to show up for my remedial lessons in mathematics and had appropriated my tutor's fees.

The weather in Normandy imposed some variety on our activities. Grown-ups and children alike had a different idea then of what made for a satisfying vacation. We did not expect to spend every day lying on the beach, anointed with oils or besmeared with creams. On many days, there were only sporadic sunbursts. We welcomed the cooler, grayer days—even the days of unremitting rain. We read, we played games. Monopoly, which was the rage, helped us learn English words other than those in the crooners' songs. We even had time to be bored and to daydream. For some reason, tennis was not high on my list of activities that summer, but that may have been because I was the only one in our gang, or *bande,* who was a regular player. We all engaged, however, in fierce bouts of volleyball, by preference where the sand was hard from the ebbed sea. I tried to show off with tennis-style smashes at the net, not always willing to recognize that volleyball was a team sport.

I was infatuated with Danielle Wolf and could think of little else. How we met now escapes me. She was part of the group. How that group came into being is now also shrouded by time. Dany was short, somewhat stocky, though her body was well proportioned. She had a smile half-tender and half-mocking. There was just a trace of light down above her full lips. Her hair was dark and combed back. She had soft hands and a melodious voice that reminded me of the mezzo-soprano timbre of my cousin Yula. It is hard for me to imagine her disheveled, haggard, thirsty, in the airless cattle train on its way to Auschwitz, clutching her two-year-old child. Yet that is how she met her end, and not so long after that summer in Deauville. The images I conjure up haunt me. I spent all my time with her—even the time I was supposed to spend preparing for the dreaded fall exam. We would occasionally get away from the group and walk alone on the boardwalk, hand in hand, our arms interlocked. Seeking greater privacy, we walked on the mole at night, and then lay on the sand with our fingers interlocked, looking at the stars when they were visible. I can still smell Dany's hair, almost sixty years later.

Our Deauville *bande* improvised activities more promptly and more harmoniously than seemed feasible for the Parisian group meeting at La Muette, where endless proposals and discussions often paralyzed us, and nothing at all happened. The summer gang, though more socially varied, seemed to agree more easily. We went on bicycle outings, taking with us a lightweight portable phonograph and some records. "Jeepers, Creepers" was the big hit that summer. I had no idea what the words meant, nor what exactly the admired "peepers," in the line that followed, referred to. "Where'd you get those peepers?" I did guess that it was a part of the feminine anatomy, but in the imperfect state of my English I chose to situate the plural "peepers" somewhat lower than was meant by the songwriter.

We also organized dance competitions, awarded prizes for the most beautiful legs or ears, looked into the Trouville casino, consumed apple turnovers in the appealing pastry shop on the main street of Trouville, and compared terms for special caresses. I still remember an older boy mentioning enthusiastically *la feuille de rose,* a caress that truly puzzled me but which I pretended to know all about. Occasionally we worried about those of us who had reached the age of being suddenly called to the army in case there was a general mobilization. The political situation seemed increasingly alarming.

I now know I learned a great deal about myself that summer. I had huge longings and desires, but the smallest favors, the slightest sign of affection and tenderness, moved me profoundly. The ultimate "favors," as some put it euphemistically, I neither received nor demanded from Dany. When I later became more expert with mature women, the physical intimacies I experienced seemed to me less thrilling than those nocturnal walks arm in arm, and the long kisses on the wharf. Dany was almost two years older than I. She told me that her parents more than once brought up the subject of a "more serious" friend. Did he exist? Was he their wishful thought? Perhaps it was their way of judging me. In any case, I felt hurt. I was made to realize that there was no future to our relationship. What would happen when the summer was over? More than ever, vacation time carried at its core the double reminder of closure and evanescence.

The other lesson was of a social nature, but it was not unrelated to my sentimental needs. When my schoolfriend Jacques came to visit me for a fortnight, sharing my room in our summer flat, it quickly became obvious that he did not fit into our little group. Jacques could not understand my relations with Dany. I was excessively "romantic," he thought. It was all so different from our expedition to the rue de Provence. I realized that people one is fond of do not automatically mix well. Jacques and I came from the same world, but by the time he arrived in Deauville, our group was already fully formed, and he remained an outsider. The group had its own tone, habits, jokes, language. Some of us stayed in Deauville, others in Trouville; these were adjacent resorts, barely separated by the narrow Touques River, though the clientele was quite distinct—worldly and even flashy in Deauville, sedate and distinctly middle-class in Trouville.

In Paris the distance between these two worlds was far greater. We belonged to separate spheres. Dany Wolf's family lived on the boulevard Voltaire, not far from the place de la République, a popular quarter; and we, in the *cossu,* or well-to-do, region of Passy. "*Cossu*" was in fact a word used by Dany almost as a reproach. When we later saw each other in Paris during the winter of the phony war, much of the spell was gone. We met, so to speak, on neutral grounds, on the Champs-Elysées. But despite my fervent love letters, shamelessly plagiarized from the poems of Musset, and her own tender replies, we had become strangers. Paris only increased the distance. Our love, born on the beaches and green fields of Normandy, no longer seemed to have any roots. On the impersonal Champs-Elysées, which knew nothing of our summer idyll, I learned the importance of emotional context. What had prospered in Deauville-Trouville could not easily survive beyond the vacation. I became aware that her family expected her to find a husband soon. And what kind of candidate was I, a mere lycée student? None of this was really news to me. But vacation time, I discovered, is a time of suspended reality. I knew all the while that I was going to lose Dany.

THE FEELING OF impending loss, that summer of 1939, was compounded by a pervasive anxiety shared by almost everyone. We were surrounded by dark signs of which even a self-centered sixteen-year-old could not be unmindful. The Spanish Civil War had ended in defeat for the Loyalist side, crushing the hopes of antifascist forces there. Madrid had fallen and Franco was in power. This had been foreseen for some time, and it lent additional poignancy to André Malraux's novel ironically titled *L'Espoir* (Hope)—that heroic account of the Spanish war about which my cousin Shura Adler, waxing dithyrambic, did not stop talking every time he came for a visit.

But that same summer brought even more stunning news. While the Soviet Union was assumed to be negotiating some kind of military agreement with France and Britain, Stalin, in fact, signed a pact with Hitler that spelled the doom of Poland, which they set out to divide between themselves. At the very beginning of September, we learned that the German army had crossed the Polish border, launching a massive attack on the ground and in the air. What followed had the inevitability of a bad dream. France and Britain declared war on the Third Reich. With that, our summer came to an end.

It was more pathetic than dramatic. A lot of confusion was in the air, and many people failed to understand why we were at war. To "die for Danzig" (the German name for the Polish port of Gdansk) was the slogan for what many felt was a silly, useless war, a war against the best interests of France. The declaration of war did not really unify the French behind a common purpose. War was seen by more than a few as an evil that should have been avoided, whatever the cost. In the meantime, the wildest rumors circulated. There would be gas attacks on major French cities; gas masks were in fact soon made available. In my family, each of us had one that could be carried in a cylindrical case slung over the shoulder. There was talk of imminent Luftwaffe attacks on the civilian population, of mass destruction coming from the sky. The fearful example of Guernica was on everybody's mind. Some remembered seeing Picasso's terrifying painting at the Spanish pavilion of the Exposition Internationale. And there was the recent example of dive-bombing attacks on Polish cities.

My father, ever cautious, decided that we would not return to Paris, that we would rent a villa in Deauville for the winter. He would spend five days a week in Paris attending to his wholesale and export business and then join my mother and me for the weekend. I was delighted. This year there would be no *rentrée* for me. I figured naively that there would therefore be no exam and maybe no lycée either. I was wrong, of course. A lycée was soon organized in Deauville for the many Parisian families who had settled in the resort for the winter. It was a branch of the lycée in the nearby city of Caen, and it occupied an entire hotel with a glittering white façade. The cheerful-looking façade promised a regime somewhat milder than the one I was accustomed to at Janson de Sailly. And I was either lucky or the examiners in the improvised lycée were especially indulgent, but I was admitted into the *classe de première*, the senior class of the secondary education cycle leading up to the *baccalauréat*.

The villa my parents rented was called San Gimignano, I do not know why. It had nothing Tuscan about it, nor did the name mean anything to me at the time. The name now amuses me, as I write these lines near Castellina in Chianti, within sight of the real San Gimignano, whose distant towers shimmer in midair through the morning mist, appearing unreal and almost magical. The house we rented in Deauville was fake old Norman. It had a narrow garden on the side of the entrance and stood on a broad street parallel to the boardwalk, a block away from the sea front. A distinct sea flavor was carried to us by the slightest wind. The house was large and not very attractive. It had two stories above the ground floor, and an attic room which we called the "tower." It was so large that we shared it with the family of my father's sister, Aunt Katya, her snorting husband, Ruvim, who must have suffered from adenoidal obstruction, and my cousins Sascha and Irène. A cat came with the house; we called it Mirza. I never established any rapport of trust with Mirza, perhaps because it would not forget that I had once pulled it up by its tail.

I have trouble reconstructing the rooms of this house. It was a complicated layout, as there were different staircases leading to different parts of the house. All I see clearly is the narrow garden, the wrought-iron gate through which one could glimpse some chairs and a round table with a large umbrella that was hardly ever unfolded. I also see my cousin Sascha's room, with a small desk in front of the window. In a prankish or retaliatory mood (I no longer recall which), one day I directed the garden hose against his open window, spraying his written homework. Sascha's anger truly scared me as he came running down after me, swearing that he would make me pay dearly for the insult and the water damage. But I ran faster than he did. Despite such occasional wrangles and confrontations, our relations were good. They were, in fact, cemented that winter. Sascha and I remained close for the following two years, which included the period of the Occupation and the Vichy regime.

My own room I remember in some detail. It was in the so-called tower. Against one wall, there was a tall armoire with a cumbersome key that would always fall out of the keyhole, and a squat chest whose drawers would often get stuck. It was no tower at all but an attic room, uncomfortable on damp and cold days. On hot summer days it must have been unbearable, but summer days were over by the time we settled in. I liked the idea of a "tower" even though I had not yet come across the poetic description of the Farnese Tower in Stendhal's *Charterhouse of Parma*. But I had heard about ivory towers, which I associated with the poet Vigny, and the previous year our French teacher had described to us Montaigne sitting in his tower, surrounded by books and writing his famous essays. It was in my own "tower" that I wrote endless love letters to Dany, and it was there, on late autumn evenings, listening to the howling wind, that I kept repeating to myself a line from a song in a Shakespeare play: "When all aloud the wind doth blow . . . " I enjoyed the poetic solitude in my garret room, a full floor above what I considered the trivial activities of the two families. I felt out of reach. Never before did I so keenly experience the pleasure of having "a room of my own." This was quite different from occupying a room on the same level with my parents. My privacy (a word that, incidentally, does not exist in the French language) became a need as of that winter in the villa San Gimignano. Jacques was quite right: I had become a romantic. I loved my lonely walks, especially when the weather was bad, imagining that I was Rousseau's *promeneur solitaire*. My favorite walks were on the deserted boardwalk, struggling against the wind and the driving rain. I relished the desolation of the beach, where late the sweet gang had joked and played, discovering for myself the special off-season beauty of what the French call "*l'arrière-saison*."

In my own way, much like all of France, I was living through the winter in a state of unreality. Early that fall, while everyone was slowly adjusting to the idea of war, Sascha and I had the preposterous idea, without any experience or special qualifications, of organizing a jazz club. On the model of the Hot Club de France, we modestly decided to call it the Hot Club de Paris. I was to be the artistic director and Sascha the business manager. We searched for a locale in Trouville and discovered a large, windowless, poorly lit room at the back of the same pastry shop our group had patronized during the summer. We felt that the darkness would provide just the right atmosphere. Sascha and I entered into lengthy negotiations with the obtuse and avaricious woman who owned the tearoom-pastry shop. We had drawn-out discussions about such matters as entrance fee, cover charge, price of fruit juices, percentages to be paid by us. We wanted live music but could not afford a small band. Instead we found a jobless Greek pianist named Papadopoulos. Alas, Papadopoulos had never even heard of Django Reinhardt and Stéphane Grapelli. His style of jazz was a rudimentary syncopation.

But nothing could squelch our enthusiasm. Determined to launch our jazz club, we trudged over the bridge to Trouville every afternoon as soon as school was out. As artistic director, I had repeated palavers with Papadopoulos. But nothing—neither entreaty, nor flattery, nor irony—would make him change his style, which remained decidedly metronomic. The opening night was finally upon us. We alerted all our school friends and even had some posters printed. We could even announce a featured presence: we were able to claim as our guest of honor for the occasion the budding starlet Corinne Luchaire. It turned out, retrospectively, to have been an ironic distinction for our juvenile enterprise—not because the starlet had little talent, which was true enough, but because she was the daughter of Jean Luchaire, a notorious pro-German journalist, friend and protégé of Otto Abetz, who became the Nazi ambassador in Paris during the Occupation. During that dark period, Luchaire received subsidies from Abetz and imposed himself as an ardent and influential pro-Nazi collaborationist. In his view, the Vichy regime was not fascist enough. He was executed in 1946, after the liberation. But I anticipate. In the fall of 1939, we were not aware of Corinne's father and his political inclinations. Somewhere in my old photo albums I have a picture of me sitting proudly next to Corinne on that opening night.

We did not know about Jean Luchaire's political extremism, but what we found out only too well was the irate reaction of a number of local citizens—the very type of self-proclaimed "patriots" who soon after became supporters of Pétain—who were extremely vocal about their sense of outrage at the "un-French" goings-on in the jazz club. Was it not a scandal that a bunch of uprooted adolescents from Paris were loudly and shamelessly indulging in decadent foreign dance music while the sons of solid French citizens were at the front? The subtext was a barely disguised hostility to cosmopolitan Jews, suspected of being potential draft-dodgers, who were contaminating the neighborhood with their corrupt imported "swing." Xenophobia did not discriminate between degrees or types of foreignness. It did not help that the club's pianist carried the *métèque* name of Papadopoulos.

Meanwhile, life in villa San Gimignano settled into a routine punctuated by occasional visits of other cousins who came from Paris, where life, contrary to early fears of air attacks, continued in a more or less normal way. Moussia appeared on certain weekends with her delicate aquiline nose straight out of a Lombard painting and her stunning long legs I could not avoid staring at. My mother was more interested in discussing bridge problems with her, and tournament partners they had shared (Moussia had been on the European championship team). Along with her came her husband Shura Behr, who for a while had stolen the show at my bar mitzvah. Shura had been to the States. He listened to Sascha play jazz tunes on his harmonica, and then told us about Harlem's nightclubs and about the unmistakable huskiness of black voices, which he claimed to recognize after a few beats. On all subjects, he sounded sure of himself. I did not like him. But his exotic American experiences made me envious. How distant America seemed, how little we knew about its history, its way of life. In my English classes only England mattered. Not a single American writer was ever studied or even mentioned. During the whole time we were learning Coleridge and Wordsworth by heart, there was not a word about Walt Whitman or Melville. If Edgar Allan Poe was at all known to us, it was because Baudelaire and others had thoroughly gallicized him, and his tales had entered into the mainstream. We had no idea that he was American.

The war in all this seemed distant and unreal. Only intermittently were we reminded that two armies stood facing each other with deadly seriousness. Some of our acquaintances, it is true, were personally affected. Pierre Littoff's father was interned as an enemy alien, even though he had fled Nazi Germany as a Jew. Such was the fear of a Fifth Column. Littoff *père* was held in the fortress of Falaise, and occasionally Pierre would take Sascha and me in his father's black Ford to Pont-l'Evêque on his way to visit him. It was an adventure each time. We knew no boy our age who was authorized to drive a car, and I am sure that Pierre did not have a license.

As for news from the front, it reached us directly once or twice, when our cousin, Shura Adler, came to villa San Gimignano on furlough, proud of his corporal's insignia. This other Shura, also quite a bit older, had retained his Russian accent, which sounded incongruous coming from someone wearing the uniform of a French infantryman. He told us, almost angrily, how silly and frustrating he found army existence. His unit was stationed somewhere in the area facing Saarbrücken. Military activities vaunted by the official radio he dismissed sarcastically as skirmishes without consequence. He was a scholar, could not take war seriously, and looked thoroughly clumsy and unheroic in his baggy uniform. But neither did the army as a whole appear heroic. It was just sitting behind the Maginot Line. The Germans also seemed determined to remain safely behind their Siegfried line, that three-mile-deep line of bunkers and tank traps extending from the Swiss border all the way to Nijmegen in Holland. Later, the overly cautious General Maurice Gamelin, commander-in-chief of the French army, was severely blamed for hesitating to launch a significant military action that might have thrown the Germans off balance and interfered with their plans for the major offensive that was to come a few months later. But hindsight has never won a battle.

Yet there were casualties. One day, in midwinter, the awareness of war became concrete for all of us. The lycée students were all mobilized to help when a train with wounded soldiers was expected in Deauville. We assembled at the *mairie,* where litters were distributed. We then proceeded to the train station. We waited for long hours, all evening. It was cold, I remember. The train finally arrived late at night. We helped carry the wounded men to the military and civilian ambulances that drove them off to a nearby hospital. Many of the men were joking, with lit cigarettes in their hands or dangling, French-style, from their lips. But even that nocturnal scene, in an eerie light provided largely by lanterns and flashlights, did not disrupt the sense of normalcy.

Everything changed abruptly at the beginning of May, just as we were again thinking of outings on the beach. We heard the alarming news of the Wehrmacht's massive offensive in Holland and Belgium, and then in quick succession of the German breakthrough, collapsing Allied defenses, fleeing armies, and the evacuation of the British forces at Dunkirk. Then, on a night far more dramatic than the one of the hospital train, came the bombing of the oil refineries of Le Havre, just across the bay, and the huge, fiery explosions we all watched from the beach with our gas masks in hand, for there was still the fear of poison-gas attacks. But even then, as the sky was lit up and the earth trembled, banality and comedy took over. We tried on our gas masks and I shook with laughter at the sight of my grandmother struggling to pull the grotesque rubber contraption over her face. My mother, meanwhile, got furious at me, for I had somehow managed to lose the stopper of my own gas mask in the sand.

The *drôle de guerre* was over, the real war had started. But during those eight months of a relatively normal life in Deauville, things had changed radically. If nothing seemed threatening, neither did anything seem certain. And nothing seemed possible, either. The future appeared blocked. Perhaps I felt this more sharply than did my parents. There did not seem to be any point preparing for the *baccalauréat*. What did degrees matter? Or planning anything? Although my father, during his weekend visits, kept talking to me of plans and possible careers, and even mentioned—should it interest me when peace returned—sending me to China to learn something about international business under my uncle's tutelage, I began to suspect that there was going to be no future for me in this or any other direction. If I thought at all of my uncle, it was not because I hoped to join him in Shanghai, but because I occasionally remembered the silk shirt he had once sent me. I had worn that shirt, with my initials inside a pagoda, on my visit to the rue de Provence. Two years had elapsed since that day, and that memory now seemed unreal. But it was kept alive by a lingering fear that I might have picked up some disease: What were those lesions on my lower legs? I kept reassuring myself, for I remembered that the infection on my legs spread when I scratched a mosquito bite. Still, I kept wondering, learning at the same time that small concerns can coexist with big events.

For the family, the semblance of a tranquil life in villa San Gimignano was over. With news of the debacle, we packed in a hurry, determined somehow to make our way to a safer region, south of the Loire.

Part

II

L'Exode

Chapter 7

L'EXODE

I t is hard to recapture the atmosphere of collective panic in May and June 1940. In quick succession, Rotterdam capitulated and the Dutch army was put out of commission. The German armored columns crossed the River Meuse and reached the shores of the Atlantic, while the Luftwaffe almost without opposition pounded towns and strafed the highways. Within a few weeks, the French army was in total disarray, with more than a million of its soldiers having been captured, and Paris was occupied. A crescendo of bad news and unverifiable rumors filled the air. Everything happened with the relentlessness of a bad dream. We were all in a state of shock. We packed our belongings and abandoned the rented villa in Deauville overnight, as one might a sinking ship. My father once again sensed the drift of things fairly early. We were among the first to make our way to Bordeaux.

I do not remember by what means we first reached Paris. Even two large automobiles could not possibly have accommodated us all, with our valises and trunks. I am fairly certain it was by train. But despite all my efforts to recall the trip, my memory is a blank. We spent at least a few hours in our Paris apartment, giving instructions to the concierge, Monsieur Émile, leaving some of our things and hurriedly gathering others to take with us on our exodus. The mass movement of civilians toward the south and southwest came indeed to be known as *l'exode*, though it was an exodus without a leader and without miracles.

People took to the highways and secondary roads by any and all means—cars, buses, carts, bicycles, trucks. Many got stuck when their vehicles broke down or when they ran out of gas. Lodgings were almost impossible to find. Some of those who fled were strafed by enemy planes. We had the good sense, or good fortune, of opting for a night train to Bordeaux—despite warnings that trains might not reach their destination. We sat up all night in our compartment. Even under those circumstances, I was pleased to be on a long-distance train again. All night, I watched the names of the stations—Orléans, Tours, Poitiers, Angoulême—on this unfamiliar route.

My parents' choice of Bordeaux as a refuge was not very original. Twice before, in situations of crisis, the French government had moved to Bordeaux: in 1870, when the National Assembly met there after Paris capitulated to Bismarck's Prussian army, and again in 1914 after the spectacular German advance to the Marne River. Bordeaux was thus a natural choice for us. Defeat was again in the air—only this time all of France was on the verge of being invaded. Some local counterattacks may have saved the honor of individual army units, but they were sporadic and uncoordinated. It was worse than a retreat; it was a rout. Soldiers fled, mingling with civilians. Officers were seen evacuating their families to safer zones. The front had been pierced near the Marne, very close to Paris. We now know that Germany had thrown into battle more than a hundred divisions, many of them heavily armored. When a general withdrawal was ordered (it had for the most part already taken place without any order), the radio kept reassuring us that these were carefully planned tactical readjustments of overexposed lines. But what we actually witnessed during those weeks, before and after the government fled to Bordeaux, could by no stretch of the imagination be described as carefully planned. It was general chaos, confusion, panic—a real debacle, involving civilians as well as the military. During the Battle of the Bulge a few years later, I again found myself in the midst of a disorderly retreat, but it was then limited to a few of our divisions, and did not involve millions of civilians.

In May–June 1940, literally millions of refugees obstructed the roads and railway stations. Entire towns were on the move. Some of the refugees were later forbidden by the Germans to return to their hometowns. Overloaded vehicles were seen with mattresses on their roofs—perhaps to protect the family against strafings. We were of course not aware of statistics at the time. I have since read that about one-fifth of the French population became nomadic for a while, which means that

some eight million people were on the run. Between Paris and Brittany
alone, it is estimated that half a million people found themselves home-
less. Such figures do not surprise anyone who witnessed the enormity of
it all. Soon trains stopped running, the postal system no longer functioned, food supplies dwindled, banks closed, and quite a few towns
were without water, gas, and electricity. We were struck by the onrush
of conflicting rumors and the volatility of reactions. Some of the
rumors sounded particularly threatening. The Gestapo was reported to
be accompanying all advance units of the German army, and immediate
reprisals were said to have begun against those known to be hostile to
Nazism. One also heard of French officers killed by their own men or
by the local population when they gave orders to defend this or that
position to the last. There were even rumors of civil war, of revolution.
Was that not what had occurred after the Franco-Prussian War? The
violence of the revolutionary Commune of 1871 and of its brutal
repression had not been forgotten.

OUR FAMILIES REACHED Bordeaux on a mild spring day. The city
appeared peaceful. We made our way, almost like visiting tourists, to
the historical center of town and settled in a small hotel on the rue des
Trois Conils. That street name made an impression on me. I did not
know then that *conil* was an Old French word for "rabbit." To my adolescent ears the word sounded funny and mildly vulgar. My room was
entirely windowless, but I did not mind. We were lucky to find any
rooms at all. From the bottom of my suitcase I recovered a battered
copy of Dostoevsky's novel *Crime and Punishment,* which I had begun
reading a few weeks earlier. The airlessness of the hotel room and the
absence of natural light seemed just right for sharing Roskolnikov's
predicament and soul-searchings. The room was quite bare: a bed, a
table with a lamp, a sink. It was probably a chambermaid's room, rented
out only because of the extraordinary circumstances. The rest of the
hotel was well-kept, though not very comfortable. Even my parents'
room was without a private toilet. We ate all our meals in the hotel
restaurant, where even the fruit and the nuts one was served at the end

of a meal were parsimoniously measured out. My room and the discolored dining area made me appreciate the southern spring sun and the many open spaces of the town.

Bordeaux has esplanades, broad avenues, tree-lined alleys, and a large public garden. Sascha's mother, Katya, took us to a park, where we waited near an artificial lake while she went to speak to the lycée principal about having us enrolled in the senior class so that we could continue our preparation for the *baccalauréat* exams. Not even the extraordinary events of the defeat and mass exodus put an end to the concern for academic competitiveness, degrees, and career plans. Katya soon returned to our station in the park. The principal had informed her with cold politeness that the *classe de première* was already overcrowded, that we would have to prepare for the *bac*, as it was called, on our own. He also informed her where and when the state-controlled exams would be held. I still marvel that in those calamitous circumstances the educational system, controlled entirely by the Ministry of Education, continued to function, that the uniform exam questions were sent out to the schools, and that teachers and proctors were available. A miracle, no doubt, of the Napoleonic legacy!

The news that we would not attend classes hardly dismayed me. It meant relative freedom. I saw only the good side of the principal's refusal to admit us. My aunt, ever suspicious as well as gullible, was of another opinion, attributing the *proviseur*'s ill will to anti-Parisian and anti-Semitic prejudice. Meanwhile, by sheer chance, Sascha and I struck up a conversation in the park with an affable young black student of our own age. He was from the colonies, spoke with a curious accent, and finished almost every sentence with a colloquial and usually quite meaningless expletive, "*Merde alors!*" We were to hear that expletive quite often during the following weeks, for he too was cramming for the *bac*, and we often met and exchanged notes. Sascha and he discussed problems in physics. I stayed out of it, ashamed of my ignorance. But we also walked together in the center of town, at dusk. Katou was his name, and he occasionally pulled out a small flask of a foul-smelling liqueur that he wanted us to taste. "*Merde alors!*"

One day I remember riding in a horse-drawn carriage on some of the city's broad avenues and open spaces. But it was hardly a pleasure ride.

My father and I were on our way to the Portuguese consulate in the hope of obtaining visas that would allow us to escape from France. At some point, we had glimpses of the broad curve of the Garonne River and the port from which so many barrels of claret had been shipped to England over the centuries. The leisurely, almost festive ride in the carriage put us in a relaxed mood. Papa explained to me how important it was in times of stress to make proper contact with officials, and then, at the right moment, adroitly slip into their hand, or place on their desk, an envelope with a few bank notes in it. I should not misunderstand, he added. He too could dream of an ideal state where this would be considered reprehensible. And he brought up the names of socialist thinkers he had often mentioned to me: Jean Jaurès, Rosa Luxembourg, Karl Kautsky. But the world being what it was, envelopes with bank notes could at times save lives. Was there not good reason, moreover, to be afraid of any regime that left no room for flexibility and compromises—what my father called "*accomodements*"?

I was surprised to hear him say that "incorruptible" was a dangerous word, that it has been known to lead straight to the guillotine. Was the great revolutionary leader Robespierre not nicknamed *l'incorruptible?* he asked rhetorically. The knife of the guillotine comes down with an inexorably clean sound. And was there not, he continued in what he must have perceived as the occasion for a lesson I should remember, was there not the recent example of Communist Russia and Nazi Germany, where people were so fanaticized ideologically that brother denounced brother and children denounced their parents for holding dissident views?

I can still hear my father's voice mingled with the sound of the horse's hooves on the street pavement, and I often think how right he was. I would not be alive today had it not been that someone, on whose whim my fate depended, had at a crucial moment accepted the tangible encouragement to be helpful, perhaps even compassionate, and grant that urgently needed permit or visa, that safe conduct, those stamped documents without which there would be no survival.

Alas, that time at the Portuguese consulate in Bordeaux, my father was not successful. He returned with the envelope and dollar bills intact. He did not seem ruffled. He merely pushed back his hat and wiped his forehead, by which sign I knew that he was worried. I never felt closer to him. And I was grateful that he had talked to me as to an adult.

IN THE MEANTIME, military and political events overwhelmed us. On June 10, Mussolini declared war on France, now on the verge of total collapse. My mother, who relished parallels between art and life, said it was like the fable by La Fontaine in which the donkey appears at the last moment to insult and kick the dying lion. On that day, Sascha and I somehow found ourselves swept along in a street demonstration. Half-willing participants, we were caught in its advancing tide, which lasted into the early evening hours. The slowly moving crowd was chanting "*Benito, au poteau!*" (To the stake with Benito!). They were carrying horizontal banners denouncing the coward who had used flamethrowers against half-naked, spear-thrusting Abyssinians and was now stabbing his neighbor in the back. Down with Fascism! they shouted in unison. Down with the Italian clown! The marching crowd—ten to fifteen people across—was both solemn and threatening. Sascha and I grew a little nervous as the cries got hoarser, the avenues became darker, and the street lights projected ominous shadows.

I had felt the threatening power of crowds before—at soccer games, in amusement parks, on days of popular festivities. But that was nothing compared with violent political demonstrations. In a flash a scene from the past came back. I saw myself as a child walking with our maid in the streets of Leipzig (was it in 1930 or 1931?), not long before Hitler came to power. Two marching columns appeared on a collision course. Large red banners and banners with swastikas moved against each other. The communist hymn "The International" and the Nazi "*Horst Wessel Lied*" intermingled in contrapuntal cacophony. Suddenly the chanting ceased. The two columns entered into each other. There were cries as clubs beat down on heads and shoulders. It was over in a matter of seconds—or so it seemed. The two columns were already marching in opposite directions. But there were bodies lying on the street, some of them motionless. Others staggered away with blood streaming down their faces. Our maid wanted me to look the other way. But I could not take my eyes off the scene. I had to be pulled away, shivering.

In Bordeaux, ten years later, there was no violent confrontation, only the mighty flow of a mass of people that made me feel quite powerless. It was almost an image of the larger current of events over which no one could any longer hope to have any control. Soon the government—if one could still call it that—arrived in Bordeaux, adding to the general confusion. And a few days later, we heard that the eighty-four-year-old Maréchal Philippe Pétain, who had replaced Paul Reynaud as prime minister, was seeking an armistice. The news was confirmed by Pétain himself, who went on the radio and in his quivering voice declared that he, the old hero of Verdun, offered himself to France in her hour of greatest misfortune to lessen the country's suffering. Sascha and I were tempted to make fun of his tremulous diction—which was due to old age, we soon discovered, for his voice continued to tremble in all his radio addresses over the next few miserable years. It was like a vocal caricature of senility. Yet one hesitated to make fun. Pétain in 1940 was a venerated figure, and the "gift" of his person to the nation was accepted almost unanimously as the providential reappearance of the World War I hero who had once before saved France at Verdun, and who now again, at a time of unprecedented disaster, stepped forward as the nation's protector and savior.

The surge and flux of the mass demonstration the day Mussolini attacked France, its spontaneous and equally unpredictable dispersal, and now the massive support for Pétain opened my eyes to the fickleness of public opinion. One day it was the rhetoric of war and vengeance; the next it was armistice at any cost. Suddenly sharp hostility was expressed against those who even talked of continuing the war. Armistice was great! The war was obviously over, everybody seemed to concur. Britain's fall was imminent. The Germans had won the war. And there was a lesson in the calamity: France deserved its defeat. Pétain, never losing an opportunity to be didactic, gave the reasons: not enough children, not enough weapons, too few allies. And above all, the vices of decadent democracy: frivolity, disrespect for traditions, betrayal of family values and morality. The subtext was clear enough. Parliamentary democracy had ruined France. It had to go. A political and spiritual purge was necessary if France was to redeem herself and become healthy again.

The shock of defeat had numbed the country into submissiveness and dependency on a father figure. Pétain appeared as even more trustworthy than a father; he was a resurrected, self-sacrificing grandfather of unquestioned wisdom and integrity who promised to guide the nation back to its ancestral virtues. The thirst for normalcy went along with a disposition for collective breast-beating. France had sinned; we were all sinners; we had all been led astray by the debilitating, corrosive precepts of democracy. Overnight, that was the tune we heard echoed all around us.

Overwhelming gratitude for the salvational presence of the aged *maréchal* made people oblivious to everything except their personal well-being and survival. The blue-eyed, frail-looking old man now watching over their destinies justified caring only about oneself and one's family. No one seemed to be aware that the war was going on elsewhere, or that General Charles de Gaulle had spoken on the BBC in London exhorting France to continue the struggle. We were not even aware that in Bordeaux, in the inner circle of the shaky and divided government, there were those—soon to be discredited and even accused of treason—who wanted to transfer themselves to North Africa and continue the struggle with the resources of the French colonies and the intact Mediterranean fleet. Even those who, like my family, did not in any way sympathize with Pétain's archconservative background and his hostility to democratic institutions felt relieved and grateful, as the German army came closer and closer to Bordeaux. Pétain was considered a lesser evil, and his prestige would probably spare France the fate of Poland. With Pétain in charge, France was less likely to be ruled by a Gauleiter—a Nazi head of a district or of an occupied territory. Even Jews congratulated themselves in those early hours of the Pétain regime. His presence made them feel almost protected. France was to conduct its relations with Germany as state to state. And up to a point, this turned out to be true—at least for a while. Its army crushed, France turned out to be a unique case of a country defeated by the Germans, yet allowed to negotiate the terms of an armistice.

The outcome of the 1940 blitzkrieg was nonetheless appalling: 200,000 dead, 500,000 wounded, about a million and a half French soldiers interned in German camps as prisoners of war. And France was to pay four million francs in daily indemnities to cover the cost of the German occupation. Most humiliating perhaps, even though this kept up an illusion of semi-independence, France was to be divided into an occupied and a so-called unoccupied zone separated by a "line of demarcation" that quickly became a sealed frontier. As for the shameful clause in the armistice by which France agreed to extradite upon request any political refugees who had sought asylum in France (a full measure of France's moral collapse), it seemed to upset only those who felt personally concerned.

Bordeaux was no longer safe for us. We were at risk even while the armistice was being negotiated. My father's aim was to reach the Spanish border by any means. But there wasn't much farther to run. We faced the natural barrier of the Pyrenees, and beyond that mountain range, the fascist regime of Franco. It felt more and more like a trap.

Somehow a car and a driver were found. Gas was obtained at black-market prices. With the overflow of our cumbersome suitcases strapped to the roof of the car, we fled toward Bayonne and Biarritz. Once inside the car, I remembered that I had left *Crime and Punishment* in the dark hotel room. I was not to read the end of Dostoevsky's novel until years later.

THE HIRED CAR rattled along due south through flat monotonous regions. The day was gray and colorless. A slight mist made the landscape glide by as in a sad dream. We sat in silence, uncomfortable, numbed by fatigue and apprehension. I was seated next to the driver, who kept pointing to the seemingly endless pine forests. He explained that they had been planted to reclaim what was formerly a sandy and swampy region of stagnant waters. This was the region known as the Landes. From my geography classes I remembered that the sands were swept inland from the dunes of the nearby Atlantic coastline. The driver went on to explain that the road we were on was one of the routes pilgrims took centuries ago to reach Santiago de Compostela. My parents and I also hoped to make it to Spain, though ours was not exactly a religious pilgrimage.

I continued to be struck by the flatness of the region we crossed. It looked drab and desolate in spite of the dense pine forests. This used to be one of the most backward regions of France. It had a disconsolate beauty. I did not know at the time that this melancholy landscape had inspired some of the finest pages in the novels of François Mauriac, as well as several painters of the Barbizon school.

When we arrived in Bayonne, where we got stuck in heavy refugee traffic, my parents heard that a line had formed at the Portuguese (or was it the Spanish?) consulate, and that there was apparently some hope of obtaining a visa. I see ourselves next, standing in line with hundreds of others, while our car and driver waited at the corner. We stood there for several hours. My father held our passports in his hand. The line did not move an inch. Wild rumors were flying. We were told that the movie actor Dalio, who impersonated the Jewish soldier in *La grande illusion,* was also standing in line somewhere. But we never saw him. Someone said he was sweating "*à grosses gouttes*" (the equivalent of sweating bullets) because the Gestapo was circulating a leaflet with his profile on it as an example of a typical Jewish face. I am not at all sure that Dalio, who later made it to Hollywood, was really near that Bayonne consulate with us on that day. But I did appropriate the image of him standing in that long line, to the point of actually seeing the beads of sweat on his forehead. How untrustworthy even the most vivid memories can be. The real and the fictitious play games on the screen of memory.

Much, alas, was real enough. Soon we heard more troubling news. Already on the previous day, it would seem, a line had formed at the entrance to the consulate. Toward the end of a long day of waiting, someone finally came out to collect passports for review in order to determine who might get a visa. People were told to come back the following day. When they returned the next morning, passports were lying in a heap in front of the entrance door. They had been found down the street, a few hundred yards away. The consul himself, or some other official, according to the account, had simply thrown the passports out of a car window.

We never bothered to verify the tale. Hearing the story while standing in this line that did not budge was enough to discourage us. My par-

ents agreed that we should refuse to surrender our passports—and in
no case leave them overnight. We made our way back to the car and
proceeded to Biarritz, a well-known sea resort a few miles away.

Here again there are some blanks in my memory. I cannot recall
where we stayed, nor how and when Sascha and his family joined us
again. I do remember coming across Moussia, my cousin with the stunning legs, and talking with her on the street in front of one of the large
hotels near the beach and the casino. What I recall most sharply is that
my feelings were hurt. Moussia immediately asked me where she could
find my mother, showing no interest at all in me. She hardly looked at
me. Whiffs of my old jealousy returned. I saw her with Shura in their
new Opel, a smart couple on a brief visit in Marienbad. Shura's very
name made me wince every time he was referred to as *"un bel homme"*
or *"un beau mâle."*

Nice under the Vichy Regime

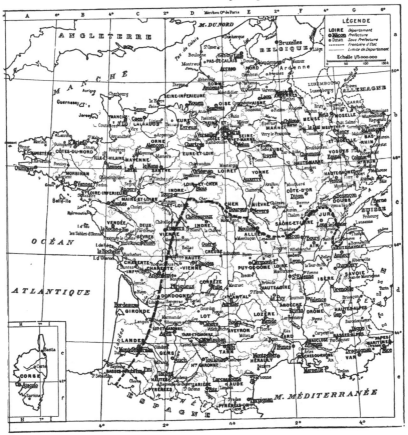

We remained at most two or three nights in Biarritz, a resort made famous by Empress Eugénie, the wife of Napoleon III, who loved to hold court not far from the rocks and reefs, and the foaming sea. On the first or second of our nights there, we left for the nearby town of St. Jean de Luz in hope of getting onto one of the small Polish warships about to escape to England. We did not even get close to those vessels; they left without us. And a good thing it was: we later heard that they had been torpedoed on their way to a British port.

When we returned to Biarritz late that night, we learned about some of the details of the armistice and the "line of demarcation." The entire Atlantic coastline, many miles deep, was to be held by the Germans, and so was all the northern half of France, not to mention all the northeast, which Germany considered as its own in the first place. We felt that Biarritz was no longer a safe place. Within hours the Wehrmacht might arrive. The problem was how to cross the newly established line of demarcation and reach the city of Pau. The situation was still fluid, but we could be sure that controls at the new border would be very tight. "German efficiency," my father kept muttering. And he set about finding a way to cross the line. My father was not, under normal circumstances, what can be called resourceful. But these were not ordinary times, and he had learned from repeated experiences of escape and exile. The next I heard was that a Swiss ambulance had been hired to take us across the line. It occurred to me that my father must have a lot of cash on him. All I recall of the trip is that we were locked up inside the vehicle and told to keep out of sight as much as possible. On what felt like an unusually bumpy road we reached the *zone libre*, the amputated "free" zone, which soon came to be known as Vichy France.

His mission accomplished, the driver of the ambulance dumped us in Pau, near the railroad station. He was in a visible hurry to disassociate himself from us. The payment had been made beforehand. We were now left to our own devices, without independent means of transportation. From Pau one has a splendid view of the Pyrenees, but we were hardly in a sightseeing mood. My parents were unwilling to remain in Pau, where the Germans might arrive after all. The nearby mountains were a sounder refuge. We would also be closer to the Spanish border. We had not given up the hope of somehow crossing over into Spain.

After some deliberation between the two families, it was decided to take a bus in the direction of Eaux-Bonnes. Getting all eight of us into the bus, together with all our baggage, was no easy matter. We kept some of our belongings on our knees and under our feet. To our surprise, the bus was not overcrowded. Even more surprising was the sense of peace we felt as the bus climbed past Bielle and Laruns and then wound its way up to Eaux-Bonnes.

Hundreds of miles, and many stopovers along the way, now separated us from villa San Gimignano in Deauville, where only a few weeks earlier our two families had lived in routine calm. Even Bordeaux—now also under Nazi control—where Sascha and I had taken the *baccalauréat* seemed far away and unreal. We would not even have to sweat it out waiting for the results, which were usually posted at the school entrance. Eaux-Bonnes, where we arrived late in the day, confirmed the sense of irreality. A mountain spa set in a deep valley, its run-down hotels surrounding a small public garden are reminders of the bygone days of the Second Empire. Almost a century later, it looked more like an abandoned movie set. We settled in a hotel where the hot water was cut off at night. Rooms and corridors with uneven floors were lit by twenty-watt bulbs. Everything was damp and dark.

The next few weeks went by as though shrouded in semidarkness. At night there was an uncanny silence. Even the daylight felt opaque. We were idle, but not in any pleasurable sense. The antiquated, off-season spa seemed dead. Not even echoes of the war intruded on the sepulchral peace of the mountain valley. My mother jokingly said in Russian that we were sitting there like dead flies. It was the end of the line, or so it seemed.

This terminal calm was interrupted one day by the arrival of what remained of a French infantry battalion, with a few vehicles and some horses. Defeated, separated from the rest of their regiment and from some of their commanding officers, those soldiers seemed quite cheerful, to our surprise. They kept talking about going home soon. Some of them were looking for civilian clothes, for fear they might be caught by the Germans and sent to a POW camp. They had heard about the armistice, but who could trust anything or anyone? Distracted from our boredom by their arrival, Sascha and I chatted with them. We kept reassuring them. They no longer needed to fear the Germans. We were in unoccupied France. But they were skeptical. What did we know? If we had seen what they had seen . . .

Of our own "escape" to Spain, there was no longer any talk. Nothing came of the vague idea of finding a place to cross over. There was the austere landscape, the forbidding wall of the Pyrenees. And my grandmother, though energetic enough to argue with anyone, could hardly be expected to hike up a mountain pass. We had heard of *"passeurs"*—probably descendants of the famous smugglers of contraband—who for a not inconsiderable sum smuggled refugees into nearby Spain. But there were all sorts of risks and even physical dangers that my parents were not willing to take. In any case, they would have been reluctant to leave most of their belongings behind.

Sascha and I were disappointed. We liked the idea of being led along hidden paths, between heavy boulders, through dark forests. Now that such a romantic flight was not even mentioned by our parents, we satisfied our need for movement and for some semblance of adventure by taking long walks in the direction of the Aubisque or Bitet passes. We kept imagining that we were exploring ways of reaching the Col du Pourtalet and the Spanish border. We were aware of playing games, and even laughed at our fiction-making. It reminded us of the time we had run away together on the beach of Blankenberghe, and our parents called the police to search for us. As we walked among the tall trees, I kept thinking of "Le Cor," a poem by Alfred de Vigny set in the region of the Pyrenees:

J'aime le son du Cor, le soir, au fond des bois

I love the sound of the horn, at nightfall in the deep forests.

I had learned at school that Vigny wrote the poem when he was garrisoned at the foot of these mountains. It recounts the medieval legend of Charlemagne's valiant nephew Count Roland, who dies with his companions in a heroic rearguard action. The dying Roland, crushed by a boulder, has just enough strength left to warn his uncle, the emperor, of the enemy's presence with several mighty horn blasts that continue to echo darkly in the valley haunted by the knight's restless soul:

Dieu! que le son du Cor est triste au fond des bois

My God! How sad is the sound of the horn in the deep forests.

I kept repeating the final line of the poem and imagined that far in the distance I could hear the long wail of Roland's ivory horn.

When we stopped along the way for a lemonade in a country inn, Sascha made fun of my poetic effusions. But he was visibly moved by my reveries, and began to bring up his own historical associations. Béarn, the region in which we found ourselves, was the home of Marguerite de Navarre, one of the great women of French history. Friend and patroness of some of the most cultivated and boldest minds of her time, fervent admirer of Boccaccio, she was herself an eminent writer and the author of the celebrated *Heptaméron*. Béarn was also the birthplace of Henri de Navarre, who was to become king of France under the name of Henri IV, one of the most beloved and enterprising kings, under whose reign France founded Québec. We had studied his agitated reign in some detail for the *baccalauréat*. Sascha's associations and my reveries were far removed from our parents' practical concerns. Yet we also knew, as we were sipping our lemonade, that practical concerns were more important now then ever.

News reached us sporadically and often unreliably while we were waiting it out in Eaux-Bonnes. Some time in July, we gathered that the center of political activities had shifted from Bordeaux to Vichy, where the government and the refugee members of the National Assembly had gathered. In the meantime the British, fearing that French naval forces in the Mediterranean would fall into German hands, attacked the naval base at Mers-el-Kébir in Algeria and destroyed most of the battleships anchored there, killing many sailors. This action outraged the French, inflaming the already strong resentment toward England ever since the evacuation at Dunkirk. In Vichy, the National Assembly, maneuvered by the politician Pierre Laval, voted, so to speak, its own demise—that is, the demise of the Third Republic—and gave full powers to Pétain, with a mandate to draft a new constitution. The *maréchal* was now no longer prime minister, but *chef de l'Etat* (head of state). It was the beginning of a new era.

We wondered about the future. But the recent developments in Vichy and the settlement of the armistice seemed to provide a measure of stability. We had felt safe in Eaux-Bonnes, but now we began to feel isolated, even lost in our mountain refuge. With the resumption of some form of normalcy, it was decided to return by bus to Pau, and from there to take a train to Nice, on the Mediterranean coast—as far away as possible from the German occupation forces. Nice was also chosen because of its proximity to Marseille, a large port with vessels still leaving for safe countries, a window onto the free world, a large city with many consulates. Our hope was no longer Spain, but perhaps a visa to the United States.

There was another reason for the choice of Nice. It was very close to Italy, and this closeness spoke of some safety in case the Germans were to occupy all of France. This latent trust in Italy may seem strange in view of Mussolini's enactment of the racial laws two years earlier. But Italians were known to be humane. Above all, and this is perhaps even stranger in retrospect, there was trust in Pétain, the venerable figure with the impeccably trimmed mustache and honest, limpid eyes. That trust did not last long, however.

I was thrilled to see my beloved palm trees again. I kept projecting their image during the two-day-long railway journey to Nice, with complicated stopovers and delays. When we finally reached our destination, however, my first encounter was not with palm trees but with swarms of nasty mosquitoes waiting for me in the hotel room.

Chapter 8

VICHY IN NICE

When I woke up, I felt burning itches and then became aware of a line of slightly elongated black dots on the whitish ceiling of the hotel room. I made no connection at first between my discomfort and the black dots on the high ceiling. Sascha was still asleep in the next bed. As soon as I was fully awake, squinting at the ceiling, I did establish the causal link. This was a squadron of mosquitoes, perfectly aligned as in a textbook illustration of Napoleon's cavalry at the battle of Austerlitz or Waterloo. Never had I seen so many mosquitoes assembled.

I had not read *Moby-Dick,* but a single mosquito could easily be for me what the white whale was for Captain Ahab: the incarnation of evil. Over the years, I have spent many a night battling this foe, like the time in Sicily when Bettina and I did not sleep a wink while I went searching for the Evil One, which after high-pitched flights of victory past our ears, had slyly hidden behind a massive piece of furniture. With time I developed an efficient battle technique, aiming a rolled towel against the wall or the ceiling. But my first epic engagement against an enemy superior in number took place early that morning of July 1940 in Nice.

Soon after, my parents rented an apartment on the rue de la Buffa, a street running parallel to the seafront just behind the monumental Hôtel Negresco. The apartment was not large but was adequately furnished. I remember sitting in the modest living room, listening to the sweet tenor voice of Benjamino Gigli coming across the airwaves from nearby Italy. There is a snapshot of me sitting at the desk in that apartment, staring at the camera with the intense, brooding look of a young Malraux posing as an intellectual hero. In the apartment above us, distant relatives had

settled, including the soprano who had sung with Chaliapin. I heard her
and her friends practice, and the bass Doda Conrad was among them. I
listened with particular care the day Mussorgsky's "The Flea" came as
from a higher sphere, punctuated by resounding stage laughter.

Life seemed normal again, at least on the surface. We were unaware
that we had found refuge in a particularly reactionary region. Nice was
the home and operating base of the extreme right-wing militant Joseph
Darnand, who was soon to head the infamous Milice Française, which,
in the name of Pétain, engaged in repressive and sadistic acts, hunting
resisters and Jews, holding secret courts-martial and summarily execut-
ing opponents of the regime. Darnand later even joined the Waffen-SS.
But we were not yet at that point. In the late summer of 1940, despite
the defeat and the occupation of two-thirds of France by the Germans,
the Riviera city of sun and cosmopolitan pleasure seemed like a haven.

My parents were not deluded. Escape, preferably to the United
States, became their steady preoccupation. My father traveled to Marseille on several occasions to investigate possibilities at various consulates. It was particularly difficult, he explained, to get into the United
States. There were stringent immigration quotas depending on where
one was born. In addition, the American authorities were extremely
fussy. An affidavit guaranteeing financial backing had to be provided by
someone residing in the United States. But that was not all. One also
needed an exit visa from France, and a transit visa if one had to cross
Spain or Portugal. And most difficult perhaps, one had to find a boat to
cross the Atlantic at a time when there was hardly any transatlantic passenger navigation. As if all these hurdles were not discouraging
enough, one had to overcome them more or less at the same time, for
visas lapsed and boats did not wait. In the meantime, money was
needed, what with restrictions and food shortages that steadily raised
black-market prices. And who knew when the Germans would occupy
the entire Mediterranean coastline, making escape virtually impossible.
Sooner or later the Germans would arrive—of that my father was convinced.

I never learned where our money came from. There was talk of "*bil-
lets verts*"—green dollar bills. Annette, my father's trusted secretary
with the thick lenses and pockmarked face, would cross the demarca-

tion line at more or less regular intervals and then quickly return to occupied Paris. I refrained from asking questions. Annette crossed the demarcation line illegally, which was dangerous business. I imagine she brought dollars from the Paris office, now managed by one of my father's assistants. Once she also brought an old school report of mine that had made its way to our Paris apartment with much delay. The report was not quite as dismal as the one that years earlier had marred my ski vacation in Megève, but it hardly added to my luster. Anyhow this was old stuff, now that the ordeal of the *bac* was behind me and, for the time being, higher education was out of the question.

I was put to work on more practical matters instead, and these became a source of unexpected enjoyment. Sascha and his family lived a few streets behind ours. We were both told to rent bikes and were sent to villages inland, to the *arrière-pays,* to find vegetables and other no longer available farm products sold by peasants for black-market prices. It was on these expeditions, often requiring strenuous uphill pedaling, that Sascha and I felt closest. We were an unlikely pair. Sascha was short, stocky, and powerfully built. He was almost two years older than I, though the difference no longer mattered, especially now that we were both out of school. He had lost a school year because of an accident to his leg that kept him in traction for many months. The leg never healed properly, and as a result it was shorter than the other. Sascha had a slight limp, or rather he walked with an awkward forward swing of the leg. The more self-conscious he felt, the more marked the swinging motion of his leg. It was almost a swaggering walk. To compensate, he doggedly trained for swimming competitions and became a junior backstroke champion. Occasionally I had watched him compete in Paris. But I did not like the steam and chlorine smell of swimming pools any more than I liked the atmosphere of locker rooms; tennis was my sport. I loved the sight of white outfits and white tennis balls against the red of the clay courts.

Our friendship was sealed in Nice. We became inseparable. Black-market bicycle expeditions were a pretext for discovering out-of-the-way places. We relished the sense of adventure, the laughter with which we responded to minor mishaps. There was that time when I pedaled with a pump in my hand, for I had to stop every few hundred meters to inflate my punctured tire. Our laughter, our lightheartedness, our delight in coming upon a hidden village or an unexpected perspective of the distant sea—all that now seems incongruous, considering the circumstances and what was to follow. We were, after all, not on a vacation.

Yet our parents, too, lived in a strange state of quasi-euphoria. It may have been a form of numbness produced by the gravity of events over which one no longer had any control, a form of mental and moral anesthesia encouraging irresponsibility and even a measure of frivolity. The beauty of the bay and of the distant mountain range added to this sense of lightheartedness. My parents made new friends, discovered the presence of old ones, walked up and down the Promenade des Anglais. They set up my grandmother in a small flat on the tree-shaded avenue Victor Hugo. The few photos surviving that period show no evidence that a war had been lost ignominiously, that the enemy was a crushing presence, that a determined antidemocratic clique had taken advantage of the Nazi victory in order to destroy the institutions and values of the French Republic, that many of us were henceforth in great danger. The photos display instead how smilingly my parents posed arm in arm with friends, some of whom were soon to go up in smoke in a distant camp; how chic my mother looked with her coquettish hat, and how carefully pressed my father's white trousers were on that late summer day. The usual resort pictures, one would think.

Many Parisian families, especially of foreign extraction, had sought refuge in Nice. In their daily life, often to their own surprise, anxiety coexisted with unconcern. It was then that I learned how easy it is to be deceived collectively, how in times of crisis human nature is disposed to hold on to illusions of normalcy, even to develop a new and intense appetite for pleasure. We did not want to admit to ourselves that we had settled in what was potentially one of the most dangerous areas of the Vichy zone. The Département des Alpes Maritimes had the immediate disadvantage of being an unproductive tourist area, highly dependent on food supplies from other regions, and not really capable of supporting such an influx of refugees. And in spite of much-needed income from tourism, it was a region whose local population was traditionally hostile to all foreigners, making it easier than elsewhere to identify anyone or any group as suspect and as "not belonging." Beside which, we were simply too numerous and too close to a sealed border. A real trap.

THE VICHY REGIME, seen from Nice, had the appearance of legitimacy. Legally speaking, the Pétain regime was not the result of a coup; there had been no official break in continuity. Pétain's new title, *chef de l'Etat* instead of *Président de la République*, was more than just a symbolic change. The key players in his first cabinet were Admiral François Darlan, head of the undefeated French navy (most of the warships were still in the ports of French North Africa, out of reach of the Germans); General Maxime Weygand, who had been commander of the French army in the 1930s and had much to do with the collapse of the democratic regime and the armistice; and Laval, a slippery politician who had engineered the suicidal parliamentary vote giving Pétain constituent powers, and who became increasingly collaborationist with the Nazis. After the liberation in 1945, he was executed for treason.

Pétain's personal prestige was played up. "Are you more French than he?" ran one of the propaganda posters with a large portrait of the benign and austere *maréchal* in his uniform. Any patriotic slogan was good if it could silence possible opposition or even skepticism. He was the super-patriot, the most French of all Frenchmen, a combination of military hero, monarch, and grandfatherly miracle worker who would heal France's wounds and lead the erring nation back to salvation. Pétain was pictured as incorruptible, a lover of children and family values. He replaced the famous *Liberté, Egalité, Fraternité* of the Republic with a new triad: *Travail, Famille, Patrie*. His blue eyes, trim white mustache, impeccably cut civilian clothes, in contrast to the sloppy, hunched figure of Laval, seemed themselves to guarantee virtue and discipline. But this aged man, posing as mentor, guide, and savior, only encouraged the collective sense of irresponsibility. Since he was in charge, since he knew the answers and lived with certainties that he preached in terse pronouncements over the radio, since he embodied national identity and national unity, why be concerned? Such was the general mood in the fall of 1940.

People were not unaware that the *maréchal* was authoritarian and anachronistic, but that, too, was found appealing. His age and apparent frailty were seen as additional reasons to be deeply grateful for what he himself presented as his self-sacrificing service to the nation. All around us people echoed his favorite themes of collective guilt and a providential punishment. This mood of self-recrimination, implacably orchestrated by the Vichy regime, welcomed the defeat as a deserved penalty and the nation's suffering as a redemptive opportunity. There was at times an almost religious fervor in the air. Jean-Paul Sartre later caught this spirit of self-laceration in his play *The Flies,* in which an entire city, amid the stench of carrion, lives in fear and with a guilty conscience. Albert Camus, in his novel *The Plague,* engaged in a similar critique: one of his characters, Father Paneloux, delivers a sermon in which he attributes the pestilential horrors to the sins of the city of Oran. In 1940, the doctrine of penitence, repeated ad nauseam over the radio and in newspaper editorials, then parroted by people in the street, was part of a political agenda. It was meant to stress the decay, whoredom, and corruption of democracy, and to give moral viability to the dream of remaking France by cleansing it of all un-French elements.

These opinions were hardly shared by the cosmopolitan refugees in Nice, but cosmopolitanism was precisely one of the decried aberrations of the Third Republic. My friends and I certainly did not share the view that American jazz had been a pernicious influence, responsible for France's downfall. We missed our records of Count Basie and Duke Ellington. But foreign influences all around us were held accountable for calamities such as short skirts, birth control, and pornography. There was talk of new laws against divorce. This especially made my mother angry. Not, as she explained to me, that she had the slightest intention of being separated from my father, who kept saying whenever the subject came up that we had other things to worry about besides new divorce legislation. I remembered that, years earlier, I had seen on my mother's night table in Paris a novel by the archconservative writer Paul Bourget titled *Le Divorce.* This was the time of her enthusiasm for Léon Blum, not because of his socialist ideas but because he had been an advocate of women's sexual freedom. My mother's politics had more to do with feelings than with abstractions.

"A woman's logic," my father would conclude in her presence, with a wink in my direction.

The logic of Vichy, meanwhile, was to use the defeat to call for a thorough housecleaning. This was done by glorifying the authoritarian state and by exacerbating all available xenophobic sentiments. The dream was to remake France by giving France back to the French. "*La France aux Français*" had long been a favorite slogan of the extreme right. This is what the Vichy propaganda machine meant by greeting day after day the "Révolution Nationale," a formula unrelated to the Revolution of Robespierre and Danton, which had led to the decapitation of the king. Yet it too was radical insofar as Pétain and his cohorts aimed at a profound transformation of French institutions and mores. The keynotes endlessly reiterated were leadership, obedience, sacrifice, respect for hierarchy, a return to atavistic roots in the French soil, and a cult of ancestors. These had all been long-standing, counter-revolutionary motifs. Mushrooming youth groups in uniform, the newly created "Chantiers de Jeunesse," were encouraged to renew contact with fields and woods.

We truly woke up to realities—even those of us who had naively trusted the *maréchal*—when, soon after we settled in Nice, a surprising "statute on the Jews" was announced. We had been aware of a shameful clause in the armistice agreement by which the shadow French government committed itself to turn over to the Germans any foreign person wanted by them. This "surrender on demand" clause, about which the French authorities wanted to make as little noise as possible, amounted to a humiliating repudiation of a proud tradition of political asylum. It meant that any non-French citizen could simply be handed over to the Nazis. In time, this would lead to other, more massive arrests and extraditions.

For a while, we lived in the admittedly selfish illusion that the infamous clause would affect only German exiles in France, mostly Jews who had actively opposed Hitler. But then, just a couple of months after the signing of the armistice, in October, Vichy began to take its own anti-Semitic initiatives. When the new statutes concerning Jews were announced, we were appalled by the list of restrictions, reminiscent of the Nuremberg laws. No Jew was to be elected to public office; no important civil, military, or judiciary position could be held by a Jew; the cultural importance of Jews was to be reduced to a minimum; Jews were no longer allowed to teach in public schools. There was even talk of excluding Jews from newspaper reporting, from radio programs, and from directing films. Perhaps it was Pétain, the victor of Verdun, who insisted that certain exceptions be made for veterans of the First World War. But I do recall that soon the famous Crémieux law, by which Algerian Jews had been granted French citizenship, was repealed. And closer to home and to my family, Jewish businesses in the occupied zone were to be, if not confiscated, then administered by Aryans. Moreover, Jews who had fled the occupied zone were not allowed to return.

The picture was not bright, even though the sun was shining on Nice. Gradually things got still worse. The Commissariat aux Affaires Juives (General office for Jewish affairs) came into being and, headed by a Commissaire Général, eventually ordered a census of all Jews in the unoccupied zone. Such a census was very much feared. It did in fact have fatal consequences, for it made later mass arrests and deportations much easier. Even more stringent new statutes concerning Jews were announced in the spring, this time imposing restrictions that affected lawyers, doctors, and dentists, and quotas on Jewish students. I came to live with the realization that there was no future at all for me. What was worse, this seemed perfectly normal.

My father was less resigned. He listened regularly to the news coming over the BBC from London. The signal of the BBC news hour in those days was the sound of Big Ben, the great bell of the Parliament clock tower, which came to represent the very sound of freedom. Papa went over to friends whose radio—a large, ornate model—caught the waves from beyond the English Channel. It was the message of the "free world," the world Hitler had not yet subdued, and my father encouraged me to come and listen with him, our ears close to the speaker. Perhaps his frequent business trips to London in the past were the reason his faith in England remained unshaken, though I believe this faith went back to his law-school days, when he developed a respect for English law and political traditions. He had mentioned to me the expression *"habeas corpus"* on numerous occasions, though my own understanding of the Latin formula remained foggy. My father, unlike most of those around us, refused to believe that England was soon going to be invaded. Almost everyone thought that Britain was doomed. His stubborn trust in the British appeared almost unreasonable. It was renewed daily by that crisp, distant, disembodied voice reporting political and military events with stoic equanimity.

We learned that the banished Russian communist leader Leon Trotsky had been assassinated in Mexico, that Roosevelt had been re-elected, that the English city of Coventry had been largely destroyed by German bombers. The announcer's voice remained imperturbable. The French, for their part, hardly felt sorry for the fate of Coventry. A lot of resentment had built up against the British ever since they evacuated their troops at Dunkirk under heavy fire, a feat that was perceived as desertion even though that evacuation had made it possible for Britain to continue the struggle against Hitler. The resentment was exacerbated when the British, at the Algerian naval base of Mers el-Kébir, after giving an ultimatum to the French naval commander to continue the fight against the Germans, destroyed a large part of the fleet at anchor there, killing more than a thousand French sailors. Then came the failed British naval operation at Dakar, in French West Africa, inspired by de Gaulle in the hope of winning the allegiance of the local French forces. De Gaulle's prestige was not high in those days, not even among those of his compatriots still willing to oppose the Germans. To many he appeared as Britain's accomplice in an effort to spoliate France of part of her colonial empire.

One day, I overheard my father say in a low voice to my mother that he had heard of an American-run committee in Marseille that helped with visas and provided escape routes for people who were especially at risk. She was not to mention it to anyone. Nothing ever came of it as far as we were concerned, but then we were not on any list of notorieties possibly affected by the "surrender on demand" clause of the armistice. Years later, I learned that there was indeed an Emergency Rescue Committee operating from Marseille under the leadership of Varian Fry that forged identification papers and visas, provided financial assistance, and found ways of smuggling endangered people out of the Vichy zone. I was given some of the details by our friend the economist Albert Hirschman, who had worked with Fry in Marseille, and whom I got to know at Yale and at Princeton. Hanna Arendt, Jacques Lipchitz, Franz Werfel, Leon Feuchtwanger, and Marc Chagall were among the hundreds they helped evade the clutches of the Nazis. Chagall's daughter did not manage to escape with her father. I seem to recall that she was with us on the Spanish banana freighter that zigzagged across the Atlantic the following summer.

But I am getting ahead of myself.

IN THE MEANTIME, no departure was in sight, and I was just as glad. I did not wish to leave and resented the endless litanies about hard-to-get visas and unavailable boats. I kept saying that I felt French, that I saw no reason to expatriate ourselves. The patriotic statements of their seventeen-year-old son must have annoyed my parents, as did many extravagant statements I made in those days—made mostly, I suppose, to annoy them. But my "French" feelings were quite real. I considered it my noble obligation to stay and share the fate of others. I was obviously quite foolish.

My father did his best to disabuse me of my beliefs. In our little apartment on the rue de la Buffa, or on a bench in the nearby garden of the Musée Masséna, he gave me what amounted to lessons in political psychology. He was patient and did not even seem irritated by my sitting on the bench with my eyes closed while he talked, lifting my face toward the sun to improve my tan. I marvel less at my adolescent vanity than at my father's determination to treat me as an adult. He took time to develop his thoughts, clearing his throat to punctuate his main points. About our predicament he was open-minded, making sure to separate cause from effect. The Jewish question in France, he explained, was part of a larger picture, part of a story that went back at the very least to the turmoils brought about by the French Revolution and that had never really been resolved. Old wounds remained unhealed. He tried to make me aware of the difficulty of finding solutions, or even of arriving at sound judgments. It is possibly to my father that I owe my disposition to seek multiple perspectives. Certainly he liked to complicate matters and disliked coming to any conclusions. He stressed that what we were witnessing was the consequence of long-standing internal conflicts in French society that had been festering and had created deep rifts. Not even the Dreyfus affair could be reduced to a spontaneous outburst of anti-Semitism, or a manifestation of endemic hostility toward the Jews. It was related to other social and ideological tensions that had remained unresolved since the political upheavals of 1789 and the Terror in 1793. Settling accounts had in fact become an obsession with the French right, and that meant getting rid of much more than Jews.

My father was no dupe, even though he had at first regarded Pétain as a useful buffer against German brutality. The *maréchal*, whom he distrusted as he did all aspects of the military, might help us, as he put it, avoid the fate of Poland. But my father also knew that Vichy and its policies were not imposed by the Germans, that they had their roots in French history, and that they corresponded to a deep-seated hostility to parliamentary democracy. The anger of the Megève hotel guests toward Léon Blum and his Popular Front came back in a flash, and that memory made my father's lesson more vivid. He explained that, contrary to what they may have taught me at the lycée, where France was represented as the home of freedom, fraternity, and tolerance, the French were really on the whole a conservative lot, attached to law, order, and their own way of cooking, and supremely afraid of another revolution.

My patience for my father's disquisitions had its limits. I had other plans for the morning and was eager to join my friends. But I will admit that it was he who helped me make some sense of the confused period we were living through. He quickly saw through the illusion of an autonomous Vichy government and was aware of its inherent collaborationist tendencies. There were daily complicities with the Nazi authorities. Soon the willingness to do the dirty work for the occupier became clearer still. Vichy was a pernicious phenomenon from the start, and not only because it responded to the worst instincts of the extreme right. It was in reality quite representative of a large body of bureaucrats and technocrats and, sadly, of the vast majority of the middle classes.

At times I felt like rebelling against my father's detached wisdom, his skepticism, his insistence on the ironies of history and politics, his lack of respect for public opinion, which he considered fickle and entirely subject to manipulations, his view that doctrines and ideologies were more deadly than vigilantes. I must have shown my boredom when he lectured me on demography and geopolitical factors. "Go read Montesquieu," he would conclude, and for once there was some impatience in his voice. I suppose he meant not the satirical *Persian Letters,* which I had read in extracts at school, but *The Spirit of the Laws,* which inspired liberal and constitutional ideas on the eve of the French Revolution. My father did not make his meaning clear. All he did say was "Go read Montesquieu."

What my father did not know, what he could not know and would not have believed, was the German plan to carry out the so-called Final Solution, the decision systematically to annihilate millions of people. What has come to be called the Shoah or the Holocaust was simply not conceivable at the time, not even in 1940 or 1941—certainly not in Occupied France. Sometimes I wonder what my father would have thought and done had he been born Catholic and French. He, too, believed in law and order. I heard him repeat ironically the smug German formula "*Ordnung muss herrschen*" (Order must prevail), but there was also a tinge of admiration in his mimicry. The full magnitude of Nazi horrors was revealed to us only gradually. For a while one could still be ignorant, if not innocent. Retrospectively, there is always the danger of conflating history. Vichy in 1940 was one thing; by 1941, it was another. In 1942 and 1943, the picture was altogether different. During the first year of the German occupation, we could not possibly have predicted events such as the large-scale executions of hostages, the enforced wearing of the yellow star, the arrest by the complicitous French police of entire families, including small children, who were herded into the infamous Vel d'Hiv stadium in Paris and then deported to concentration camps in Eastern Europe. All this was still to come, and not even my father, who had been left with few illusions after the atrocities of the Russian Revolution, could in his most pessimistic moments imagine what was to be carried out in Treblinka, Theresienstadt, or Auschwitz.

What we did know was bad enough. The news was inexorably gloomy. In October 1940, Italy attacked Greece. Soon, in quick succession, an Italo-German offensive was launched in North Africa, the Germans entered Belgrade, and Greece was forced to capitulate. Then came the arrest of foreign Jews in Paris. The accelerated rhythm of distressing news, their banal unreality, had a numbing effect. It was this numbness, I suppose, that accounts in large measure for the uncanny lightheartedness that was in the air, stimulated by the resort atmosphere in Nice during that first year of the Vichy regime. Everything that happened seemed perfectly normal. We were not even surprised one day when we saw Leni Riefenstahl, the sporty film director who had made the Nazi documentary of the Berlin Olympics, walk in splendor on the Promenade des Anglais, laughing and gesticulating, surrounded by flirtatious German officers.

IS IT BECAUSE Nice and the Côte d'Azur were associated with holidays? There was indeed a vacation mood that weakened all sense of responsibilities. *Vacances*—the word itself signifies an emptiness, an unfilled space, an interlude, a reprieve from duties. Softness surrounded us. The French call it *"douceur."* But vacations also carry a sense of measured time, of the fleetingness of things. And in 1940–41 there was an especially acute awareness of the finite, of an impending end. We all knew that the *douceur* was deceitful, that it could not last. For some, it meant the intuition of their doom was made more ironic because it would be met in what was known as *la douce France*. I had read about the psychology of collective crises, about unheard-of orgies taking place precisely because the opulent empire was about to fall, the barbarians were about to arrive, the plague was transforming the city into a charnel house—or simply because people thought the end of the world was at hand. French newspapers would occasionally propose a question to their readers in peacetime: What would you do if you knew the world was coming to an end in two weeks? How would you occupy the remaining time? I knew even then that the answer would be colored by the hypothesis of a collective catastrophe.

Nice seemed to me lovelier than ever. Memory has its moods. On certain days images come back in black and white, as though reproducing the picture postcards and guidebook photos of that period. On other days I see very clearly the shimmering liquid shades of blue moving in uneven strips and the gray beach pebbles, to which the soles of my feet

never quite got accustomed. I still see, at about the center of the bay, the gaudy Moorish architecture of the Casino de la Jetée—a cross between the Brighton pier and the old Palais du Trocadéro—which the Germans later destroyed to cull scrap iron for their war effort. The Casino de la Jetée, jutting out into the sea, had been for many years a landmark of Nice. Though quite garish, it did not spoil the view of the distant castle at the extreme point of the amphitheater of hills, behind which lay hidden the old port that goes back to Greco-Roman times when Nice was known as Nikaia.

I developed a taste for solitary walks past the Bellanda tower, where

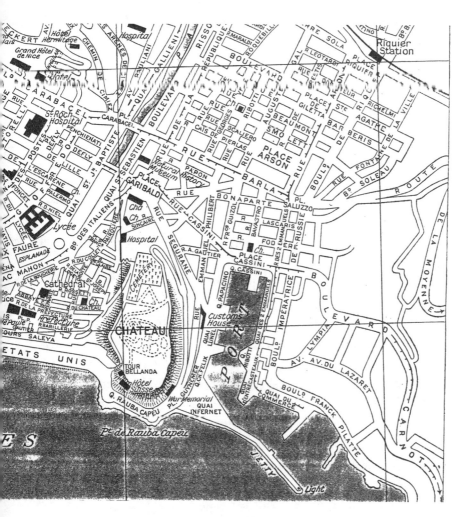

Berlioz had stayed, and enjoyed the balmy air of the orange groves. I would walk several miles around the cape of Nice, until the natural harbor of Villefranche came into view, and beyond it, the elongated line of Cap Ferrat. There were hardly any vehicles; fuel was severely rationed. The road belonged to me. At other times, I would take off in the opposite direction, also along the sea, past where the international airport is now located, until I reached the River Var, which was often quite dry. Beyond it, I could glimpse the hill of Cagnes, known as the Haut-de-Cagnes, with its medieval castle surrounded by cypresses and olive trees, for years a favorite haunt of painters.

I had recently discovered the poetry of Paul-Jean Toulet and had memorized a short poem about the remains of the Provençal necropolis in Arles, a lovely avenue of marble tombs. The poem evokes the bewitching hour of the day when deep shadows fall under the rose bushes. I kept repeating one line:

Prends garde à la douceur des choses

Beware of the sweetness of things.

The whispered warning seemed very appropriate as I walked and day-dreamed. I was thinking of Dany, who was by now married in Lyon. Bittersweet sensations came over me, and I felt sorry for myself. But even that feeling was not unpleasant; it was part of the "sweetness of things."

In my solitary moods, when not on one of my long walks, I liked to settle in the garden of the Musée Masséna with a book. I don't know where I had obtained the sentimental novel by the Hungarian writer Lajos Zilahÿ, translated into French as *Deux prisonniers*. The story of these two "prisoners" takes place just before and during World War I. I was deeply moved by the young couple separated in wartime, when the hero was made prisoner by the Russians and both started new lives (he deep in Russia, where he now lived with another woman), and by the irony of the end when they almost—but not quite—met again. Maybe I saw a romantically aggrandized parallel to my own separation from Dany, and her new life. I had heard, from common acquaintances who had passed through Lyon, that she was expecting a child.

Another book that made an impression on me was Axel Munthe's *The Story of San Michele*, which describes at great length life on the island of Capri, and which strengthened my early enthusiasm for an Italy I had yet to discover, filling my head with stereotypical images of the bay of Naples and anecdotes enhanced by much local color. As I looked out of the museum garden toward the sea, I kept thinking that the same Mediterranean whose sound I could hear was washing the blue grotto and the Faraglioni rock of Capri.

But there is no doubt that the book that made the most powerful impact on me was Victor Hugo's *L'Année terrible*, a collection of poems about the year 1870–71—the terrible year of the Prussian invasion, the siege of Paris, and the violence of the Commune. I had found this volume by chance in a secondhand bookstore. It was a sturdy, leatherbound edition published just a few years after those events. I acquired it for just a couple of francs, and I still have it; it sits on a shelf in my study, within arm's reach. When I take it down, it opens by itself to some of the pages I learned by heart. I loved especially Hugo's acrid lines denouncing those around him who spoke of brotherhood with the Germans. "*A Ceux qui reparlent de fraternité*" inveighs against submission and collaboration. It takes on prophetic tones, predicting disaster to the invader:

Et je prédis l'abîme à nos envahisseurs.

In vehement terms, Hugo summons his compatriots to seek strength in contempt for the enemy. Only after offering resistance and winning the war can there be room for forgiveness and love. I read those lines over and over again. I recited them to myself aloud as I walked at a military pace along the seashore. I could not understand why this poem, which seemed to me so relevant to our situation, was not broadcast daily from London to inspire the French to react against Vichy. The voice of Hugo was for me the voice of resistance, pride, and dignity.

NOT ALL MY moods were so heroic, and not all my recitations so grandiloquent. My readings, like my walks, took two directions. Political awareness led to daydreams of resistance. But I also felt the temptation of poetic reverie, of epiphanic surrender to the moment. My reveries were associated with cypress trees and the little I knew of Italy from books and pictures. A recurrent otherworldly fantasy was one that now, with hindsight, I call my "Berenson dream." I had never even heard of the American Renaissance art expert who settled near Florence. But as a seventeen-year-old in Nice I often had a mental image of myself as an elderly gentleman with a trimmed beard walking with a stylish cane on a flowery terrace or in a sloped garden—and this decades before I was a guest at Villa I Tatti, Bernard Berenson's abode near Settignano, in a setting I instantly recognized as a place I had fantasized about as my ideal home and ideal landscape. Tuscany has remained just that, with its cypresses, olive groves, and the cool shade of its loggias. The memory of a longing has given a fuller meaning to nostalgia. Now that I am on in years, even if not bearded, and catch myself acting like my father, I suspect that my mind foreshadowed aging as a way of protest, perhaps as an escape. Perhaps it is the same yearning that later made me look backward to the child I had been, even if as a child I had been sometimes chided and made to feel insecure. But the backward glance, much like the future-oriented dream, allowed me to believe that the present was not overwhelming, that even my flaws were not serious.

Not all my occupations during that uncertain period in Nice were so self-centered. Sascha and I explored the region on bike as well as on foot. Our calves were solid. We would take off for Cap d'Antibes, find ourselves a pebbly nook, and eat our baguette sandwiches listening to the suction of the seawater that followed each successive small wave. Most of the properties were shut. Everything felt abandoned. This sense of desertion was even stronger when we pedaled in the other direction, all around Cap Ferrat. Here the estates were more sumptuous and largely hidden by lush vegetation. We sometimes left our bikes under a tree, walked between thick bushes, climbed over a low wall. On one of these transgressive expeditions we picnicked beside an empty swimming pool in visible disrepair, with one of its sides all cracked. All was silent, and we had the impression of discovering a world that was no longer inhabited. The owners had probably not returned since the outbreak of the war.

Sometimes we pedaled into hilly regions—toward Vence when we were in search of black-market farm products, or toward Èze when we were just lusting for adventure. I still do not know how we made it all the way up to Èze on bicycles. Perched on a sharp peak like an eagle's nest, this ancient Celto-Ligurian stronghold had seen the Phoenicians, the Romans, the Saracens. I don't remember ever encountering a human figure in the narrow shaded streets of this medieval village, after we passed the fortified gates with their battlement features. We found

vaulted passages and stairs everywhere. What has now become an animated tourist attraction was then empty, dead. Only the stones seemed
to be alive and speaking. Sascha and I felt a rare inebriation as we gazed
down from one of the belvederes and caught a dizzying view of the
entire coastline. Coming down late in the afternoon was easier on our
legs. But they felt wobbly when we began walking home in Nice after
returning our rented bikes.

Since we were no longer going to school, nothing prevented us, even
on winter days, which were often sunny and mild, from settling for several hours in one of our haunts, the Lido Beach. It was the beach closest
to the Casino de la Jetée, where, only a few years earlier, my mother
had taken me to a performance of *Le Pays du sourire,* as Franz Lehár's
Viennese operetta was called in French. It was in that same casino that
as a boy I had watched a variety show featuring as its chief attraction
Charles Rigoulot, proclaimed on the billboards as the strongest man in
the world, capable of lifting and holding two men with each arm. These
memories were still vivid as I sat in my swimming trunks at one of the
tables at the Lido, next to the pebble beach and the wooden planks
installed to make walking easier. There were ping-pong tables at beach
level, recessed underground below the promenade in what felt like a
grotto. There Sascha and I would play epic matches, interrupted by fits
of uncontrollable laughter, for we had gotten to know each other's
game so well (my tricky, tennis-style drives, his unstylish but successful
retrievals) that we could predict all the moves, and volleys were seemingly endless. Ping-pong became an addiction. I even enrolled in a local
tournament and reached the semifinal before being beaten by a hollow-
chested Hungarian with a mean service and a meaner backhand.

The Lido rented beach chairs, rowboats, and two-seater *pédalos,*
paddleboats resting on floats and propelled by blades that we turned
with our feet. That was fun, especially when the sea was slightly agitated. But we were mostly content to sit and read, anointed with odiferous tanning creams, joined by newly made friends with whom we were
beginning to constitute a little "Parisian" group. A tiny photo of that
period taken by my cousin shows me in profile, with a book in hand, my
wavy and shiny hair clearly saturated with brilliantine, the oily hair
product whose use so sickened my mother. There is not a hint in that

snapshot that those were grim times, that food was scarce, that we were all living with a threatening cloud over our heads, that the Germans could—as they would—suddenly occupy our region as well, bringing to a brutal close the illusion of an independent Vichy government.

Some odd characters gravitated to our group. There was a self-styled Irishman in his late twenties, a real adult in our eyes. Ireland was not at war with Germany, and his presence in Nice therefore seemed perfectly reasonable. All the same, it was not at all clear what he was doing there. He was handsome in a way I later associated with James Bond as portrayed on screen. What were his occupations, if any? Why did he take such interest in our group? We were vaguely baffled by this tall, athletic figure, who at times looked a little like Cary Grant. In retrospect, I am suspicious: was he interested in adolescents in a personal way, or was there some other reason? I recall also a gap-toothed young woman, Didi Andrieu, with excessively blond hair and provocative breasts, who flirted with each one of us in turn. My romantic imagination endowed these two figures with an espionage mission—though why we young Parisian refugees would be worthy of the attention of any spy I was at a loss to explain.

Much as I now marvel at our surface insouciance in the face of looming danger, I also wonder at the mixture of frivolity and seriousness in my personal life. If philosophizing is an adolescent avocation, I was mightily given to it during those long months in Nice. Surveying the starry sky, seated at night on the Promenade des Anglais, I pondered about being and nonbeing. "Why me?" I insistently asked myself. Why in the trillions of unlikely possibilities did I at this point emerge into existence? I recalled Aunt Anya's disquisitions about the vagaries of sperm cells. What I felt was akin to vertigo. And with it came a corollary anguish: the fear of losing life. Why *not* me? Years earlier, Papa had told me one morning that he had had a nightmare about seeing himself dead. He claimed that upon awakening his hair stood on end. At the time I found this rather funny, for my father had hardly any hair left. Now I understand the hair-raising nature of that bad dream.

In this same philosophical mood, under the guidance of Philippe Andler, a slightly older friend who had finished his *classe de philo*, I came to read some Henri Bergson, notably his essay on the intuitive grasp of human experience, and began to make distinctions between objective time and psychological temporality, between time and duration. This same Philippe Andler also wrote pornographic verse describing in graphic detail the acrobatic skills and circus-like flexibility required to fellate oneself. Bergson's essay on time, however, made a more lasting impression. I began to cogitate about conflictual temporal schemes, about immediate, mediated, sequential, and cyclical times, about continuity and recurrence, about the operations of memory as well as the retrieval and survival of experience.

This intellectual mood now surprises me. It had nothing to do with class stimulation, homework, or exams. We were free, after all—but this very freedom, it would seem, weighed on us. Perhaps it was some form of nostalgia that made us attend courses at the Centre Universitaire. (Nice did not at the time have a real university.) Some of this was interesting, some of it was fun. I don't know what imp of perversity (or of protest) made me go to German classes and, when called upon to read a passage aloud, to pronounce the words (I, who spoke German fluently) with a thick and almost incomprehensible French accent, which made Sascha, who was seated next to me, double up with laughter and disappear red-faced under his desk.

Sascha is no longer. And where are my other friends? What happened to André Baumann with his sad, long face, to baggy-trousered Jean-Pierre Helft, to effeminate Pierre Casnati, whose father was a second-rate opera singer, to Didi Andrieu, to Suzanne Ivaldi, to Annette Schwab, to my Bergsonian initiator Philippe Andler, to crop-haired Naftalion, whose nasal hum I remember but not his first name? How many of them survived the war years and the deportations? Not one of them reappeared on my horizon. What happened to Andler's close friend, Sébastien Lucas, who was the only one of us living with a woman, about whom he said, as though to explain a bondage, "*Elle me tient par les couilles*"? I could not get out of my mind the image of being held by one's balls, and tried to literalize the figure of speech as I imagined her grabbing him in the privacy of the room they shared.

The image bothered me during daylight hours and tormented me at night. I decided to repeat the experience of the rue de Provence. Someone had pointed out near the Jardin Albert I a house with closed shutters. I presented myself one evening, alone. The door opened a few moments after I rang. But I was refused admittance just as quickly: "*Voyons, tu n'as pas l'âge.*" Perhaps because I was alone I did not have the courage to protest that I had reached the legal age. There was no use arguing, in any case. Police controls were no doubt stricter in Nice. Or perhaps the new "moral" concerns of the Vichy regime made establishments of this sort more cautious. This was not a time to get into trouble with the authorities. I left ingloriously, yet I was relieved in a sense. I did not mention my unsuccessful initiative to anyone. It was ironic, I kept thinking, that I had been refused entrance at the age of seventeen, whereas in Paris, more than two years earlier, no questions had been raised, and I had been made to feel so welcome. These were evidently different times.

Being seventeen had an additional meaning for our group during that winter after the fall of France. To keep ourselves busy and to have a purposeful pretext for getting together, some seven or eight of us decided to rehearse a play. After much debate, we settled on a juvenile comedy some of us had seen performed in Paris just before the war started. *J'ai dix-sept ans* (I am seventeen) was the title; I have forgotten the name of the author. The play dealt with a group of adolescents trapped in a ski lodge after an avalanche, and the ensuing emotional entanglements between them. The sentimental complications seemed to us loaded with meaning and the situation of entrapment symbolically relevant. We decided to begin rehearsals. We found in a hotel a large, empty room that was made available to us for a small fee. The hotel was at the far end of the unfashionable Quai des États-Unis, the seafront just next to old Nice. Where and for whom we would eventually perform remained unresolved. The more immediate problem was to decide who among us would direct the play. Some of us had acted in amateur productions, but no one had any experience directing. The difficulty was solved in what we thought was a fair and democratic manner. We decided simply to take turns, to rotate director and assistant director every few days, giving everyone a chance to be in charge, and no one an opportunity to become tyrannical. No wonder we never got through with our rehearsals! Scenes with only two characters worked fairly well, but as soon as there were three or more characters on stage, arguments and chaos followed, compounded by the discovery that each successive director had an altogether different notion about where the actors should stand or sit, and how the scene was to be played. There were constant interruptions, loud protests, but also frequent bouts of laughter. We remained good friends.

I don't recall any professional theater in Nice during that year. But there were performances at the local opera house to which I went, alone or with my friend Naftalion. It was Naftalion, who was taking voice lessons, from whom I learned the importance of singing *du masque*— from the head, not from the throat. He also demonstrated for me the exercise of humming with one's mouth closed, an annoying habit that he practiced no matter what he was doing. The opera performances were of a provincial quality. *Manon,* which was a discovery, charmed me with its story of juvenile love and infidelity and Massenet's fake eighteenth-century music. *Tosca* was another matter: it was sung in French, and the tenor squealed. As for *The Barber of Seville,* I was sufficiently acquainted with Rossini's staccato recitatives to be bothered by the monotonous and silly-sounding French version. Moreover, someone had announced, in front of the still-lowered curtain, that the baritone was indisposed with a cold, though he would valiantly perform nonetheless. When the baritone entered to sing Figaro's famous aria, he held his hand to his throat to make sure the public understood that he could sing much better if only he were not afflicted with a sore throat. All his artistry on that night went into the expressiveness of his hand.

At other times, Naftalion and I, seated in front of the roofed bandstand, listened to concerts in the Jardin Albert I. The program, rich in brassy sounds, consisted mostly of waltzes, marches, and light operetta overtures by Jacques Offenbach (no one seemed to mind that he was both German by birth and Jewish), whose music reflected the glitter and underlying cynicism of another disaster-bound period.

BEWARE OF THE sweetness of things . . . Toulet's warning about the *douceur des choses* ran like a basso continuo in my inner music, a reminder of the impermanence and vulnerability of life. I have since

relived periodically—on vacations, on army leaves, on sabbaticals—
this sense of measured-out time. As I gazed at the Mediterranean from
Nice's Baie des Anges, the Angels' Bay, recalling classroom discussions
of Ulysses's travels, aware of no longer being at home myself, I developed an exile's sense of longing. I do not quite dare speak of a spiritual
longing; "spiritual" is a big and, today, much-overused word. But I did
have the dim perception that there was, or must be, something else. In
Nice, during those months of waiting and uncertainty, I got to know
myself a little better. Though attached to the here and now, I was
unwilling to believe that this was all there was to it. Much in the same
spirit, I was unwilling to confine a book I read to its literal meaning; I
wanted instead to see it transmuted and transformed into an exalted
realm. But this reluctance to accept unadorned reality, much like the
habit of looking at scenery through colored glasses, was surely also a
form of pleasure-seeking.

Meanwhile, harsh reality pushed itself to the foreground. A family
my parents had known in Paris was released from the French camp at
Gurs, where so-called enemy aliens were interned. They were refugees
from Nazi Germany. After their release I befriended their dark-haired
daughter, Rita, with whom I carried on heated arguments. She had
come out of the camp experience a confirmed communist, and she tried
to convert me. She had acquired rudimentary skills in Marxist dialectics.
Our arguments were often bitter and quite personal. I defended my
position, though without any dialectical skills. But I had learned from
my parents not to justify communism just because Hitler was its enemy.

All around us small and large signs spelled reasons for worry. Even
our lethargy was ominous, for it reduced the ability to resist and bounce
back. The great concern for most people was not the war and its ultimate outcome, nor the ubiquitous Vichy propaganda, nor even the
Vichy government's attempt to "collaborate" with Germany, but food
shortages that quickly led to much-resented rationing. By the spring,
even bread was rationed, and oil and butter sold for outrageous prices
on the black market. Prices and weights made up much of the adults'
daily conversation. We were at times on a hated diet of rutabagas—
which, for some reason, seemed inexhaustible. Preoccupations were
largely practical and selfish. Transportation became a problem because

of the absence of gasoline. Cars and buses ran in limited numbers on long, metal *gazogène* tubes, affixed to the roof or the side of the vehicle, that oxidized coal and wood into combustible gas. These cumbersome cylindrical fixtures gave a new and somewhat grotesque look to the buses. The smaller vehicles seemed altogether crushed by them.

A major practical concern was the line of demarcation established between the occupied and the unoccupied zones. It was a sealed frontier and it allowed for only limited postal service, which was subject to censorship. There were very few authorized crossings. Permits could be obtained only for special reasons. And persons given official permission were not authorized to carry more than a few hundred francs with them.

As for the German presence during that first year of Vichy France, it was largely a threatening absence, for the Germans at that point were not yet occupying all of France. But this absence-presence exercised a strange fascination. It is hardly an exaggeration to say that more than a few among the French experienced during that period an almost sexual admiration for German discipline and power.

My father was surely not among those mesmerized by the virility of the Third Reich. Nor did he succumb to lethargy as others did. I never saw him more active. As of the spring of 1941, he took off quite regularly to the American consulate in Marseille, carrying with him documents, letters, affidavits. He contacted any number of shipping agents. He stood in line at the Nice post office sending off telegrams to New York, where my uncle from Shanghai had landed—the uncle who had managed my father's business in China and who had given me the silk shirt with a pagoda on it that had made such an impression on the rue de Provence. It was he—my mother's brother—who helped us secure the visas, who provided the required statements of financial guarantee. Countless telegrams went back and forth between Nice and New York. My help was often enlisted, for when it came to sending off documents or even ordinary mail, my father liked to have a witness, not quite trusting himself to have dropped the letter in the right box or submitted the document at the proper counter. He would ask me to copy, in extra-neat handwriting, texts to be submitted at the telegraph window. On one occasion, he even got angry at me because, in copying his draft, I had crossed with one line two unadjacent t's in the same word. My father considered this a provocative fantasy on my part, likely to indispose the telegraph operator and mess up things. This kind of paternal silliness indisposed *me* instead. It induced a vaguely rebellious mood and confirmed my suspicion that my father was generally inept. I recalled his many manias and anxieties, but I was unfair and, as it turned out, overly critical.

Through most of 1941, telegraphic communication with the United States was still possible. This was months before Pearl Harbor, and Washington still had an ambassador in Vichy. In fact, the United States, where there was no shortage of isolationists, seemed determined to maintain good diplomatic relations with Pétain. We hoped of course that Roosevelt would come to the rescue of Britain in its now-lonely struggle against Hitler. Roosevelt's cheerful and self-assured face, with which we were familiar from newsreels, seemed to promise succor and salvation. What we did not know was that under his watch, as though the stringent U.S. immigration quotas did not make it hard enough, one of the top officials of the State Department had given instructions to all consuls in Western Europe to raise every possible administrative obstacle so as to delay or impede the granting of visas. Only recently did I come across Breckenridge Long's original letter to the consuls when it was on display at the Los Angeles County Museum of Art. At that same exhibit, dealing with intellectuals and artists who escaped from Nazi Europe, I also read a letter written by Helena Rubinstein, the cosmetics magnate, refusing to contribute even a modest sum to rescue Marc Chagall's daughter. She explained that, having made a contribution for the painter's rescue, she had done all she could do. I felt almost more offended by Helena Rubinstein's letter than by the directives sent from Washington to the consuls. My indignation was doubtless increased by the fact that my cousin Moussia had by then been remarried to the son of Helena Rubinstein. What I felt was akin to family shame.

Nothing in any case would have discouraged my father in his efforts. How he eventually managed to put together and synchronize (for that was of the essence) our American immigration visas, the French exit visas, the Spanish transit visas, and boat tickets at an exorbitant cost, I shall never know. By the summer of 1941, however, we were ready to leave. It was fortunate, because the situation was rapidly getting worse.

Anti-Jewish measures had intensified. Systematic arrests of foreign Jews were taking place in Paris with the help of the French police. The ugly mood spilled over into the Vichy zone. The military situation looked grimmer than ever. In June, not long after the capitulation of Greece, Germany had invaded Russia on a 2,000-kilometer front, throwing into action an army of two million men. As a result of this sudden attack on the Soviet Union, my father found himself in new danger. Born in Moscow, he was now considered an enemy alien and placed under surveillance. Indeed, Vichy joined the German anti-Soviet war effort seemingly overnight. A special legion of French volunteers was organized to fight Bolshevism side by side with the Germans. The lightning-quick advances of the German army deep into Soviet territory dismayed us. Leningrad and Moscow seemed about to fall.

The underground French Communist Party, silent and inactive until then because of the unholy Hitler-Stalin pact that had dismembered Poland in 1939, now slowly swung into action. Isolated terrorist acts were spreading. The German reaction was swift and relentless. Soon after a young Communist killed a German soldier in a Paris *métro* station, ten French so-called "hostages" were executed in retaliation. A month later, more than two dozen random "hostages" were executed in the town of Chateaubriant, and even more elsewhere. Collaboration began to be a dirty word. None of this bode well. Developments as of the beginning of the Russian campaign made us fear that all of France would soon be occupied. We felt cornered in the Département des Alpes Maritimes. Our only hope was that this region, close to the Italian border, would be occupied by Italian troops. And this is what happened eventually when, late in 1942, Hitler ordered the occupation of all of France, and Mussolini's forces took over the region around Nice. For a while, the Italians looked almost like a liberating army to the refugees; they set up a regime of human decency that saved many from deportation to Nazi camps. Alas, this clement interlude did not last very long. The day Italy signed a separate armistice with the Allies in the summer of 1943, it too was treated as an enemy by the Germans. But for a brief, fragile period of Italian military presence, even though the Italians were officially the fascist allies of Hitler, the region of Nice was transformed into a privileged enclave. Italian soldiers sang amusing and amorous songs. They were seen marching in a deliberately casual or even disorderly fashion in total disrespect of the goose-stepping model. With their departure, however, the full horror began. That was when my Aunt Anya vanished, together with many others who were sent off in cattle trains.

Of our own departure I have only disconnected memories. I clearly see the shed and the platform of the Nice train station, which in the past had cheerfully greeted us at that time of year, when Paris was chilly, damp, and morose. Now it meant neither an arrival nor a return home, but exile. We struggled with our bags and suitcases. Our luggage was heavy, even though quite a lot was left behind in storage. I felt dejected, and my parents did not offer me solace. All my friends were left behind, and I had no one to look forward to on the other side of the Atlantic. Yet I recognized my parents' wisdom and our good fortune. What we avoided is obvious in retrospect: ostracism, grim measures, the mandatory wearing of the yellow star, denunciations, quotas set by Heinrich Himmler for deportation to death camps, the zealous collaboration of the French police to meet those murderous quotas.

The train kept rolling toward Spain, but this time the rhythm of the rails did not punctuate the excitement of feeling irresistibly carried toward a desired destination. At the frontier, men in unfamiliar uniforms scrutinized our papers with visible difficulty. A little over a year earlier we had given up the hope of crossing the Pyrenees on foot. We were now crossing the border legally. Yet we constantly feared that some unforeseen technicality would stop us, that some whim or new regulation would invalidate our permits. My father was questioned at great length before we were allowed onto the night train for Madrid. We had to separate because the train was so crowded. I sat in another car, in a stifling compartment, staring at sweaty faces. This time I gave up the old game of trying to guess the professions, the habits, the love lives of other travelers. The night was uncomfortable, the toilet at the end of the corridor was without water. At the Madrid station, we changed to a train for Seville, after a long wait during which we were assailed by swarms of beggars. It was in Seville that we were to board our ship, which seemed bizarre to me. I knew enough about Spanish geography to realize that Seville was on an important river, the Guadalquivir, but at quite a distance from the ocean.

Chapter 9

NAVEMAR

The Floating Camp

We did not really know what "south" meant until we reached Seville that July. Nice and Marseille were southern all right, but only in relation to the temperate French climate, and they were barely a few degrees warmer than Lyon or Orléans. Andalusia in the summer was a different matter. My first impression was that of blazing sun and constant thirst. The heat and the glare of the light forced the inhabitants to seek shelter behind thick walls and shuttered windows. In the afternoon the streets, empty and silent, reminded one that it was siesta time. Even the dogs, sprawled in the rare shade, were asleep. Never before had I seen a city come alive only during the evening hours, when the sound of seguidillas could be heard from courtyards and at street corners, accompanied by the rhythmical clapping of hands and the sudden raucous utterances of the *cante jondo*.

Seville was unlike my early bookish notions of Spain. I had imagined a land of arid landscapes, rugged mountain ranges, dusty country roads on which an ascetic-looking knight and his emaciated horse proceeded toward encounters with windmills and unsavory inns. But Seville was not in the least a quixotic place. It seemed positively opulent compared with what we had left behind in Vichy France. The stores were filled with merchandise and produce we had not seen for quite a while. And we discovered the delicious cool fruit drinks called *batidos* that were served at stands in the streets.

Franco's dictatorship had not succeeded in getting rid of the hosts of beggars, whom we encountered everywhere. They were the visible festering wound of the recent civil war. These beggars made themselves especially conspicuous when they saw foreigners, hoping to arouse their sense of compassion and guilt as they sat in a café or near an open restaurant window, or came out of a store. One quickly learned to avoid the tables near open windows. Our sense of guilt was minimal, however. Having been deprived of many delicacies for so long, we indulged without remorse in constipating orgies of candied fruit, and mastered the expressions for the smooth, refreshing drinks of cold, sugared milk, the *leche fria con azucar,* and the ubiquitous *horchata di chufa.* At the hotel restaurant, we also discovered the highly seasoned cold soup made of summer vegetables, *gaspacho andaluz.*

We did not expect to remain in Seville beyond a couple of days. But no ship could be sighted in the harbor, and no one could tell us when ours would appear. All we knew with some certainty—but even that certainty no longer seemed unshakable—was that the ship we expected was called *Navemar,* and that my father had purchased three tickets, which were then as precious as a passport and a visa. It became clear that we would have to wait. The hotel in which we had settled was patrician and picturesque. It was, we were told, an old ducal palace. Its chief attraction was an inner roofless courtyard with potted flowers and a gently murmuring, sculpted fountain. The rooms were disposed with a certain monastic order on the two floors above the central patio. The hotel restaurant became the scene of some linguistic controversies and embarrassments. My father, who insisted that his meat be prepared in butter, brought out the Italian expression "*al burro*" in the belief that Spanish and Italian had trustworthy common roots, only to find out, after prolonged parlays and repeated expressions of consternation and disbelief on the part of the waiters, that "*burro*" in Spanish means not "butter," but "donkey."

From day to day we kept inquiring about the arrival of the *Navemar.* My father managed to locate an agent of the ship's company, but the man turned out to be evasive and ill-informed. Various rumors circulated among the other hotel guests, many of whom were to be fellow passengers. My parents befriended a Belgian couple, as well as a family of Parisian refugees who had spent the year in Montpellier, and a jeweler from Antwerp with a myopic and excessively shy daughter. All of us began to understand that German submarines in the Atlantic made schedules unreliable.

So we had time to explore Seville. It was not easy to figure out the layout of its labyrinthine streets. Itineraries remained tentative. There were constant surprises. Some of the walks I took with my father had a purpose. We found our way to the post office, and more telegrams went off to my uncle, waiting for us in New York. But other walks were random. Certain images and sensations remain vividly imprinted on my mind: the teeming commercial street, the Calle de las Sierpes, covered with stretched canvas to keep the sun out; other narrow streets that felt like paved corridors, where men in somber costume stood smoking stubby cigars whose smell blended with that of frying olive oil and of freshly whitewashed plaster; some unidentified smells I later came to associate with Moroccan markets, or souks. The Moorish influence was indeed perceptible all over Seville, in the shaded patios that were an Arab legacy, or in the pink-and-white cathedral bell tower known as the Giralda, in reality a minaret of Moorish origin.

The sound of music came from invisible sources as we walked. Inspired by some private associations, my father kept humming, off-key as usual, Carmen's song "*Près des remparts de Séville*. . . . " At the time I was not aware of any rampart, nor did I identify any cigarette factory from which a sexy, provocative gypsy might emerge. I did notice, though, some parks and gardens, and the yellow tower, the Torre d'Oro, reflected in the murky waters of the Guadalquivir River, where day after day we kept looking for the boat that was to carry us to a new life. As for the huge bullring, it was only years later that I saw it, when Bettina, in a holiday spirit and fresh from readings of Ernest Hemingway and Henri de Montherlant, dragged me to witness the bloody ritual. I now find it difficult to separate the two Sevilles, the one of 1941 when my parents and I were escaping from the Nazis, and that of 1955 when, in an amorous mood, I was touring Spain in a capricious Renault with an adventurous companion.

The grand ducal hotel felt cool and reassuring. Its stately, austere architecture suggested not a place of transit for refugees but a residence promising stability, even permanence. It is remarkable that an edifice can have such a soothing effect. Whether the boat would appear tomorrow or next week did not really seem relevant when we sat on the cool patio, momentarily lulled by the gentle trickle of the fountain. Yet we had every reason to be anxious. Our visas would soon expire, and surely the money my father carried in a special belt hidden by his underwear was not inexhaustible. About that money, I never asked any questions. Having so often run out of cash myself, I still marvel over where it all came from. My father tried to hide his fears, but his vacant stare into space and the beads of perspiration on his forehead betrayed him. One day he was called to the police station, where he had to spend the night, for anyone born in Moscow was suspect in Franco Spain. His courteous release the following morning allowed us to relapse into a semblance of lightheartedness.

I discovered a ping-pong room on the side of the central patio, opposite the dining room. The sight of the ping-pong table made me think of Sascha and his family, left behind in Nice. Soon I was playing hotly contested games with the Belgian whom my mother dubbed the Seducer. She also called him *le bellâtre,* which designates a smug and insipid type of masculine beauty. The Belgian had the gift of gab and probably, I now think, made a pass at my mother. He was prodigiously annoyed when I repeatedly beat him at ping-pong. This pleased me greatly, for he reminded me of Moussia's husband, Shura—a *bellâtre* of the first order, who always had to be the center of attention, especially when there were women around.

Mama had other notions of Don Juanesque stature and vitality. In the theater of her consciousness, Don Juan represented, I believe, a quest for some unattainable absolute. Dashing, bold, fully committed to his self-destructive selfhood, he somehow came to be united in her mind with the death-bound Tristan of Wagner's opera. Such notions, strangely, did not seem incompatible with the fact that she was a convinced monogamist. Monogamy, she once explained to me—she probably meant any exclusive passion—was so beautiful because it inevitably resulted in tragic loss. I remember her words, though at the time I did not grasp her idea that real love has death at its center. How could the Belgian Seducer comprehend the beauty of the irretrievable and the need to transcend the appetite of the senses?

It was in this same spirit that, sitting in the roofless part of the hotel lobby, Mama spoke to me admiringly of Dostoevsky's *Crime and Punishment,* the novel I had left behind in the windowless hotel room in

Bordeaux. She was especially impressed by the end of the novel, the developments of the epilogue I had not yet reached: how Sonya, the noble prostitute, follows Roskolnikov when he is condemned to forced labor in Siberia, how this sacrifice represents an expiatory and redemptive act of supreme love. I remained somewhat embarrassed by Mama's sentimental mood, as when she cried at the movies. I was taken aback by this glorification of Dostoevskian love in a Seville hotel lobby, and by the implicit suggestion that it was her own role to follow my father no matter where. Certainly my father was no Roskolnikov, any more than he was a Tristan or a Don Juan. I could not imagine him, even in his juvenile days, consider wielding an ax to murder a mean, old, money-lending woman. My father would not have approved of anyone wantonly killing a fly. (One of the rare times he got very angry with me was when he saw me, as a child, squash a fly and scrutinize the yellowish stuff that oozed out of its tiny belly.) But between my father and my mother there was obviously a pact that had led them, in joy and in mourning, from the early days of the Revolution to exile in Denmark while on their honeymoon, then to London, to Germany, and finally to France. They were on their way again.

NEWS BROKE ONE morning that the *Navemar* would be in port on the following day. The *Navemar*—those two words for ship and sea, carried an almost mythical sound. Our departure had indeed taken on a mythical, slightly unreal dimension. Rumors had it that the boat was damaged, that it was docked in Cadiz, that it did not really exist, that it was all a hoax. There was certainly nothing mythical or unreal about the cost of the tickets, which were paid for from funds available in New York. Papa confided to us—he normally did not mention money or cost—that he had paid $1,000 per passage, an almost unimaginable sum in 1941, the equivalent of at least $10,000 in today's money. Some passengers, we learned, paid even more. It was a scandalous exploitation of individuals and families in distress. We never learned the details of the shameful operation. We heard that the boat was formerly German, that it now belonged to a Spanish shipping company, and that it had recently been chartered by Portuguese entrepreneurs. There was even an ugly rumor that the chief entrepreneur was a Portuguese Jew.

A more shocking surprise was in store for us when, on the following day, we saw the ship that had finally docked in the tidal river port from which Spain normally exported sherry, oranges, lemons, olives, and cork. The slightly listing, very long, very large, very high ship—bulky, massive, and morose-looking—was not a passenger ship at all, but a banana freighter. But there was a worse surprise. Though the freighter had cabin accommodations for 15 passengers, we were 1,200, crowded into the hold of the ship. We were the bananas! Only now did the magnitude of the chartering racket become clear. The exorbitant sum paid per passage by my father had to be multiplied by 1,200. A simple calculation comes up with the staggering figure of $12 million in today's terms. No bananas ever proved so valuable.

The morning of our departure, the dock was unrecognizable. Every time we had come there in the hope of glimpsing our ship, the place had been quiet, almost desolate. Now it was a scene of great confusion. When we appeared with our valises in two large, horse-drawn carriages, we saw baggage and boxes everywhere. People were arriving visibly agitated, running, gesticulating, getting into one another's way. The dock had become an obstacle course. Calls, screams, curses could be heard in French, German, Russian, Polish, Yiddish—in all the languages of Europe. Angry arguments erupted, while the Spanish gendarmes, the *guardia civil,* with their three-cornered hats, looked on impassively, seemingly unconcerned by the cacophony, watching from a distance the masses of human figures climb slowly up the gangplank like laden insects and disappear behind cranes and thick ropes into the bowels of the ship. Where had all these people stayed while we were waiting in our hotel? The only other time I was to see such endless crowds march up a gangplank was on the troop ship carrying me back to Europe—but that was a far more orderly procession. The boarding of the *Navemar* was a frantic scene. The confusion and dismay became even greater as we were directed down narrow stairs to our bunks in the semi-dark hold.

Many of us quickly emerged again to daylight, pretending that what we had seen below did not exist. Soon the *Navemar* began to move, imperceptibly at first. I watched the landscape on both sides glide by. I had always loved to see landscapes unfold from a moving train. But the rhythm of the train was joyful. This river navigation, in spite of the bright sun, was mournful—quiet, smooth, ominous. It took hours to reach the sandy delta of the Guadalquivir. Beyond either bank of the river lay monotonous stretches of grassy marshland. Here and there a herd of cattle could be seen at a distance. A sense of emptiness and desolation descended on the boat as we steamed down the river under a leaden sky. Someone pointed out a pink flamingo and knowingly explained that this was an insalubrious swampy region known as Los Marismas, filled with insects but also with some lovely long-legged wading birds, such as flamingos and herons.

At some point, the big boat began to rock—slightly at first. We had reached the point of encounter between river and ocean, the sea reach filled with tidal currents. In years to come, I would never teach the opening pages of Joseph Conrad's *Heart of Darkness* without associating the turn of the tide and the interminable waterways leading to the end of the earth with our own departure from the extreme western tip of Europe.

Once on the open sea, we returned to reality. We began to understand that this was going to be a long and uncomfortable journey. We learned that, for reasons not explained to us, we were to stop over in Cadiz and Lisbon, then in Cuba, and next in Bermuda, before approaching the shores of America in a most roundabout way—without being allowed to go ashore until we had reached our final destination. We saw ourselves as prisoners for weeks on this absurdly overcrowded and unhygienic freighter that was obviously not prepared to convert its usual cargo of bananas and crates into human merchandise.

The hold was stifling. Coming down the steep stairs that felt more like a ladder, one had trouble at first distinguishing anything. Coming up, one was blinded by the light. These were more than separate levels, they were separate worlds. The Latin word *inferi*, or nether regions, began to make sense; it was no longer merely a word to be translated from a dead language. Caught between the relentless bright sun above and the damp, airless stench below, we were like restless souls moving up and down a floating underworld. My father referred to the jammed and shadowy area of the bunks and the washrooms as *ad,* the Russian word for "hell."

Groups tended to form, largely according to national or linguistic background. There were exceptions, such as the Italian physician who had fled Fascism, and who joined our French and Russian-speaking group. The Germans and the Poles tended to remain by themselves. Language counted for more than social and professional status in promoting group solidarity. It did not seem to matter whether one was a lawyer, a doctor, or a merchant. People apparently wanted to be with "their own." Our group, or subgroup, huddling in a nook on the deck, was largely Franco-Russian. We shared much, even reserves of chocolate bars and precious drops of condensed milk. Food and sanitation were chief preoccupations. The smells that came from the boat's invisible kitchen were so repulsive—rancid fried oil blending with whiffs of crude machine oil—that hardly anyone bothered to find out where and when food was distributed. We relied largely on the provisions we had brought with us, which we hoped somehow to replenish in one of the ports of call.

Personal hygiene was a more vexing affair. One had to descend "below" to wash or to use the toilets. Water came in trickles. My father, the high priest of cleanliness, found his ritualistic habits severely thwarted. Instead of soaping his hands three times, abundantly and ceremoniously, he could do so only once, and even that was frustrating. What came out of the faucets and shower was seawater, from which ordinary soap would simply not produce any lather. Somehow my father managed to procure a special saltwater soap, which, at certain hours when the facilities were not overcrowded, he would share with me as we stood showering together in the dark, standing on wooden planks that covered a hole. To the so-called toilets—army latrines were civilized by comparison—one had to bring one's own paper, which turned out to be as precious as the special soap, the condensed milk, and the chocolate bars. There was no assurance that any of these items would last for the entire journey.

After ablutions and other necessities we would reascend as quickly as possible to that part of the deck we claimed as our own. Our group occupied a spot just behind the smokestack, which turned out to be a good position because it protected us from the wind. We were afflicted nonetheless by spray and even showers from the escaping steam, as well as by grimy particles flying out of the funnel and by the sickening smell of fuel. Below deck, on the level of the bunks and the toilets, the smell was worse. Fortunately, the weather allowed us to remain above most of the time, even at night, when we lay on deck, covering ourselves with some extra clothes. This on-deck camping under the stars, with occasional descents to the bowels of the ship, was not a feasible regime for the many who were aged, feeble, or sick.

Sanitation and health problems were more serious than the offenses to one's personal hygiene. All around us were people in need of medical attention. We heard of diabetics running out of insulin. A growing number of passengers suffered from diarrhea or downright dysentery. There was fear of spreading communicable diseases. The ship's doctor, a neatly uniformed, middle-aged man with an underslung jaw, paid perfunctory visits to the sick and quickly disappeared, attentive only to the three families who occupied the few passenger cabins near the captain's bridge. Some of our fellow travelers were doctors, but they had no instruments and no medicine. At best they could diagnose, at times reassure. A few of them tried to treat the sick, but these improvised treatments were mostly palliative. They predicted that the ship would be quarantined upon arrival. A number of aged people died during the crossing. Upon hearing that their bodies had been buried at sea, I conjured up a romantic literary reference: the burial sack in *The Count of Monte Cristo,* thrown into the waters of the Mediterranean—only to realize more keenly that there was nothing romantic about the *Navemar.*

As time passed and the heat increased, conditions below deck became increasingly hard to take. Diarrhea and dysentery were spreading. We would go below deck only for pressing needs or to look for some article in our baggage. Tempers inevitably flared. Someone reported that the Yiddish poet Sch—— (his wife kept referring to him as "the famous poet Sch——") had threatened to deal physically with a dysentery-stricken neighbor who spent much of his time on a chamber pot. He wanted the crew to remove him. "Else, I'll throw him overboard myself."

Uncivil behavior and outbursts of minor violence were additional problems. The passengers included a contingent of former inmates of German concentration camps who had been liberated recently, we were surprised to learn, as a result of a circuitous deal, via a Balkan country, involving trucks delivered to the Germans in exchange for a certain number of prisoners. We called them *"les sauvages"* (the wild ones). They were an angry lot, uncouth, pushy, bullying, quick to take advantage of a situation, quick to annex what did not belong to them, fighting with others and among themselves for a desirable spot on deck as though trying to follow the militant German ideology of *Lebensraum*— territorial expansion—on this ship of refugees. These liberated inmates had been contaminated and corrupted by camp mores. The Nazis were experts at human degradation.

We might have felt sorry for them, but our immediate concern was to protect ourselves. We could not count on the crew, who remained utterly indifferent to our various discomforts. We organized our own police, composed largely of French, Belgian, and Russian contingents, mostly younger men. We patrolled the deck in teams of two or three to keep *"les sauvages"* in check. In this we had the blessings of the captain, as the ship's doctor told us in his heavily Spanish-inflected French. Both the captain and the doctor seemed more concerned with possible "disorder" than with sanitation. Patrolling, I must confess, was fun; it gave us young people a sense of purpose and importance. Thefts and threats diminished as a result of our roving presence and vigilance. We mainly saw to it that quarrels were not allowed to escalate into acts of physical violence.

Reflecting on the aggressive behavior of those freed camp inmates, only recently themselves the victims of violence, helps me make even better sense of what Primo Levi, in *The Drowned and the Saved*, meant by "the gray zone." Perhaps the worst crime perpetrated by the SS guards in the camps was to transform victims into accomplices. The first blows often came from fellow inmates who were, quite diabolically, made to do the dirty work for the Nazis. This cunning corruption of the victim's humanity was something we could not comprehend. And so we "judged" the wild ones. A dialogue with them was not possible. They knew something we did not know, and they held it against us. And what they knew was the shame of having been made to realize that we are all weak in the face of power.

⌒

DESPITE ALL THESE conditions, couples could nevertheless be over-heard, sometimes in broad daylight, giggling in lifeboats that served as trysting places. My mother, who was always amused and reassured by the appetite for love, commented that life does not give up: "*La vie con-tinue.*" Stimulated by what I imagined took place, I made it my business to walk past the lifeboats at night, hoping to overhear telltale sounds. On a few occasions, I became aware of commotion, but subtler sounds were drowned out by other noises and the churning of the engines. It was obvious, though, that something was going on inside. Once, it seemed to me that I briefly saw two bare feet in the air. How I wanted to be with an eager partner in one of the lifeboats! It might not have been the most comfortable place for intimacy or lovemaking, but under the circumstances it was probably the only one. Years later, during my time as a professor at Yale, Claude Lopez, who has written so well of Ben-jamin Franklin's life in Paris, told me that she, too, had escaped to the United States on that same *Navemar*. It created a bond between us. We exchanged memories. When I spoke of the lifeboats, she teasingly said that it might have been her I overheard amorously engaged in one of them. I should have joined, she added.

Among the machinery and the cranes, next to protruding ventilators below the captain's bridge, a little clan of bridge-players gathered, presided over by my mother, who had somehow talked a sailor into pro-viding a semblance of a table. Mama sat, her back quite erect, with a light shawl wrapped around her neck because of the wind. These are mental pictures, of course, as are all the pictures of that voyage. Only one material piece of evidence has survived, a snapshot of my father, the only one I have of the *Navemar* crossing. Papa stands in front of some hoisting machinery; there are wheels, drums, coils, levers—all made of dark metal. He is hatless, unshaven (there are shadows on his cheek), looking pensive behind his horn-rimmed glasses. His face is pale, emaciated, his cleft chin more prominent than usual. His short-sleeved shirt seems particularly delicate against the grimy machinery of the deck. He wears funny-looking striped, baggy, pajama-like beach trousers that are kept from falling by a tightly closed cord belt. In his left hand he holds what looks like a small white towel or washcloth. He might have just come up from the washrooms because his trousers are rolled up to his calves to avoid the puddles down below. He stands there, all thin, in a Gandhi-like pose. Behind the black, oily machinery, a shirtless, bespectacled, hollow-chested man can be seen. His left hand, held up to his face, has a large bandage on it. Behind him, what looks like white underwear is hanging from wires or cords. One can partially see the railing of another bridge on which hangs a dark towel. All of daily life took place in public. In the background, the monotonous sea. The expression on Papa's face is arresting. An unconvinced smile, struggling against the serious look, suggests resignation.

Not for a moment during those six weeks at sea did my father lose his evenness of temper or give up his consideration of others. Yet he was skeptical about human nature and pessimistic on the whole about the course of events. Both my parents somehow managed not to appear affected by discomforts or downcast by the unusual surroundings. Stretched out on a strange contraption she kept calling her "deck chair," her legs elegantly crossed at the ankles, Mama was surrounded much of the day as though she were the center of a salon. A sailor by the name of Ruy had taken a fancy to her. Ruy had in the past worked on passenger ships, and he showed pride in giving service. In this he seemed unique among the crew. It was he who had provided the table-top and put together the weird-looking but serviceable chair on which Mama was reclining. The name Ruy reminded me of Victor Hugo's play about Ruy Blas, the noble valet who was in love with a queen. This melodramatic mental association corresponded, I now realize, to an old fantasy. In childhood, I often thought of Mama's demeanor as regal. I later continued to appreciate her unaffected sense of decorum and her self-control, evident even in the way she would repress a sneeze, reluctant to provoke the unavoidable and perfectly silly "*A vos souhaits*," "*Gesundheit*," "*Na zdarovia*," "*Salute*," or "Bless you." Even her laughter was unobtrusive; it was silent, so to speak, more like a whispered smile than a spasmodic outburst. On the grimy deck of this banana freighter, she continued to take delight in witty conversation, making amusing observations about the foibles of various fellow passengers, including our own group—shrewd but always tolerant observations that reminded me of our early morning discussions of La Fontaine's fables, when she was helping me prepare my class assignments.

I had my own private conversations, and some of them made a lasting impression on me. One of the members of my parents' group, one of those adults who like to explain things to the young, took a didactic interest in me. At night, before we prepared to lie down—we had decided to sleep on deck—he would draw my attention to the stars that shone with unusual brightness against the Atlantic sky, singling out the Big Dipper, perhaps in order to display his linguistic skills. He first named the group of stars in English, explaining that these seven constellations are called that way because their disposition suggests a cup with a long handle. But he quickly added that they were also known as the seven visible stars of the Ursa Major. Did I know what *ursa* meant? *Ursa*, I realized from my Latin studies, meant not at all "dipper," either big or small, but "female bear." Big Bear indeed. And my mentor added that, sure enough, the constellation was *Grande Ourse* in French and *Große Bär* in German. But then he pointed out with a chuckle in his voice that both in Italian and in French it was also known as *Il Carro* or *Chariot*, and in English as the Wagon. My astronomer evidently enjoyed impressing me with a profusion of linguistic designations. The Big Dipper, he added for good measure, was also known in English as the Plow.

I remember being not so much impressed as intrigued. The same constellation could be seen as dipper, plow, wagon, bear. These were of course metaphors, all of them. What struck me is that these metaphors pointed to correspondences as well as divergences in different languages and cultures. My teacher's slightly self-satisfied linguistic display had somehow brought home—but was that his intention?—the complex and arbitrary relation of language to reality. For hours, as I lay facing the sky, I kept thinking about the nature and function of figures of speech. These conversations made me reflect, perhaps for the first time, on the relation between language and cultural context. It was almost more dizzying than cogitating about constellations and celestial spheres.

Another subject that came up in casual conversations had a greater personal impact. One of our fellow travelers was a Belgian architect who had done some advanced work on city planning in an American university. He asked me about my career plans. I was embarrassed and had to admit that so far I had none. I hoped that the United States would enter the war, that I could then return with the American army to liberate France. He laughed, observing that this was not likely. At best, the United States would provide ships and war materials to England. He then urged me to consider getting into an American college. I was just the right age, nearly eighteen. I would have four years ahead of me to discover myself, to discover what I really wanted to do and to be. He and my astronomer friend, who had overheard this conversation, both then spoke glowingly of the American "campus"—a word I had never heard associated with any university in Europe. They spoke of bucolic settings, of the Anglo-Saxon habit of sending their children off to board in schools and distant universities, of campus life and fraternities. (I knew of *"fraternité"* only as a revolutionary slogan.) I heard from them that one could choose one's courses, that teachers were friendly and accessible, that discussions took place in what was called a "seminar atmosphere." Discussions I may have had with friends, but in class we only answered questions; at best we were asked to develop a theme. We knew of lectures and regurgitations, we were taught to write compositions according to set rules, and we filled long exam papers. But what I now heard was all new: student freedom away from families, generous allowances, student dates and dances. The combined observations of my two interlocutors left me reflecting. I saw myself in a distant never-never land, on a campus (accent on the second syllable), in a spellbound park surrounding a palace of joyful studies. I remembered what we had been taught in France—but, oh, how pedantically—about Montaigne's ideas on education, how he felt that a student's brain should not be stuffed with knowledge but be trained to think, how he valued a *"tête bien faite"* (a well-formed head) over a *"tête bien pleine"* (a well-filled head). Thinking rather than cramming. Better still, I thought of Rabelais's notion of merry studies in the mythical abbey of Thélème, from which all pedants and all boredom were banished, and whose motto was that of the freedom to do as one pleases. *"Fais ce que voudras."* As the ship's mast swayed from one constellation to another, I wondered: Could it really be that a college or university resembled such an enchanted citadel of free thought?

The movement of the mast often helped me fall asleep. But even in my sleep I was aware of the vibrations of the ship and felt the occasional brief showers from the funnel. The gentle rocking was sleep-inducing but also conducive to drowsy meditation. Here I was between two worlds, not yet in a country where I did not want to be, and forced to leave an adopted country which was not really mine—already yearning for Europe in mid-Atlantic. Never before had I felt so powerfully a sense of multiple exile. I did not even have a true mother tongue, nor did my parents have a country they could claim as their own. I was to learn that nothing is slower than finding one's home in the world.

I was not insensitive to the poetic nature of the circumstances, and I even indulged in poetic associations. In a state of half-sleep, I spent stretches of time watching the moonlit clouds. The spray that came from the flue I chose to attribute to the sea foam. I recited to myself lines from Coleridge's "Rhyme of the Ancient Mariner" which we had learned at the lyceé:

> *Water, water everywhere,*
> *And all the boards did shrink.*

And more pleasurably still, because of the alliterations I so loved, and also because the images seemed appropriate:

> *The fair breeze blew, the white foam flew,*
> *The furrow followed free;*
> *We were the first that ever burst*
> *Into that silent sea.*

We were of course not the first. I thought of the legendary voyagers, the intrepid explorers, and later the pilgrims aboard the *Mayflower,* which took two months to make the crossing—only fifteen days longer than the *Navemar*. For we had now been told that it would take six weeks, what with the ports of call and the detours to elude the German submarines. In my reveries, I began to see us as what we were: pilgrims on a journey to a distant land on which some of us, with almost religious fervor, had pinned our hopes.

In the meantime, down below deck, "the famous Yiddish poet" with the forked beard was inveighing like a Biblical prophet against the scandalous presence of the dysenteric old man. All of the world's evil seemed embodied in the offensive victim of an intestinal disorder. Less poetic thoughts—of illness—began to gnaw at me. After a couple of weeks at sea, I began to feel a steady, insidious pain in the lower right side of my abdomen. Perhaps it came from having lifted heavy loads, I kept telling myself. But I was not reassured. The horror of appendicitis in mid-ocean, without an operating room, without even an adequate dispensary, struck me—especially in the early hours of dawn, when it required some determination to arise from the improvised bedding and face the routine of the day.

I experienced what was perhaps my first real crisis of hypochondria. There were to be many others later—above all my syphiliphobia and my chronic fears of latent, slowly destructive diseases. The idea of dying young appalled me. Ever since my sister Nora's death, I had been encouraged to view myself as immensely precious. Fear of death is a heavy price to pay for self-love. Over the years, I have learned to bring palliative thoughts to the rescue: So many better people than I have died at an early age; so many Holocaust victims did not even have the comfort of medical help and died without dignity; I might not have been born in the first place. It did not help. Nothing alleviated my sense of panic. Things have not changed much. In the past, it was the fear of not getting there; now, it is the fear of losing it all.

On the *Navemar* there was not even a reassuring mirror available. The absence of mirrors seemed to put identity itself into question. I am not ashamed to admit that mirrors have always been important to me. I believe that this is so for reasons more valid than simple vanity. Mirrors can be deep metaphors. Memory itself is a form of reflection, and so surely is the writing of memoirs. This mirror of writing is filled in depth with surprising discoveries, for not only the future is unpredictable; the past can be unpredictable, too. We rewrite our past as we go about meeting the uncertain future. I have always been bothered by St. Paul's statement in one of his epistles that when he was a child he thought as a child, but when he became a man he "put away childish things." It seems to me that the child is still in me, with me, and conversely, that this child is in large part a creation of my present self. I see no clear discontinuity, nor do I wish to.

Because mirrors were missing we had to shave by touch alone, which was not easy with a Gillette razor and cold water. But the absence of books was also disturbing. Until that Atlantic crossing, I had not fully realized how important books were to me. Over the years they had come to mean privacy in the midst of family life, secrecy, intimacy with myself. They also unleashed dreams. As a boy, at a time when I could barely read, I would drag down a heavy volume of an encyclopedia from my father's bookcase (it might have been a volume of the Larousse or the Brockhausen encyclopedia) and stare for hours at the images that accompanied the text: the flags of the various nations; the maps of distant regions; the anatomical, geographical, nautical illustrations; the representations of exotic flowers and strange-looking animals. I would leave for long voyages while sitting on the rug next to the bookshelves. Now I was on a real voyage, and it was a long one—but without the incentive of a book. As my eyes roamed over the ceaseless repetition of the sea, however, I did recall some readings that had left their mark. Baudelaire's lines in "Le Voyage" kept echoing in my mind. (Baudelaire, in the days I went to the lyceé, was not recommended reading—a good reason for loving him.) I remembered his lines about true travelers who leave in order to depart, about the soul as a three-master in search of an unattainable utopia. Most telling, perhaps, was the link between voyage and death:

O Mort, vieux capitaine, il est temps! levons l'ancre!

But this literary death, versified and rhyming, did not at all have the smell of mortality. Reconstructing portions of the poet's text in the absence of the text itself was most reassuring. It provided a pleasure that was new.

༠—

OUR FIRST PORT of call after a brief stopover in Cadiz was Lisbon, which we reached within a day or two after leaving the estuary of the Guadalquivir. We were still on the old continent, though at its extreme western end. The delaying stopover turned out to be a blessing for a number of us. Because of the long wait for the boat in Seville, our immigration visas were about to expire, which caused not a little anxiety. We were told that the American consulate in Lisbon had been informed, that they expected us to appear in person to apply for extensions. But getting off the boat on our own was out of the question. We were prisoners of the *Navemar* and undesirable on Portuguese soil.

A solution was found in the form of a sealed bus that transported us in midday heat, under police guard, first through narrow, winding streets, then to the broad avenues of the embassy quarter, which years later I would come to know so well on various holidays. It was stifling in the bus. We were made to wait inside the bus in front of the consulate under the blazing sun, doors and windows closed, having arrived at lunch or siesta time. Finally the doors opened. The procedure in the consulate was slow, but the personnel, both American and Portuguese, were friendly—certainly more friendly than any officials we had had to deal with during the past year. We returned to our banana freighter with our visa extensions in the same airless bus, feeling rejected by the city even more keenly now that we had caught glimpses of its joyous, appealing streets. For the next few days, like prison inmates looking longingly at the world of the free, we stared at the terraced city shimmering in the distance, all aglow in the late-afternoon light. We were at anchor on the Tajo River, and the landmarks of the city of Lisbon were never quite where we expected to find them. The tides and flow of the river made the boat turn on itself. We were moving in circles, getting nowhere, yet gaining new perspectives as we changed positions imperceptibly. Even time became perplexing, for sunsets and dawns seemed to play hide-and-seek, as we kept circling in view of the city that did not want us.

The sense of being outcasts, politically if not medically quarantined, was even stronger when, after a few weeks at sea, having eluded the

subs that induced our captain to proceed in devious ways, we finally
reached the port of Havana. In contrast to Lisbon, the human bustle of
Havana seemed to come to meet us where we lay at anchor. Dozens of
small rowboats and motorboats literally surrounded the *Navemar* as for
a many-sided assault. The men in the boats kept yelling their wares,
hoisting them by means of ropes adroitly slung over the boat's railings.
Money was lowered by the same means. The scene was boisterous and
joyful. Condensed milk seemed to be much in demand. But it was
amazing how many different articles were available.

There were also representatives of various Jewish relief agencies in
those little boats, who communicated with the passengers leaning over
the railings, screaming out names and exchanging information about
families on the ship or left behind. Some of these representatives were
allowed on board, carrying special messages, money, or documents to
be signed. The noise and agitation, the movement of the small boats,
the sight of the rooftops under the deep blue sky—all this was very different from the way I had imagined Havana. I must confess that in my
ignorance, much like the simple-minded old servant in one of
Flaubert's stories, I had mental pictures of an entire island enveloped by
thick clouds of cigar smoke.

When we next sighted land it was, briefly, the American continent.
The impression was elusive, even weird. We were gliding along the
coast of Florida—so near, yet not to be approached—on our way, we
knew not why, to Bermuda. We could clearly distinguish the tall buildings all along the flat American coastline. So this was America! It was
all rather frustrating. Here was the promised land, yet we were still so
far from landing. Endlessly, as in a dream, the agglomerations shining
in the morning sun kept moving by against a background without relief.

There was nothing dreamlike about our stopover in Bermuda. We
were once again prevented from getting off the ship. The British
authorities inspecting the boat and our documents were at best matter-
of-fact. The officers—looking trim, moving about briskly, and addressing us in a cutting manner—made us feel like an unsavory, contagious
lot. The British police, in their impeccably neat shorts, had contempt
written all over their faces. There was contempt in their gestures, their
silence, their way of handling our passports and our tickets, as though

we and all that belonged to us were infected. If I remember correctly—but I may be carried away by a fitting metaphor—these supercilious and uniformed officials wore gloves. It was obvious that in their opinion we were hardly better than vermin. It did not seem to occur to them that under other circumstances this was not at all the way we looked, that some of us were used to wearing smart summer clothes and belonged to attractive tennis clubs. Instead, one could read in their eyes and demeanor that we deserved to travel like tramps because we were tramps.

THE *NAVEMAR* STEAMED out of Bermuda harbor, now on a course due north. One morning, as I still lay half-asleep on my bedding, I became aware of a great commotion all around me on deck. Something special was going on. I put on my trousers in a hurry and got up. The boat was almost motionless, the waters unusually calm. People were at all the railings, pointing excitedly in the same direction. We had reached the waters of New York harbor. At a distance we could see the glistening skyscrapers of downtown Manhattan. Someone explained that this was the area of Wall Street, also the area of the great market crash. The buildings, erect and proud, had a kind of geometric beauty. It felt hot and humid even though it was early in the day. The boat was barely moving and the air was still. The moment was at the same time oppressive and exhilarating. To our left, at a distance, I could clearly distinguish the Statue of Liberty, with which I was familiar because of the smaller copy standing on the little island near one of the bridges over the Seine. In school I had learned that the original statue in New York harbor, commemorating the American and the French Revolutions in the shape of a woman on a huge pedestal holding a torch, was a present from France to the United States, and that it symbolized the friendship between the two nations, going back all the way to the days of Lafayette.

We docked in Brooklyn, far from the wharves for the transatlantic liners. The humidity and the heat on that September day, as we waited in long lines on deck to disembark, was unlike any I had ever experienced.

It was nothing like the dry, inebriating heat of Seville. We were drenched from the effort of carrying our heavy valises up from their places near the bunks in the hold. Immigration and health officials appeared, as well as representatives of various relief agencies. We were told that the newspapers had referred to the *Navemar* as "the floating concentration camp." The discomfort of the heat and the confusion of disembarking made it difficult to rejoice that the journey was over.

The pier, next to the gangplank, was crowded with officials, photographers, and journalists. Further back, families were waiting for relatives. There, behind a police line, stood my uncle, Lyolya—tall, dapper, and long-legged, with his elegant narrow trousers and fashionable straw hat: a figure out of a sophisticated spy film welcoming us with his slightly husky, bass voice. His strong, clean-shaven chin and the silver collar bar under the knot of his tie were in harmony with his immaculate white shirt, which might have been the envy of the Bermuda police.

The ride in two taxis to our hotel on upper Broadway left few traces on my memory—barely enough to recall that I felt disappointingly empty of emotion, numbed by fatigue. Our two taxis arrived together. I climbed out, aware all the while of the sultriness of the air. And then, just outside the hotel, I was rudely bought back to my senses. Clumsily, distractedly, with a sudden turn of my head, I bumped into a metal sign, cutting myself above the eyebrow in this, my first physical contact with the big city where we had found refuge.

Chapter 10

TO THE BANKS OF THE SUSQUEHANNA

My self-inflicted wound was hardly serious. Once we were in the hotel lobby, my mother asked for some cold water. Ice cubes were produced, which she applied above my eyebrow to stop the bleeding. I was embarrassed by this public spectacle, but no one seemed to pay the least attention. Clutching my blood-soaked handkerchief, I felt irked by my inglorious entrance into the new world.

The rude encounter with the signpost left a gash, but I quickly forgot about it as I surveyed my hotel room: the large bed, the brightly lit bathroom, the view from the window high up, the movement of the street seen from an unaccustomed height. Vehicles and pedestrians looked like toys. I could still feel the rocking of the boat. I undressed. The shower felt voluptuous, with its forceful stream and the soap that produced abundant lather. This was no salt water. I prolonged my ablutions until I almost fell asleep under the shower. I had not slept in a bed for six weeks. I slipped between the sheets, naked. They felt cool and soft. I tried to tell myself convincingly, "I am on another continent. I am in America, the land of Gary Cooper and Katharine Hepburn. Far from the war zones. We are safe." But I was too tired. I dimly knew it was so, but could not sense the truth of it. I could not even feel estranged.

Recognition of newness came during the following days. There were small and big surprises as I gradually explored parts of the city. Even some of the hotel mores made an impression. In the elevators, men took their hats off ceremoniously in the presence of a woman but continued to chew gum or smoke their cigar. In the street, I stepped on chewing gum, which stuck to the sole of my shoe. I had preconceived notions of the big city, largely derived from Hollywood films that glorified the miracles of concrete, the upward thrust of buildings, the vertiginous perspectives, the rhythm of the thoroughfares punctuated by the film's syncopated soundtrack. But my mind had also retained less-pulsating images. I remembered angry pages in a Céline novel that presented New York as a grim metropolis, stiff and unyielding—very unlike European cities that spread languorously along riverbanks or the sea. As I stared at the famous skyscrapers, the Empire State and Chrysler buildings, it occurred to me that they might just as well have been called "sky-climbers" or "sky-aggressors." I recalled the biblical story of the Tower of Babel in the land of Shinar—that tower of overweening pride whose top was meant to reach unto heaven, and how God had decided to put an end to its construction by confounding the language of its arrogant builders.

Manhattan was not only vertical but, as I noticed, insistently linear and rectangular. Its geometric patterns called for the reign of numbers. I was used to streets and squares carrying the names of political figures, scientists, saints, writers, historical dates, and even the less-reputable professions. More archaic designations pointed to crafts or functional landmarks (wells, markets, slaughterhouses), or even utensils such as scissors, keys, ovens, pumps: rue des Ciseaux, rue de la Clef, rue du Four, rue de la Pompe. In New York, I was struck by the overwhelming rationality of numbers running north, south, east, west. Even the subways hurried along in straight lines up and down the elongated island. These rectilinear designs were altogether different from the convoluted network of the Paris *métro*, which, much like the old sewers of the capital, constituted a labyrinthine mirror-city below the city above, with its own tortuous arteries. The New York subway ran up and down Manhattan in parallel fashion but at different speeds, the express trains overtaking the locals with a particular lurch that delighted the train lover in me.

On my walking explorations of Manhattan (I needed to be on my own, away from my parents), I did not tire of counting and recounting the floors of the tallest buildings—rarely coming up with the same numbers, but always ending up with a stiff neck. I noticed that banks often had monumental columns that brought to mind ancient temples, whereas churches were dwarfed by nearby skyscrapers that seemed to look down on them as anachronistic presences. Walking up and down past huge department stores on Fifth Avenue, I gazed longingly at smartly dressed women carrying shopping bags, moving at a brisk pace, with an almost masculine gait. Not one of them seemed to notice me. But then, people were not looking at one another. They all seemed to proceed with a sense of purpose. These were not strollers. And there were no love couples embracing in the street, kissing interminably as they did in Paris, oblivious to what was going on around them. I missed those love couples who transformed the sidewalk into an erotic spectacle, as I also missed the sidewalk cafés, the smells of the *métro*, and the smells coming from the bakeries where the freshly baked *baguettes* stand in rows, still warm, waiting to be carried away by people who would then nibble at them on their way home. So far, New York was a city without smells of its own.

A certain uneasiness came over me during those walks. I was escaping for hours, aware of not helping my parents get settled. But there was something more to it than the uneasiness of filial guilt. I asked myself whether I really saw New York through my own eyes. It was an unexpected crisis of honesty. I wondered, if ever I got there, would I not see the isle of Capri through the writings of Axel Munthe, Rome through Stendhal, the American Midwest through Mark Twain and Sinclair Lewis, and China through Pearl Buck? Even now, as I write about first impressions of the linear cityscape of Manhattan, do I not carry, already lodged in my mind, the image of Melville's "insular city of the Manhattoes," with its streets taking one right and left straight to the water? Similar suspicions about the imp of inauthenticity assailed me when, recently, in St. Petersburg, I encountered shades of Dostoevsky and Gogol on any number of bridges astride the city's canals. But it was in the late summer of 1941, ambling along on the sidewalks of New York, that I was first asking myself, perplexed, whether my reactions were genuinely my own. I was scandalized by the string of clichéd opinions my parents and their friends kept uttering. When I tried to communicate my misgivings about preconceived ways of seeing reality (I must have sounded intolerably pretentious), they simply could not understand what I was talking about. They made it clear that they had other concerns, and that I had also better busy myself with practical matters instead of theorizing about inauthenticity.

My parents found an apartment on West 72nd Street near Riverside Drive. It was a building into which several expatriate families from Paris had already moved. Our apartment was on the tenth floor. We were surprised that the building had no watchdog-concierge such as we were used to, who in his ground floor lair expected you to cry out your name when you came home late at night. On the other hand, there was a uniformed elevator man such as I had seen only in department stores. Another novelty was the mail chute on every floor, as was the incinerator—which did, however, worry my father, who was so afraid of a fire that he never failed to place already extinguished matches under running water. The greatest surprise for me was to find the toilet in the bathroom, next to the bathtub and shower. I was used to the *cabinet de toilette,* the famous W.C. or water closet with the dangling chain, an intimate retreat, an exiguous, poorly lit space at the far end of some corridor, windowless and ill-ventilated but providing a sense of privacy. Here, the toilet stood in a bright, open space offering no sense of intimacy even when one was alone. I felt exposed. It was not a place for lingering.

I don't know how or from where my parents acquired some furniture. But in no time my narrow room looking out on a wall had a bed in it, a small desk, and a modest bookcase with glass doors. I remember that a thick volume of O'Henry's short stories and a biography of George Bernard Shaw were the first books I placed in it. Our new furniture was at best functional, lending the apartment a provisional look. But at the age of eighteen, I was hardly troubled by impermanence.

Little daily discoveries kept me busy. I became addicted to crunchy Kellogg's Corn Flakes with cold milk and heaps of sugar. I got to enjoy cold milk so much that I drank glass after glass, sometimes adding ice cubes. I tried Coca Cola, too—that quintessentially American drink—but as I always drink too fast, it inevitably made me hiccup. My most passionate consumption, however, was that of dense, foamy milkshakes, which in short order led to a double chin. In the drugstores, where to my astonishment one could also eat and drink, I watched boys and girls about my age sip out of the same tall glass from separate straws, and I felt vaguely envious. Hamburgers and cheeseburgers on buns were also a revelation, though I did not go in for ketchup. And I was taken aback in restaurants by the addition of cranberry and other sweet sauces to meat dishes. As for the cafeterias, the automats, where one served oneself, I had never seen anything like them, and I was fascinated by the little glassed compartments that displayed a salad or sandwich that one could free from its enclosure by introducing coins into a slot.

In the weeks after our arrival, we met a number of people through my Aunt Liza and her husband, Simon Millner, who knew successful businesspeople and also had contacts at Columbia University. Simon prided himself on being president of a foundation devoted to Spinoza. He enjoyed being called "Dr. Millner." My parents, along with the rest of the family, liked to make fun of him. They recognized his charm and the elegance of his silver cigarette etui. But they thought that he was something of a fake. The truth, as I found out in time, is that he was respected by well-known scholars. I later inherited from him a rare book that had belonged to Spinoza and carries his signature on the title page: a volume of reports by one Antonio Perez, secretary of state and minister of King Philip II of Spain, dealing with inquisitional accusations of "judaizing." From my Uncle Simon's library I also have some early editions of the works of the philosopher Moses Mendelssohn, the grandfather of Felix, the composer. Simon Millner's great talent, and the source of his financial success, seems to have been the ability to bring people together, which is how we met a number of colorful personalities. The tone at such meetings was jovial. I noticed that, during the ritual of greetings, when asked the prescribed "How are you?" guests tended to respond with an emphatic "Just fine"—or, more wondrous to my ears, with a sparkling "Like a million dollars." Everybody smiled benignly and looked exceedingly friendly when told that we had just arrived from Europe. No one seemed to shake hands, except upon being first introduced. After that, one was immediately called by one's first name.

It was irksome to be repeatedly congratulated for having been allowed to enter the United States. It was bad enough to hear people talk smugly about our "good fortune," and to listen to their predictions that mine would soon be another "American success story." More annoying was the shaking of heads about what happened in June of 1940. People harped on France's defeat and humiliation. I was upset by the unavoidable question "Why didn't the French fight better?" followed immediately by condescending remarks about the inadequate Maginot Line and the immorality and laziness of the French people. It sounded like a caricature of Pétain's pronouncements about the sinfulness of the Third Republic. The idea of America intervening in the European war and helping stem the tide of Nazism seemed out of the question. The mood was distinctly one of nonintervention. "Isolationism," some called it. I tried to point out (but who was I to argue with the adults gathered at the Millners' suite in the Hotel Delmonico on Park Avenue?) that France had lost two million men in the Great War of 1914–18. Since the population of the United States was roughly four times that of France, one would have to imagine what it would be like for the United States to have eight million of its young men disappear in a war. The will to fight might indeed be somewhat diminished. My reasoning did not seem to make much of an impression, nor did it affect the benevolent smiles.

Though radiantly friendly, people could also be quite blunt. "Where do you come from?" "Are you Jewish?" These questions seemed to me less than tasteful ways of starting a conversation. My mother was taken aback by some people's crude ways of talking about money. When she expressed her astonishment over the steep fee on a doctor's bill, the specialist she had gone to consult explained in a matter-of-fact way that he had incurred large debts while in medical school, and that he now had to make up for them.

But there was something reassuring and downright moving about the belief expressed in many ways that all ills, whether personal or social, can be cured if only one takes the trouble to understand their causes and applies proper remedies. This faith in solutions I found summed up in a story I read years later to my children about Rupert the Rhinoceros—the mean, aggressive rhinoceros who attacks any moving shape simply because he is myopic. Overnight Rupert becomes a gentle animal and a good citizen when his nearsightedness is properly diagnosed and corrected. This ophthalmological taming of violence and belief in cures made me understand better than anything else the incurable American brand of optimism, so radically unlike the resigned and ironic skepticism with which I was brought up.

If I found street life in New York erotically unstimulating in daylight, it was different at dusk, when I stared at the lit-up windows of apartment buildings. Then, especially on sultry evenings, I imagined scenes behind the drawn curtains. Everywhere I saw enticing shapes and shameless postures. From the day after we landed, I could not protect my mind for long from such phantasms. Every morning, at the hour testosterone is most prankish, I would awaken with the hope that some adventure, aware of my need, would come my way.

The lush covers of magazines on newsstands, featuring the parted lips of movie stars and starlets already ensconced on the firmament of my dreams, held me as if by a spell. I did not dare buy any and bring them home, for fear of my mother's knowing smile. As for the sports headlines, next to these magazines, they puzzled me: I knew nothing about American football and baseball. The very names of the teams seemed outlandish to me: the Senators, the Cardinals, the Pirates . . . So did the glossary of the sports verbs for "victory" and "defeat": to trounce, to whip, to punish, to clobber, to wipe out, to maul . . . I had visions of Senators whipping Cardinals; the thought of it seemed to illustrate the very separation of church and state about which I had heard so much in school.

Other newspaper headlines were not much easier to decipher. But I liked the word "headline" for front-page news, and I was struck by the like-sounding term "deadline," which I had never heard before. When I looked it up in a dictionary, I discovered that it was a line, drawn around a prison, that the inmate transgresses at the risk of being shot. I understood that by extension the term referred to a terminal date beyond which a document or an article would not be accepted. My mind reverted to more threatening deadlines we knew only too well: the date when a visa or passport expired and there was no hope left for escape. Our new acquaintances were indeed right: we were fortunate. But we worried about those we had left behind: my grandmother, Sascha and his family, Aunt Anya, and the friends who were still waiting for immigration papers in Nice.

⌒

A SHORT WHILE after our arrival, we went on an excursion. Mr.
Slepak, a Russian lawyer-friend of my parents who was doing research
at Harvard, offered to drive us to Pennsylvania on a radiant early fall
day—one of those days when the light gives depth to the landscape. He
said that he had a little surprise in store for us. About an hour after we
left the city, he turned off the highway and drove into a small, residential community. Soon we were on what looked like a main street with
many shops. Our guide stopped close to an intersection. "We are in
Princeton," he declared with some solemnity. I now recognize that he
parked his car at the precise point where Witherspoon and Nassau
Streets meet, across from the triumphal gateway beyond which lies the
broad lawn of the campus. Past the lawn, through the iron bars and the
gate topped by two imperial eagles, we could see a large, rectangular
building with an elongated cupola. The stone façade was partially covered by ivy. It was my first concrete encounter with American history.
Mr. Slepak explained that this colonial building was Nassau Hall, and
that in 1783 it had served briefly as the seat of the Continental Congress.
Pointing to it with a courtroom gesture, he said with pride and conviction, "This is where Einstein teaches."

He was wrong, of course. Einstein did not teach at the university; he
was a member of the nearby Institute for Advanced Studies. But regard-
less of the misinformation, the brief stopover in front of Nassau Hall
made a lasting impression on me. So this was an American university.
This is what I had heard about during the slow crossing on the *Navemar*. I took it all in: the ivy-covered stone building, the tall trees, the
expanse of green, the carefree young people who seemed to be ambling
in a vacation atmosphere, the youthful look of the not-so-young moving more briskly with their briefcases—students and teachers such as I
had never encountered in the gray environment of French academe.
These fleeting autumnal impressions later accompanied me during my
army training, and then occasionally re-emerged during the campaigns
in France and Germany, until one late-summer day of 1945, in devastated Berlin, they came back to me in a flash—only this time the image

included me. I knew then, with a four-year delay, that the scene would have to be mine, that there was nothing I would rather be than one of the students on just such a campus—and then, perhaps, one of the figures in tweed jackets hurrying along, their briefcases filled with books and papers.

On that September outing in 1941, I was still far from imagining that this would one day be my resolve. Nonetheless, soon after the stopover in front of Nassau Hall, I took an initiative that was to have far-reaching consequences. College, for the time being, was out of the question. It was too late to apply, and anyhow, I did not feel ready. Maybe I was afraid of the experience. I secretly hoped that the United States would get into the war, that I would become a soldier and be carried back to Europe by events. I was also unsure of my English. Instead, I hit on an intermediary solution. I do not know what impulse led me to Rockefeller Plaza, where I found an agency specializing in educational institutions. I looked through their catalogue listing junior colleges. That schools would advertise like ordinary businesses was new to me. But a school was a business, I learned, one that could prosper or fail. The one I selected was in fact in financial trouble and would eventually have to close its doors.

Harrisburg Academy probably appealed to me because of my recent day trip to Pennsylvania. I inquired. Though it was late, there was an opening. A day or two later, we were off on another family expedition, this time in my uncle's Chrysler. I still remember my room in the Harrisburg hotel, and my vivid, troubling dreams about the well-endowed blonde I had glimpsed in the hotel bar, smoking through a long cigarette-holder. My mind was not entirely focused on school.

We were received cordially by the headmaster, Mr. Baldwin. My father took an immediate liking to him. The sympathy seemed to be mutual. Mr. Baldwin was a courteous, fair, gentle person—the kind of person ("a fine American," my father later decreed) who made one trust him because he himself seemed so full of trust in others. This was no cold, French lycée administrator dismissively invoking rules and regulations. Even the word "headmaster" sounded so much warmer and more humane than the French *proviseur.*

It was the first time I was to live away from home. In France, students commonly lived with their families. My only school experience away from my parents had been in England, during a brief summer, and that was largely in the company of French-speaking boys, basically vacationing. Harrisburg Academy, in the heart of Pennsylvania on the banks of the Susquehanna River (honored as "noble" in the school song), promised to be a truly Anglo-Saxon experience.

Yet it was, as we were often reminded, a home away from home—almost excessively so. There was something sugary, paternalistic, over-protective in the prevailing spirit of good cheer and kindness. It felt Christmas-like long before Christmas, long before we were assembled to sing "Jingle Bells" in the common room. Our regular assembly began with prayers; Harrisburg Academy provided daily opportunities for the soul. But it also offered more worldly amenities, such as I did not associate with school: a gym with a swimming pool, cement tennis courts (for lack of good players, I became captain of the team), planned excursions with cookouts to the Pennsylvania hills (I still recall the smell of the woods and the oblique rays of the afternoon sun), walks around the small lake nearby, cozy quarters. A life-size photograph of Loretta Young's face and upper body covered almost the entire inside of my door. Her face had a voluptuous expression, and I explained knowl-edgeably (a fellow from Paris would surely know!) that hers was with-out a doubt an expression of sexual pleasure. My room became popular, and students would come to examine Loretta Young's languorous eyes and glistening lips.

The dining-hall ritual with the postprandial announcements and the rotation of student-servers was a new experience. I could not believe how much cold milk was consumed with the meals—industrial quanti-ties, it seemed to me. The tone was never boisterous, as it would unavoidably have been in a French refectory. Faculty wives ate with us. (I had never before met the wife of any teacher.) Grace was always said at the beginning of meals. Conversation was subdued, languishing. A certain prudishness hung in the air. One day, I mistakenly used the French word *physique,* meaning to say "physics." I was given a stern look by Mrs. Davis, the wife of the history teacher, who then hinted that "physique" was a slightly scandalous word that referred to the shape or shapeliness of male and female bodies, and that it should be avoided in decent conversation. Mrs. Davis did not know about Loretta Young's picture on my door.

Her husband insisted on being addressed as "Dr. Davis." He was, so it seems, the only Ph.D. on the faculty, and he made sure that we were aware of it. His subject was American history, but he also taught a class in music appreciation. We were regularly exposed to one of the "three B's," as he formulaically referred to them: Bach, Beethoven, Brahms. But he would also go on at great length about how even a popular song such as "Blues in the Night" obeyed certain basic rules of form. Dr. Davis was not the only teacher who exercised multiple functions. Mr. Smith, the math teacher, was also the football coach. Mr. Ferguson, the Latin teacher, coached the tennis team.

In the dormitory, we were less well behaved than in the dining hall. We indulged in traditional pranks involving water and insects inside the beds, as well as the temporary disappearance of personal belongings. Some of the games were more cruel, and I am ashamed not to have protested. We had our whipping boy, a pale and balding English fellow whom we called Limey. He was defenseless. We made him go on the floor, face down, and imitate the movements of copulation. Later, I would never hear about the scapegoat Akaki Akakyevich in Gogol's "The Overcoat," which my mother had read to me aloud when I was a child, without being reminded of Limey and his meek expostulations. He was also called "The Jerk"—a word that I had recently learned, together with the expression "to jerk off." School talk began to enrich my English vocabulary, though it was mild compared to the kind of English I was soon to learn in the army.

The one friend I made whom I continued to see for a while after leaving Harrisburg Academy was a refugee from Yugoslavia, Ivan Laric. He was also on the tennis team. He had broad shoulders and slender hips and boasted to me of his sexual encounters with one of the female employees who sometimes acted as assistant physical education instructor. Perhaps to give credibility to his descriptions of their feverish bouts, he one day confided how, after a strenuous swimming session, he experienced a total fiasco in bed. From him I learned the words "*kurva*" and "*pička*" (pronounced pitchka)—the Serbo-Croatian equivalents for whore and the female pudenda, or bluntly, cunt.

I did, however, learn more than colorful language at Harrisburg. To my great surprise, I became a serious student. Whether because I had taken the initiative of finding a junior college, or because of the shock of newness and a fresh sense of responsibility due to our wartime escape from Europe, I no longer wanted to be a *fils à papa* and rely on my father. I did well in all my subjects—even in mathematics. For Dr. Davis I wrote a research paper on immigration to the United States in the late nineteenth century. I myself marveled at the transfiguration of the *cancre* who cut classes at the lycée into a motivated fellow who ended up valedictorian of his class. I have no detailed recollection of my speech on that occasion, except that I had learned it by heart, that it dealt with the American involvement in the war, and that I referred to Pearl Harbor as a happy event—a qualification of the disaster that was not exactly appreciated.

Academic success in these new surroundings encouraged me to aim at other successes in the future, but when they came, I could not believe that I really deserved them. I feared that sooner or later someone would find out about my inadequacy. My self-awareness as the underachiever of Lycée Janson de Sailly never deserted me, even when, after returning from the war, I finished Yale with an average of 92 and Philosophical Orations (the Yale equivalent of *summa cum laude*), and my undergraduate essay on the criticism of T. S. Eliot won a prize and was published. A residual doubt remained. Not even when I got tenure and then became chairman of a department could I take myself seriously. Part of me watched in disbelief. The *cancre* followed me on lecture tours. Unsure that I had any real substance, I continued to feel light to myself. Eventually, I came to value that sense of lightness. It has saved me, I believe, from boring myself.

Harrisburg, spread out along the Susquehanna, was hardly a thrilling town. The capitol seemed to me the only significant building. But for several school visits to the public library, a few late afternoons at the movies, and a dinner at the hotel where my uncle once stopped overnight on his way from Washington to New York, I had hardly any contact with the downtown area. There was one notable exception, when I was invited for lunch at a women's club. It was vaguely political, if I remember, but I don't recall if it was Republican or Democratic. I was given to understand that I should consider it a signal honor to be their guest, and that I would probably be asked to say a few words about my experiences as a refugee from Europe. I gathered that I was expected to stress how grateful and happy I felt to be in the United States.

I had never been to anything like a ladies' club or ladies' lunch. All the women in the room looked alike to me. They wore white gloves and small hats that only partially concealed the bluish tint of their hair. All around me I saw wrinkled faces and smiles displaying perfectly aligned teeth. The bread on the tables was as white as the tablecloths. No wine, of course, but the tall glasses were constantly refilled with water and ice cubes. The condiments were even sweeter than the ones I had tried in New York. The conversation, however, proved laborious. The ladies at my table quite clearly—though politely—had difficulty believing the "horrors" I reported. I told them about the Nazis, their ideology of hatred, their concentration camps, the strafing of fleeing civilians on the highways of France, the disgrace of the armistice and of the Vichy regime, Marshal Pétain's anti-Semitic legislation, the zeal of the French in making arrests, the shameful extradition of political refugees, the collaborators. I noticed kind smiles. Then came well-meaning reactions. I had gone through a lot for a young person; it was only normal that I should feel emotional . . . and exaggerate somewhat. When I was asked to stand up and say a few words to the entire group (my first and faltering attempt at public speaking), I did not forget to say that I indeed considered myself grateful and happy to be safe with my parents in the United States. But I could not prevent myself from adding that I very much hoped that this country would get into the war and help defeat Hitler.

The mood briefly changed; the smiles vanished. This was clearly not what they had come to hear. I sensed discomfort. Did my little speech confirm the suspicion that European Jews, for obvious reasons, were warmongers? When dessert was served, everyone was again all smiles. America was the best place, all concurred. And it felt good, so I was told, to meet such a promising refugee-student. The ladies also felt good about themselves, I gathered. They went on at great length about their interest in world affairs.

I came away from the lunch with the uneasy feeling of having breached good manners. But I was more determined than ever to follow military and political events on the Russian and North African fronts as if they were a personal matter. I obtained two large maps as well as tiny flags that I could stick on my maps and displace at will to keep up with defeats, retreats, victories, and advances. For the time being, in the late fall and early winter of 1941, there were, alas, mostly retreats and defeats. The Germans had reached Leningrad, and Odessa, on the Black Sea, was in their hands. The battle for Moscow had begun. Then came Pearl Harbor. I was sure that now even my luncheon ladies were preaching the war effort. Soon, at the beginning of 1942, more defeats and retreats were recorded on my maps. The Japanese occupied Singapore. In Libya, Field Marshal Rommel launched a powerful offensive and reached El Alamein in Egypt. Tobruk fell. Later that year things slowly began to improve. But by that time I was back in my parents' apartment in New York, together with my maps and little flags, following the events with even greater intensity: first came Field Marshal Montgomery's offensive in Egypt, and then, in November 1942—just in time for my nineteenth birthday—the Allied landing in French North Africa and the German defeat at Stalingrad. More than ever I looked forward to joining the army.

The news of Pearl Harbor was the most exciting moment of my year at Harrisburg Academy. The report of the Japanese attack spread rapidly through the corridors, the dormitories, and common rooms. For me, December 7 was not so much a day that would live in infamy as a day of renewed hope—especially as Germany immediately declared war on the United States. I came home to my parents elated at Christmas time. I could think of nothing else. On the train to New York, as I watched the winter landscape glide by, I kept singing to myself, in rhythm with the wheels on the track, the lyrics of two recent hit songs dealing with railway travel. One of them was "The Chatanooga-Choo-Choo":

You leave the Pennsylvania station 'bout a quarter to four,
Read a magazine and then you're in Baltimore.

The other was more evocative of the rhythms and sounds of trains. Dr. Davis was quite right when he praised "Blues in the Night":

Now the rain's a-fallin',
Hear the train a-callin'

Now that America was at war with Germany, I began to feel at home.

When I later prepared my valedictory speech, I was no longer afraid to be accused of warmongering. Unashamedly, indeed pompously (I have no record of my precise words), I orated about the need to crush Nazism and liberate Europe. This time everybody agreed—though I had hardly said a word about Japan.

Part

III

OMAHA BEACH AND BEYOND

Chapter 11

THE WAY TO CAMP RITCHIE

Throughout the months preceding my induction, my desire to be in the army was hardly a secret. During the summer days of soupy hot weather, when I stayed with my parents in a guest house on Long Beach run by a Russian lady, getting a taste of the dog days and dreary flatness of Long Island, this question of the army became a subject of repeated arguments. My parents were dismayed that I did not wish to begin college. They hoped that as a college student I might be spared the draft, or at least that the inevitable might be deferred. I, on the contrary, eagerly anticipated events. I did not dare enlist; my parents had already lost one child. Torn between the desire to volunteer and the realization that I simply could not do this to my parents, I preferred to resort to delaying tactics. I knew that if I waited long enough, the inevitable was bound to happen.

I could understand my parents' fears, but I resented their sentimental blackmail. They were resigned, of course. Long-standing pacifists, they knew that this war was a necessary one. But they did not see why I would want to rush ahead of events. They, on the other hand, lost no time in trying to have me exempted from service. I subsequently learned that they were collecting evidence from our family physician, Dr. Binkin (who had also turned up in New York), that I had an "enlarged" heart—whatever that meant.

In the meantime, my grandmother also arrived, avoiding by just a few weeks the dragnet operation of the French police that turned over to the Germans foreign Jews still living in the Vichy zone. Though Babushka did not escape until a year after we did, my parents somehow succeeded in having her come over from Lisbon to New York on a regular Portuguese passenger ship, which, I think, was called the *Serpapinto*. When she joined us on the Upper West Side, she was a little more unsteady on her feet but had lost nothing of her feistiness. She immediately enrolled in an English class and before long was proudly declaiming adages such as "A friend in need is a friend indeed." She was by now over eighty and looking forward to becoming an American citizen.

To placate my parents and to appear fully responsible, but also to give myself something to do, I came to an unexpected decision. A newspaper advertisement drew my attention to the New York School of Mechanical Dentistry. I went to inquire, though I had no particular interest in other people's teeth, and not the least mechanical aptitude. The secretary explained that the course of study would teach me how to make dental prostheses—false teeth, or dentures. In a couple of months, I would learn a useful trade. I reported my findings to my parents. My uncle was appalled and made no effort to hide his distaste for such a prosaic occupation. My parents were surprised but ended up approving the project. Not that they viewed "dental mechanics" as a noble vocation, but they considered it a skill that, if I were to be drafted in the near future, might protect me from the dangers of the front. After all, soldiers also need to have their teeth fixed or replaced.

I was, in truth, adrift, very far indeed from knowing what I wanted to do. Even the army, I now suspect, held out not just an opportunity for heroic adventure, but for postponing important decisions. And so I enrolled in the New York School of Mechanical Dentistry. My parents provided the money for the tuition, and I began to master a new vocabulary made up of words like "plaster cast," "acrylic," "vulcanize," "bite," "bridges." We sat at partitioned desks, on little stools, each student wearing an apron, our tools spread out in front of us. The instructor, wearing a more generous apron, moved with quick steps from desk to desk, briefly stopping behind each student to correct this or that mistake, showing us how to mix the plaster more efficiently, how to set the teeth straight, how to polish the bridge. We studied the nomenclature and characteristics of human dentition in both the upper and the lower jaws: incisors, canines, bicuspids, molars. We learned about the parts and composition of the tooth—the crown, the neck, the roots, the pulp. We heard at length about enamel and dentine. This theoretical information I was able to handle. The trouble began when we moved from words to procedure. I mixed the plaster all right, but that was the high point of my dexterity. For the rest, my hands fumbled. I constantly dropped teeth on the floor. And I showed scant gifts when it came to matching teeth and setting them straight in the model of the jaw.

The truth is, I was distracted. Every morning, on my way to my work table, I passed by the dark-haired secretary, seated behind a glass partition. She hardly ever looked up to see who was going by. My view of her, on the contrary, was very precise. I imagined her coming out of the shower, her body still moist. I was haunted by what I glimpsed of her as she walked past our desks—by the shape and the rhythm of her buttocks. "*Un cul de rêve*," I kept muttering to myself. I wanted to glide my hand between her thighs. I could hear her moans of pleasure. I figured out exquisite caresses. I even believed that if only I were bold enough to ask her out, she would agree to meet me. She of course did not even notice me, in my silly apron. And so I continued to dream of moist limbs and complicated embraces. No wonder I mismatched the teeth.

When I ingloriously finished the course, I was nonetheless offered a job. The owner of a dental laboratory interviewed me, seemingly interested in my background. The providentially named Mr. Gold had immigrated from Eastern Europe decades earlier and perhaps felt that it was his charitable duty to give a refugee from Nazi Europe a break as an apprentice. For a minimal sum—ten or fifteen dollars a week—I was allowed to mix plaster, but mostly I served as an errand boy, picking up rows of teeth in specialized supply stores and delivering finished dentures to various dentists in midtown Manhattan. Mr. Gold's modest laboratory was near Times Square, and I often used the lunch hour, and some delivery time as well, to stand in line for cheap tickets at the old Metropolitan Opera on 39th Street. Mr. Gold seemed to like me. He expressed the desire to meet my father. He did not tell Papa that I had no talent for laboratory work. As plaster mixer and errand boy, I could hardly have given him any sense of what a misfit I really was in the dental trade. Instead he told my father that I was a "good boy."

This good boy had other longings, however. The image of the dark-haired secretary kept pursuing me in my loneliness. I had few contacts.

Occasionally, I saw my Yugoslav school friend Ivan Laric, but we now had little to say to one another. Some Parisian lycée friends had turned up: Jacques Blum, who was joining the Air Corps; Jacques Calse; Jacques Leviant, whom I had known from the time I had attended the Lycée Claude Bernard; and Leo Lamont—the same Leo from whose window we used to peer into the girls' gym with his parents' binoculars. Leo seemed equally in need of female company. We decided to rent for a brief period what we called with Parisian nostalgia a little *garçon-nière*—a "bachelor's flat," the purpose of which was clear enough. We found a shabbily furnished studio on the same street where my grandmother had settled, which added piquancy to the affair. I don't recall who gave us the telephone number of the call girl who appeared at the appointed hour, and whom we shared. This transcontinental bond between Leo and me was enhanced by early evidence of globalization. We laughed when we realized that the condoms sold in New York drugstores carried the same trade name as in Paris.

I soon tired of these sessions. Besides which, we were running out of cash, and I yearned for something better. Sex and fancies of love seemed further apart than ever. I tried to meet suitable girls my own age, "suitable" being one of my mother's favorite adjectives. I was out of tune. The girls I got to know seemed to me exceedingly naïve—preoccupied with dances, proms, early marriages. And the boys' notions of sex struck me as rudimentary, limited to more or less coarse images of the missionary position. I thirsted for suave delights. Dany came to mind—tender Dany who was now a mother in Lyon and whose idealized image was already transformed by the alchemy of remembrance. I recalled a sentence she used to murmur to me in Italian:

> *Perduto è tutto il tempo*
> *Che in amar non si spende . . .*

For a long time I thought that what Dany so often whispered was a wise old proverb. "Lost is all the time that is not spent in loving . . ." Only years later did I discover that these were two lines from Torquato Tasso's sixteenth-century pastoral poem "Aminta." I never knew how Dany came to know these words in Italian. Was it some older relative or some teacher who imparted them to her? I will never find out. But I did come to associate this poetic message of love with a voice that now reaches me from beyond Auschwitz.

It was during my brief career as an errand boy for Mr. Gold that I began to learn Italian opera buffa arias and recitatives. They became the foundation of my spoken Italian. When I stood in line at the Metropolitan Opera during lunch hours, the performances I was most eager to get tickets for were Mozart's *Le Nozze di Figaro* and *Don Giovanni*, which I saw repeatedly and soon knew by heart. They were a revelation. The magical casts included the great Ezio Pinza, Bidú Sayão as Suzanna or Zerlina, and the portly basso buffo Salvatore Baccaloni as Dr. Bartolo and Leporello. Bruno Walter was conducting. Not only were the casts magical, the distance was magical, too. From all the way up in the rafters, everything about the singers seemed to have mythical proportions. The sensuous vibrato of Pinza's voice filled the house. The elegance of his singing and of his movements as the crafty servant or as the dynamic seducer held me in thrall. I learned several parts almost entirely: Figaro, the Count, Don Giovanni, Leporello. What amazed me most, once I got wise to it, was the tension between the urbane irony and cynicism of Lorenzo da Ponte's librettos and the tender lyricism of Mozart's music. That tenderness and lyrical sweep seemed protected by the irony of the recitatives. I never tired of listening to the records I had bought and with which I endlessly rehearsed Figaro's mock-heroic "*Non più andrai,*" the bitterly sly "*Se vuol ballare,*" and the stylized outbursts of misogynic jealousy and wounded male pride "*Aprite un po' quegli occhi,*" which Pinza sang so delightfully in the mysterious semidarkness of the final act, wrapped in a melodramatic cape, with one foot on the prompter's box. The explosive enthusiasm of the delighted audience brought tears to my eyes because it meant a very special moment of communion in my loneliness and felt like a tribute to my private emotions.

During that same period I spent many hours, especially on weekends, at the Public Library on Fifth Avenue at 42nd Street. Its majestic stairs and façade reminded me of monumental edifices in Europe. I was especially fond of the little public garden behind the library—an intimate oasis close to the tumult of the traffic—where I would sometimes continue reading on a bench. Inside the library, seated at a long table, I read all I could find by, or about, the eighteenth-century French playwright Beaumarchais. Perhaps I was drawn to him because he was the author of the original *Barber of Seville* and *Marriage of Figaro*. Beyond the wit of his dialogues and the resourcefulness of his plots, I learned something from his works about pre-Revolutionary France and the hostile claims of the Third Estate, the commoners, as expressed by Figaro's cutting remark about the Count (but with all aristocrats in mind): "You merely took the trouble to be born." Reading about Beaumarchais's life I also learned something about an exceedingly litigious age. He was involved in endless legal entanglements. I even learned about a minor aspect of American history: Beaumarchais had at one point supplied weapons to the American Revolutionary army but was never properly compensated by Congress.

LATE THAT WINTER of 1942—the Allies had by now landed in North Africa—the long-awaited summons for the Selective Service medical examination finally arrived in the mail. I had worked for Mr. Gold for only a few months. I vaguely remember that I was instructed to report to some armory. My parents insisted that I take with me the X-ray evidence of an enlarged heart that Dr. Binkin had provided. To placate them, I agreed, but with no intention of showing the pictures to anyone. My head was filled to the point of giddiness with bits of poems by Victor Hugo and Charles Péguy about the glory of fighting for a righteous cause. The latter's line "Happy are those who died in a just war" now seems perfectly shocking to me. In truth, my eagerness for military glory was not altogether genuine. I also looked forward to being away from my parents. The antiwar literature they had made me read when I was a boy—the novels of Erich Maria Remarque and Henri Barbusse—no longer seemed relevant. As for my parents' request, it turned out that there was no opportunity to display my X-rays to anyone during the medical examination, even had I wished to.

Of that experience I recall only fragments: bunks in one room, naked bodies, other rooms through which we were herded, people busy at paperwork, eye tests, and a whole range of auscultations. At some point, blood was drawn from my arm. The fellow ahead of me explained that this was called a Wassermann test, which people who were getting married also had to have.

Shortly after, I received my induction notice. I was to report to the induction center just a few blocks away from my parents' apartment, on the same street where my grandmother lived and where Leo and I had rented our shabby studio. I left my room on the tenth floor of 72nd Street to the sound of a Mendelssohn symphony coming over WQXR. I said good-bye to my little desk, to my phonograph, to my bookcase. I felt both moved and apprehensive, and indulged in a moment of sentimentality. My parents tried not to make me feel their distress, but their faces were drawn. They chose not to accompany me to the induction center. I left with a small bag containing essentials, as well as slim volumes of La Fontaine fables, La Bruyère maxims, and selected poems of Keats—not, as I would learn, standard provisions for a serviceman in any army. I was carrying part of my lycée baggage with me.

The train ride to Fort Dix left the dimmest of memories. For some reason, I was riding backwards—and that seemed to fit what was going on in my mind. The car was filled mostly with young men my own age, nineteen or twenty. There were a few older men. It was a noisy group, and everyone was trying to sound cocky. Their calls were uniformly loud, coarse, and scatological. My silence drew no attention, no hostility. But I felt very much out of it all. The shouts were mostly jarring background noise, for I was relentlessly focusing not on what was going on around me, but on three words I had seen stamped in large letters on my induction record: SYPHILIS INADEQUATE TREATMENT. Anguish and disbelief filled my mind. The throbbing beat of these three words is all I remember with precision from that train ride. That beat was harder than the rhythm of the rails. Even now, over half a century later, I would find it difficult to pronounce these words, or write them down, had they not been negated (though hardly erased!) by repeated reassurances that it was all a routine error. The words lingered on for years. The power of words is lasting, perhaps irradicable, for words are events.

On my way to Fort Dix, I tried in vain to cancel the words I had seen stamped. They kept flashing in my mind like a distress signal. Or rather, they were as though branded in my flesh. That flesh had taken chances, I knew. I also knew that the words would follow me, that they were part of my record. True, the record was to be cleared. Eventually, I found out what had happened. The explanation was simple, and quite typical of army bureaucracy. My Wassermann had been "doubtful," and anyone with a doubtful result was automatically sent for further examinations together with inductees who had tested positive. Indiscriminately, all were provisionally identified under the same label, until a proper diagnosis could be made.

My state of anxiety was prolonged for an entire week, maybe longer. But the shock waves lasted, with varying degrees of intensity, far beyond that period. Upon arrival at Fort Dix, several of us were separated from our group and sent to a special barracks. It was the VD ward—the ward for venereal diseases. We were confined like prisoners. The majority of the inmates struck me as unsavory types. They spent all day playing blackjack and poker, or shooting craps. My mind ranged feverishly from despondency to panic, to despair, to resignation, to shame. At some point, we were confined to our beds for an entire day. The word circulated quickly: we were to be given a spinal tap. Orderlies with needles and tubes made their entrance. A needle was introduced into the spine to collect the spinal fluid that slowly dripped into the test tubes. An incongruous image came to mind. I thought of trees being tapped for resin. I thought of natural rubber, and rubber was necessary for the war effort. The procedure was painful, certainly uncomfortable. It was followed by imposed immobility in an awkward position. But neither the discomfort nor the pain was as distressing as the sense of powerlessness, the fear, the apprehension of what was to come next. The worst of it was that for days—I lost count—no doctor ever talked to us. They were invisible, inaccessible. They were the hidden divinities. No questions could be asked. The orderlies dealt with us, and they themselves were uncommunicative, acting as the placid intermediaries—though hardly the intercessors—between us and the absent authorities. "You'll get your instructions when the time comes," is all we heard about our fate.

The real misery came once I tired of self-blame and became convinced that the diagnosis was correct. I tried to reconstruct past events. Did I catch the disease in New York? It seemed more likely that I had contracted it a number of years earlier, in Paris, on the rue de Provence, but then the disease would be in an advanced stage. I remember that in Deauville I had suffered from skin lesions on my arms and legs, which I attributed to an infected bite or a cut produced by a sandal. I never showed them to our doctor. I felt helpless, remembering what I had heard about the three stages of the disease caused by the dreaded spirochete: the original chancre, the subsequent skin eruptions, and finally the tertiary stage with damages to internal organs and degeneration of the nervous system. I recalled my father's warnings about locomotor ataxia and possible insanity.

In my misery, I escaped into a world of fantasies and fiction. Once the ordeal of the spinal tap was over and we were again free to move about, I walked in circles within the four walls of the courtyard, imagining that I was a famous prisoner. I remembered stories of heroic escapes, including recent wartime exploits. I saw myself as General Henri Giraud, who was captured by the Germans in 1940 and who later made a dramatic escape and landed with the Allies in North Africa. I saw myself in a heroic role, combining suffering, military glory, dramatic exploits, and noble failure.

When I was finally discharged from the VD ward, relieved to find out that I was neither in need of any treatment nor of further tests, my army life really began. After the venereal scare nothing, it seemed to me, could possibly bother me. But I was not so easily allowed to forget the episode. Almost immediately, the group I was now part of was herded into an auditorium and shown a film about the dangers of venereal infection and how to protect ourselves. An officer clumsily demonstrated the use of the condom and later pointed with a rod to enlarged medical illustrations of chancres, lesions of the mucous membranes, and gummy tumors. By now I thought that I was relatively immune to the scare. Nonetheless, years later, panic seized me periodically, and I rushed to consult medical dictionaries in the reading rooms of libraries. I never lost my fear of blood tests, or false diagnoses, or for that matter of any medical examination. Whenever I have to undergo any kind of diagnostic test, I live for days in suspended animation, waiting for the results. Superstitiously, I try to propitiate medical authorities and diagnostic laboratories by leading a "clean life" in anticipation of the tests, knowing perfectly well all the while that my self-denials are use-less. But research in the libraries also divulged that even when it comes to the fiendish treponema, poetry has its claims. I learned that the word "syphilis" was the invention of a doctor-poet from Verona, Girolamo Fracastoro, the author of a sixteenth-century didactic pastoral poem in Latin, "*Syphilis sive de morbo gallico*" (the latter two words mean "French disease"), in which he describes in hexameters the devastating symptoms of the dreaded infection.

My army dog tag brought different thoughts to mind. After all those years, I can still rattle off my number—32906913, one of the few bits of information I was to provide the enemy if I were captured. The letter J that appeared on the dog tag drew my attention. I must at some point have given "Jewish" as my religious affiliation, even though I was not in the least religious; I was indeed hostile to any form of dogma. The "J" bothered me, and not only because of what it might mean if I should fall into the hands of the Germans. There was something else. Ever since my arrival in the States, I had repeatedly been questioned about my religious affiliation, whether in applications or official questionnaires. This sur-prised me, unpleasantly. I had also heard about quotas in the colleges and universities. It was obvious that one was expected to "belong," and that there was a need to do so. I had been warned that not to identify oneself as part of a religious group, to answer "none" to questions about reli-gious affiliation, was not a good idea; to be considered an atheist was only one step away from being a suspected communist. As for the "J" on my dog tag, it also bothered me because I imagined undercurrents of anti-Jewish sentiments, which I thought I had left behind, undercurrents that I had already sensed in the repeated questions—"Where do you come from?" "How do you spell your name?" and in the more blunt "Are you Jewish?"—questions that were put to one as though motivated by well-meaning curiosity or simple human interest.

SEVERAL KEY WORDS and exclamatory phrases sum up the early morning routine of basic training: "Reveille," the traditional sunrise bugle call, the unwelcome signal to "get your ass up"; loud screams to "rise and shine"; the command to "fall out," the jarring order to rush out of the barracks "on the double" and take one's place in the first military formation of the day. In my early morning confusion, stiff and more than half asleep, I often stumbled out wearing the wrong headgear instead of the prescribed "fatigue hat" that was to be worn with army fatigues for exercise and manual work. Corporal Danci, our stocky platoon leader, would scream at me, laugh angrily, and put me on KP duty. KP, as anyone who has served in the army knows, stands for "kitchen police," namely the periodic assignment, also a form of punishment, to work on a detail to assist the cooks in the mess hall. At best, it could be an all-night or all-day adventure in camaraderie and good fun. And depending on the mood and disposition of the cooks, it could also mean a bonanza of extra food and unlimited quantities of cold milk. Most often, however, it was degrading and disgusting work under the command of a head cook bent on exercising his power and on humiliating us. The most hateful work on KP was the cleaning of pots and pans and the unclogging of the grease trap. One of my chief joys when I was later promoted to the rank of master sergeant was to be liberated from this repulsive task.

The routine inside the barracks imposed its own demands. We had to learn to make our bunk-beds perfectly, with impeccable hospital corners and with the blanket so tightly drawn that a coin would bounce off it. My hospital corners were never impeccable, and my blanket was always sagging. I remembered that when I was in camp as a little boy, the monitors made fun of me because I was not good at tying my shoelaces. Only now, there were no parents I could complain to, there was no one I could ask to come and rescue me. The image of my grandmother helped, as did the echo of her voice. No self-pampering. Be tough. I could hear her remonstrances to my parents who, she was convinced, unconscionably spoiled and overprotected me.

Inspections kept us on the alert, requiring a sense of group responsibility. We cleaned the barracks and the latrines with what was called "elbow grease," an expression I had never heard before. We stood at attention in front of our bunks when the ape-necked first sergeant appeared, together with a young officer whose features resembled those of a gentler primate. Occasionally a medical officer showed up, and we were made to stand, quite divested and much less dignified, for what was known as short-arm inspection (the expression being patterned on "small arms," the generic term for hand-held firearms), signifying the medical inspection of the genitals for signs of venereal disease. ("Milking" is a word I had not until then associated with the examination of the sex organ.) Corporal Danci seemed particularly cheerful on those occasions and did not cease to crack jokes after it was over. I got to like the corporal, despite his propensity to send me to KP. He was a good egg after all, and we were all sorry when he announced one day that he had to leave us for a stay in the hospital—"To fix the can," as he put it. We understood that he was going to be operated on for hemorrhoids.

The GIs in my barracks showered every day, sometimes twice a day. That amazed me. I kept thinking of the offensive smell of feet in the Paris classroom. Our barracks were well ventilated, and we regularly scrubbed the floors. My manner of speaking surprised some of my comrades. They called me Frenchy. I, in turn, had difficulty with some of their rural accents. The Alabama beat and intonations of our drillmaster made his commands almost incomprehensible to me. I had never heard anything like it. I had also never heard before (though I turned out to be a quick learner) expressions such as "fuck up" (for blundering, or spoiling something, or simply wasting time), "fuck it!" (an expostulation of annoyance and dismay), and snafu (referring to typical army confusion and stupidity), an acronym formed from the initials of "situation normal—all fucked up." Perhaps the most common expression, sometimes reduced to the initials TS, but usually articulated in full with varying degrees of intensity, was "tough shit," conveying supreme disinterest in another guy's problems, as well as the refusal to provide any aid or comfort. I soon incorporated these vivid expressions in my personal lexicon.

The close-order drill commands were less metaphorical but had their music too—the highly rhythmical sound of the platoon or company after they "fell in" and stood at attention, when they began their martial evolutions to the hoarse but chanted sound of the commands I loved to utter full voice when, later, I myself occasionally drilled the troops: about face! forward march! hat, hop, hip, hoar! by the right flank, march! by the left flank, march! left oblique, march! to the rear, march!

companeee . . . halt! The more guttural the sound of the commands, the more raucous the counting of the beat, the more purposeful appeared this rudimentary choreographic exercise, which otherwise, as far as I could tell, had no military function whatsoever.

Taking apart, cleaning, and oiling our weapons at least had some practical value, though there was also sheer aesthetic satisfaction in the smooth operation of the parts and the decisive sound of the metal when we reassembled them. Training on the field was less pleasurable. It was meant to toughen us: practice on the rifle range in the rain; running the brutal obstacle course; climbing, jumping, crawling under simulated or real fire; endless sessions of push-ups and sit-ups until one's belly felt like one huge cramp; thrusting bayonets on the run into sagging dummies; instruction in hand-to-hand combat. My hands were full of scratches and cracks, my fingernails were black as though in mourning.

One day, news came that I was to be transferred to the Medical Corps for additional training as a medic. The news did not thrill me. I felt disappointed and vaguely humiliated. Why was I not to be a fighting soldier? Was it because of my brief stint in Mr. Gold's laboratory? But who knew about my fleeting association with the world of dental prostheses? When I joined my new group, I noticed that quite a few of the trainees were also European refugees—recent arrivals who, like myself, had not yet become U.S. citizens. I began to suspect that my assignment to the Medical Corps was perhaps part of a deliberate decision not to put foreigners in fighting units. We were not to shoot—though we could be shot at. Some of our training struck me as remarkably silly. We were practicing simulated battlefield rescues in teams of two litter-bearers. After lifting the wounded "body" onto the stretcher and covering him with a blanket, we were instructed to place ourselves, one in front, the other at the back of the stretcher, and then to synchronize its upward motion (so as not to dump the wounded man on the ground) by having one of us crisply utter the command "prepare to lift, lift!" My Austrian-born co-trainee and I could not help laughing. Who in the noise, confusion, and terror of the battlefield would take the trouble to give such a neat textbook command? But we were wrong to laugh, just as I was wrong to feel demeaned by my assignment to the Medical Corps. For there was nothing silly about the medics: some of the greatest acts of heroism, as I found out in Normandy and during the Battle of the Bulge, were performed by medics—doctors and enlisted men alike—whose presence of mind and disregard for personal safety under heavy enemy fire and across minefields made it possible to evacuate and save many badly wounded soldiers.

My training as a litter-bearer was soon interrupted. Gallantry in the Medical Corps was not what I was destined for. Someone in the Pentagon, it would seem, had the bright idea that those foreign types in American uniform could be put to a different use. They spoke other languages, thus they were linguists. They had lived in other countries, therefore they must have insights into the mentalities of those we fought or liberated. And so, quite a few of us were sent to Camp Ritchie for training in military intelligence.

CAMP RITCHIE IN western Maryland, a former training center for the National Guard, was situated in the picturesque landscape of the Blue Ridge Mountains. The camp, complete with a parade field, was surrounded by woods, brooks, significant elevations, some rather rugged terrain, and even, if I remember correctly, some artificial lakes. On rainy days, this setting of natural beauty looked bleak, remote, forlorn. With the sun out, one understood why, at the turn of the nineteenth century, the camp site had served as a resort area for the rich of Baltimore, Philadelphia, and Washington.

Camp Ritchie's past as a National Guard installation was still visible in its stone headquarters, built in a style known as National Guard gothic. This building had the somewhat comical shape of a miniature castle featuring stylized crenellations that suggested battlements. The miniature castle-headquarters was itself patterned on the miniature castle-shaped insignia of the Army Corps of Engineers. The building did not seem quite real.

There were other forms of unreality about the installation. Camp Ritchie had only recently been converted into a military intelligence training center (MITC), a fact that was hardly kept secret. This MITC function was in fact made known explicitly in so many letters over the camp gate. Everyone in the region knew about it. If not for their olive-drab U.S. Army uniforms, the soldiers moving about with a thoroughly unmartial gait, conversing in languages that had never been heard in the Appalachians, might have been taken for Central European vacationers at a spa, gossiping about the effects of their cure and the latest news from Vienna or Prague. Their movements and gestures seemed particularly incongruous when contrasted with the massive, bearded figure standing beside the PX store where we bought toiletries and other supplies. This human hulk in an ill-fitting noncommissioned officer's uniform was said to be the wrestler Man Mountain Dean, whose presence or function in the military intelligence camp was never made clear but who seemed to be there like a fixture to provide local color, a living emblem of the remote hillbilly world, a bit of Americana to remind all those foreign types that they were on American soil.

The specific purpose of Camp Ritchie was to train "combat intelligence specialists." The core of the training had to do with front-line interrogation of prisoners of war or civilians in the immediate combat zone. We were also told that some of our work might entail reconnaissance operations ahead of the main body of our troops. Special attention was also given at Ritchie to aerial photography intelligence, order of battle assessments (known as OB), and combat-zone psychological warfare. German speakers were generally assigned to a two-month PWI course, which trained them in the techniques of interrogating prisoners of war. French speakers were placed in a similar course specializing in the interrogation of civilians and tactical contacts with the French resistance. I was assigned to such an MII course. It now appeared that I would surely be sent to the European theater of operations when the invasion took place, and most likely to France. I put my best efforts into the course, looking forward to speedy assignment to a military unit in England preparing for the landing. But then someone at camp headquarters, going over my record, discovered that I was also fluent in German, and I was put through another course, this time to train me as a front-line interrogator of prisoners. This additional course, which extended my stay at Ritchie, later also extended the war for me. When my armored division reached Belgium in the fall of 1944 and I was recalled to military intelligence headquarters in Paris, I naively thought that the war was over for me, that I could henceforth stroll along the banks of the Seine. I was soon disabused of that dream. Within weeks, I was reassigned—this time to an infantry division positioned in the murderous Hürtgen forest and that would soon after be badly mangled in the snows of the Ardennes. By that time my zest for *la gloria militar* had considerably dampened.

At Ritchie I was still full of enthusiasm. I enjoyed the class work and the field exercises. I did not mind the long hours of study and practice. Conscientiously, I memorized the organization of German and Italian army units, the military terms and abbreviations used, the classification and characteristics of their armored vehicles, the capabilities of their weapons, the nature of their ordnance and of their supply system, the emblems and insignia of the various military branches, the hierarchical structure of their chain of command.

Refugees from Nazi Europe kept arriving at Ritchie, giving the camp the extraterritorial character of a foreign enclave. Most of them were older than I was, and quite a few had had a higher education. I participated in conversations on politics, history, even philosophy. The camp was in a sense my first university experience. I befriended a dark-haired Viennese by the name of Beno, with whom I discussed the respective merits of Toscanini and Furtwängler. It was he who first mentioned to me the name of Piero della Francesca, whose frescoes he had seen in Arezzo with his parents. We also had our tiresome camp joke about the term "military intelligence," which we considered the perfect oxymoron. Our group was made up mostly of enlisted men who were to be promoted at the end of the training program. Some of them, especially the ones who had been away from studies for a while, found class work quite arduous. They had trouble memorizing so much material. For some, it was also difficult to keep up with our occasional marches in the countryside, slowed down by their heavy infantry packs and the blisters that quickly developed on their feet.

Classes could be fun. The instructors made us interpret captured documents. Enemy morale was studied in letters written by German soldiers at the front. I still don't know if these were authentic letters or if they were fabricated especially for the program. Much of our training was indeed staged; the instructors sometimes even disguised themselves in German uniforms and acted out with us the ritual of interrogation. The letters we examined were often intimate, even scabrous. One, in particular, grabbed our attention. Writing to his wife or sweetheart, a German soldier nostalgically evoked precise moments of their love-making: "*Wenn ich mein steifes Glied in deine weichen Teile stoße . . .*" (When I thrust my stiff member into your soft parts . . .). I am not sure what precious military information could be gleaned from this image. But it certainly led to guffaws, endless jokes, and even to some pointed comments about the difference between words and deeds, as well as the nature of obscenity and pornography.

Our inventive instructors also lectured us on the nature, purpose, and uncertainties of front-line interrogation. We were told to interrogate civilians as close as possible to the front line, and always as soon as we came in contact with them. The information had to be fresh, given under the impact of immediate events, and if at all possible, not yet filtered and rearranged by selective memory. Young people were said to be the best informants. To avoid lethal mistakes, we were urged always to ask several people about the same road crossing, the same bridge, the same machine-gun installation. Even when they do not intend to misinform, and some may wish to do so, witnesses are famously unreliable, especially when it comes to location and numbers. We were not to waste time on "high-level" questions such as guesswork about strategy, intentions of the enemy high command, and diagnoses of national morale. Our task was to provide our regimental and divisional commanders with concise tactical information: What units were facing us? What was their strength? How many men were defending a particular farmhouse or village? What were the immediate reserves in men and weapons? What concentration of armor had been observed and where? What emplacements of artillery could be identified? What machine-gun nests had been sighted? Of particular interest were natural and man-made obstacles: canals, sunken roads, felled trees, minefields, tank ditches, and wedge-shaped concrete antitank defenses known as dragon's teeth.

Even those of us who were not specializing in aerial photography had to learn how to read and interpret stereoscopic pictures taken from high above ground of military installations, signs of troop movements, camouflaged artillery, ammunition depots. We also studied the Morse code, and I remember being called "frivolous" by the instructor when I compared the dots and dashes that stand for the letters of the alphabet to trochaic, iambic, and anapestic beats in poetry. As for terrain reconnaissance and map reading, they had the merit of getting us out of the classroom into the fresh air. On certain occasions, we were driven a distance away and let loose in the countryside, sometimes at night, and had to find our way back to a designated area with just the help of a map and a compass. We not only studied but drew topographical contour maps, connecting on paper the points of a landscape having the same elevation. To this day, when planning hikes in the Chianti region with Bettina, I consult military contour maps to determine which itinerary is most suitable to the weather and the mood. From a military point of view, as a matter of sheer survival, my ability to read maps and solve map problems came in extremely handy at the time Field Marshal Gerd von Rundstedt launched his counteroffensive in the Ardennes and my team was desperately seeking an escape route in the vicinity of Bastogne.

Few distractions interrupted our camp routine. A short leave allowed me once to spend an entire day in Washington. I walked alone aimlessly for miles past monuments and public buildings and along the Potomac River, impressed by the gridiron arrangements of the streets, the radiating diagonal avenues and open vistas. I needed to be alone. No museum tempted me. Perhaps I still remembered the tedious Sunday visits to the Louvre with my mother. That long day of solitary strolling in Washington exhausted me more than our forced marches at Ritchie with occasional accelerations in double time. I was relieved once I got back to camp, where the only private moments were those I spent listening to records in the recreation room. The collection there was small, and I listened over and over again to Toscanini's recordings of Brahms. The music created a link with my room on West 72nd Street.

That narrow room was briefly revisited when I took the train from Baltimore to New York to say good-bye to my parents shortly before being shipped over to England. On that train ride, the opening of the hit song "The Chattanooga Choo-Choo" once again kept beat in my mind with the relentless syncopated rhythm of the rails. I didn't even mind that American coaches had no corridors, no compartments, and that all the passengers were facing forward, largely unaware of one another. The familiar, almost musical elation was still there as I watched the landscape race by, giving me the sense of music's joyful thrust as each successive note and each beat seemed to press forward. Trains of thought nostalgically connected the Gare Saint-Lazare and the Gare de Lyon in Paris with all the other stations and stopovers I had known— Leipzig, Marienbad, Montreux, Genova, Nice, Madrid, Seville . . .

And then, on a sweltering September day, I was taken on a bus, together with a few others, to nearby Hagerstown, and sworn in as a U.S. citizen. The date of September 9, 1943, appears on my naturalization papers, as does a photograph of me with closely cropped hair and a determined look. I greeted the event as a sign that I was soon to be sent overseas. Our first move as a group of freshly naturalized citizens was to proceed to a local bar filled with advertisements for various brands of beer. We sampled diverse chilled cocktails—manhattans, martinis, daiquiris—which tasted particularly good on that occasion. On the bus returning to camp, we were all fast asleep.

The end of my double-course training at Camp Ritchie was now in sight. But before it was over, we still had to undergo the initiation rites of an uninterrupted forty-eight-hour field exercise during which, in groups of two, we were instructed to find our way to a sequence of stations set up in remote parts and at considerable distance from one another. These stations were for the most part hidden or camouflaged. Once there, we had to solve a number of problems and demonstrate our skills at interrogation, map-reading, and order-of-battle assessments. We also translated documents with hardly more than a dim light to see what we were doing. The most difficult part of the exercise was to cross hazardous terrain and find the stations in the dark. Nonetheless, my companion and I thought it all rather entertaining. We took in the pungent smell of the woods and the reassuring smoke of wood fire whenever we came close to a human habitat. Fatigue gave us a sense of *déjà senti* as we advanced in the dark. At no point did we feel that we were in hostile territory. No maneuver or field exercise can provide that sensation. We joked about our mistakes. When we chanced on other teams, we laughingly reported our minor mishaps. It was all like a good group game, not like preparation for war. We got lost and found our way again. We wanted to be back in our heated barracks, yet much like weary travelers, we did not wish the journey to end.

A final exercise out in the fields kept us busy for several days with some rather pointless activities, as though to demonstrate that even intelligence personnel were subject to unaccountable army ways. Pitching a pup tent in muddy terrain and then trying to sleep in it with an equally drenched tent-mate are feats I never saw repeated in actual war zones. We also received more combat training. To play war games with us, our German-speaking instructors disguised themselves as gun crews in Wehrmacht uniforms. And we were given instruction in hand-to-hand combat by commando experts. We were shown how to sneak up behind a guard and kill him without making any noise. The instructor used one of us for his demonstration. He firmly held a short stick in his right fist, with the stick protruding on the right side of the fist. From behind, with a quick snap of the wrist he struck the victim across the Adam's apple, from left to right, and immediately grabbed the protruding stick in a criss-cross manner with his left hand so that the two fists, both pulling tightly, were now in a criss-cross stranglehold position. With this hold, it was "nothing," as he put it, to choke the Kraut, break the cartilage of his voice box, and have him sag dead to the ground "without as much as a peep." That's fine, I thought to myself. But what if it doesn't work? I kept my thought to myself, determined then and there that I was not going to try out his neat little trick.

I MUST HAVE done well in my two courses, for at the end of the training period I was promoted from private to the rank of master sergeant. It was a huge leap. Master sergeant is just about the highest noncommissioned officer (noncom) rank in the army, usually attained by career military after years of service. I was not yet twenty and had six stripes on my sleeve after only a few months in the army. I remember top-ranking American noncoms at an army mess in England doing a double take when they saw me walk past their table with my tray and my stripes. Even by the way I walked, they could tell I was a fraud. I cannot begin to guess what they thought when they heard the European inflections of my speech. Even the four-letter words I used in the hope of abolishing barriers sounded incongruous coming from my mouth; they only drew more attention to me. I wore my six stripes with some pride, and within the confines of the intelligence units they did not upset anyone. All of us Ritchie graduates were seen as somewhat anomalous with regard to regular army structures, and at times we must have looked like impostors in American uniforms. Eventually the combat units got used to us. We shared their dangers. But our accents and untypical demeanor did on one occasion almost cost us our lives . . . Again, I am getting ahead of myself.

We had been organized into teams of six, with two jeeps at our disposal. In addition to the captain in charge, a first lieutenant, and a master sergeant, who were the chief interrogators, the table of organization provided a staff sergeant for the translation of documents, and two technical sergeants who served as combined linguists, typists, and jeep drivers. But this table of organization was strictly theoretical. In reality, we all shared the tasks. The captain would often type the reports, we all interrogated, and I did much of the liaison with the French resistance, interrogated French and German civilians, and was frequently at the wheel of one of our jeeps, as on the day we landed in Normandy.

We were shipped on a convoy to England, to be assigned to a combat division. Our boat left from Brooklyn, not far from where the *Navemar* had docked with its overload of refugees two years earlier. It occurred to me that there was a certain symmetry to this arrival and departure. But the crossing back to Europe was very different. On this journey we slept on clean bunks, in well-aired spaces. Everything was neat and orderly on the boat. We were protected by warships. The submarine threat was still very real, but no one seemed to worry. The convoy moved almost imperceptibly, always in the same formation. We played poker for hours to while away the long days. Except for repeated fire and abandon-ship drills, we had no duties. It was time out.

I befriended a fellow master sergeant, also fresh out of Camp Ritchie, an Alsatian with a broad open face by the name of During, who had emigrated a few years earlier and who was a little older than I was.

We conversed in French. He told me about his wife, and how she had been so good to him when he was sick. Standing on the deck near the railing, looking out at the other ships and the angry winter sea, I indulged in silly talk about fighting, liberating, heroic action, and the noble side of military servitude. He looked at me. "*Tu as le virus,*" he commented sarcastically, "You've got the bug." He, unlike me, knew what it meant to leave behind a woman he loved.

Chapter 12

BEYOND THE BEACHES OF NORMANDY

"You've got the bug." During's words kept echoing in my mind. It is not clear to me when I was cured. Was it shortly after D-Day, when I lay at night on the bluff above Omaha Beach? I had been too tired to dig a foxhole. A flare lit up the sky, and I heard the shriek of a Stuka plane diving toward me. I felt exposed, naked. I hugged the damp earth, digging my nails into the ground, all my muscles tense. I wanted to press myself into the soil. So that's it, I heard myself think. I imagined the line of bullets cross my back, tearing my flesh. I did not know how to pray, but I did know how to make a promise: I promised myself that if I survived this moment, I would never complain, as long as I lived. Never. All of life would be a precious gift, no matter what happened.

Perhaps the cure for my bug of heroism came in late December of that same year, in the Ardennes. Paralyzed by fear, I was crouching, together with two comrades, in the cellar of a house in a Belgian village. A mortar and Nebelwerfer barrage was shaking the building as the Germans stormed the village. I had slashed my knee jumping down the steps, and blood was streaming down my leg. But I did not feel the pain. I only heard the infernal whistle of the screaming meemies. I heard the wild prayers of the poor villagers who felt, as we did, that our number was up. We were all alone and encircled. We had to make a decision: get caught in a few minutes by the Germans, get exterminated by a grenade or a burst of tommy guns, or take a chance and expose ourselves to the mortal barrage, jump into the jeep, and try to escape. The mental agony was terrible. Feeling trapped was worse than taking risks. We made the decision. Up the stairs, across the street, into the jeep, out of the village, away, away from this hellish place. Trembling, bleeding, totally exhausted, we joined the rest of our team two miles farther south. That very night, we were ordered to face Tiger tanks with our carbines. But nothing I experienced before or after can compare with those desperate minutes in the cellar. I can still hear the Belgians' prayers. God knows what happened to them. The Germans made short shrift of civilians suspected of hiding U.S. soldiers. A grenade or two would have taken care of them and their prayers.

What is certain is that I had definitely been cured of my heroic illusions by the time I saw the dismal dawn light of the following day. I see myself at the edge of a wood, in the fog and snow, on a field near Bastogne. General Cota, with anger and determination on his face, is addressing the remnants of our division. I cannot believe that I hear him say, looking at me, "I'll shoot any bastard who runs." Could it really be that he holds his pistol to my head? I am in the thick of a nightmare. I feel abject fear. I am drunk with fear. I hear his voice as in a dream's echo chamber. So this is the terrible Norman Cota—tough "Dutch" Cota. And this is my last day. I shiver. He does not see the panic in my eyes. He looks at me but sees only my six stripes. He has never encountered a master sergeant like me. "Take your men and dig in. Let the tanks pass, and take care of the following infantry." What men? Dig in? In the frozen ground? Take care of the infantry? I carry only a carbine, almost a toy. This is my last day—not even a full day. I think of my parents on West 72nd Street. Why not push fat Slezak in front of me, or make myself invisible? Too late to hide behind the jeep. I try to pull my head inside my shoulders. I look at the ammunition truck on the other side. The heavy rumble and clatter of tank tracks can be heard. The Panther appears near the edge of the wood facing us. It stops, pivots its long, obscene snout in our direction. One shot. The ammunition truck explodes, lighting up the dim scene. Fragments are flying. I am dazed. When I look around me, there is no one; I am alone. No one else, not even the general. I run for the jeep. Slezak and Lukács are already there. They rev up the engine and skid away with a few other soldiers hanging on. Safe again—but for how long?

These memories come back in discontinuous frozen images— intense, isolated moments that resist being part of a reassuring sequence of events. Instead, they blend into a jarring simultaneity. The sight of animal and human carcasses in the mud of Normandy is hardly distinguishable from the sight and smell of death in the Hürtgen forest or during the Battle of the Bulge. Except that dead cows were strewn all over the Norman landscape. Dead livestock—a bitter oxymoron—covered fields and roads. The cows lay bloated in grotesque positions, their legs all stiff, their tails raised as for defecation. Their bulk served at times as a parapet for our riflemen. Nowhere could one escape the smell, the unbelievably sweetish smell of death.

As for the bodies of dead soldiers, I tried to avert my glance. But that was not possible. I, who always crossed to the other side of the street when approaching an unsightly cripple or a retarded child, could not resist looking. One image continued to haunt me. It was that of an embrace in death of two American soldiers—almost a love couple. One of them, a medic, had fallen over the body of the other. Their hands were close together as though ready for a loving clasp. Their wristwatches were visible, though not their faces.

Other poses were more outlandish. Some of the corpses seemed to have been caught by surprise in attitudes of ordinary activities—getting out of a vehicle, bending over a map. They reminded me of human figures mummified by volcanic lava in pictures I had seen of the ruins of Pompeii. Others were more dramatic still, lying between hedgerows or by the side of the road, in contorted positions, one arm raised as though to implore or accuse the sky that showered such devastation.

The most horrific were the corpses close to tanks or on top of them—tank drivers, their bodies folded over the turret, or gunners and mechanics who had crawled out of the escape hatches but did not make it. They had tried to get out of their tank when it was hit and set aflame. Half-burned, they had been finished off by shells or machine-gun fire. They were often burned beyond recognition—barely human forms. Even the demolished tanks looked like mutilated animals, their underbellies gutted, leaning on their side like extinct prehistoric beasts. The stench of the dead cows and of the spilled fuel mixed with that of burnt human flesh.

I recall the first lines of a poem I wrote in Normandy about images of war and sent to my cousin Sascha:

Les chars blessés, les hommes troués,
Images de la guerre que personne n'a voulue . . .

I had interchanged, or crisscrossed, the expected couplings of wounded flesh and pierced armor, so that, in my opening image, it was the armored vehicle that was wounded and the frail wounded body that was pierced by bazooka shells. But I knew even then that my poem was wholly inadequate. In reality, everything blended, everything was sharp and fuzzy at the same time. My poem did not account for the uncanny way in which images and fragmented moments conflated like double-exposure photographs.

I have often wondered why my war memories are so lacking in continuity, so full of gaps, why so much vagueness is attached to what lies between splintered moments. Is it because in war passivity is the rule, even in the midst of action? Someone else decides, plans, moves, inflicts. Little if any margin is left for the exercise of the will. Except perhaps when one is left to one's own devices, in situations of extreme crisis, or on the run when one improvises to survive. Then, later memory is keen, activated by successive epiphanies of fear.

THE BRIEF MONTHS in England while training for the invasion had not really prepared me for what was to come. Nor could I anticipate my own reactions. When we reached Liverpool after endless poker sessions on the troop ship, I was sent together with my team to Tidworth barracks in the Salisbury plain, in southern England, not far from prehistoric Stonehenge, to join the 2nd Armored Division, known as "Hell on Wheels." That division, formerly commanded by General George Patton, had distinguished itself in Sicily. It had captured Palermo. It was soon to lead the spearhead in France all the way to Belgium and the River Meuse, and later helped save the day during the Battle of the Bulge. Its high spirits were contagious.

For some reason, my teammates and I were not quartered in the Tidworth barracks but stayed in a nearby village. I was billeted with a local family. The husband, a rural craftsman in the old style, took great pride in his work. Their notions were narrow, but they loved music, and every morning I could hear the sounds of Bach or Telemann come over the kitchen radio. They were quite reserved at first, but when they realized that I behaved in a civilized manner, that I did not make savage noises and did not destroy their furniture, they became very attentive to my needs, trying their best to make me feel at home and part of the family. I was allowed to take warm baths whenever I wanted; I could borrow the husband's bike for rides in the countryside, and I was welcome to have tea with them. In good weather, they even moved an old armchair to the garden so that I could read there. Occasionally—this was the supreme accolade—they invited me to share their dinner, at a time when food was rationed in England, and German buzz bombs were flying overhead toward larger cities and industrial targets. In exchange, I shared with them the candied fruit, California dates, and chocolate bars my parents kept sending me.

My division went on road marches, special drills, then on extended maneuvers on the Salisbury plain, which was considered a good terrain for armor tactics. Parts of the division participated in practice landings. During that same period, I learned how to drive using one of our team's jeeps. In those days few twenty-year-old Europeans knew how to operate a car. My crash course involved neither driving lessons nor a driver's test. My driving habits to this day are perhaps attributable to the fact that I taught myself to drive on an army jeep. As for armored vehicles, though a member of an armored division, I was fortunately not expected to know anything about the functioning or handling of a tank. I was most thankful not to be a tanker. Tanks looked reassuring enough when parked and lined up in long rows. They reminded me of unsold vehicles standing in extensive formations on some dealer's lot. They certainly did not seem vulnerable. But when I was given a demonstration and climbed inside one, I was gripped by intense claustrophobia. I imagined being trapped inside one of them, unable to get out—asphyxiated, blinded, burned alive. I was not far from the truth of what happens, or can happen, in battle.

One of my first longer jeep excursions, once I was in full command of one of the jeeps, led to Salisbury, where a few members of my team had planned an encounter with some "willing broads," as they put it. I was not especially eager to join them when they walked up the stairs of the house, which they identified without much difficulty. My memory of that special ward at Fort Dix was still vivid. I was teased, of course, for chickening out. While waiting for them, I went to have fish and chips, which I had become fond of, even though they came greasily wrapped in old newspaper.

In these early spring weeks, during war games and hours of leisure, I got to know the other members of my team. Captain Lyme, with his bland baby face, and Lieutenant Tarasco, whose hooked nose and sharp features brought to mind a mixture of Hispanic and Maya, were both easy-going, with limited college-level linguistic abilities. They held commissions as artillery and infantry officers. The others had a European background. There was Sergeant Scott, a laconic Englishman—scholarly, witty, and skeptical. And there was the unforgettable, mercurial, unpredictable Sergeant Andrew (was that his real name?), by far the most colorful, wildest member of our intelligence team. How wild he really was became evident later, once we had landed on French soil.

It was in an army installation on the Salisbury plain that I had my first experience as a lecturer. I had been given the assignment of talking to a group of officers about what we might find in a typical French town upon invading the continent. I took out a map of the French coastal region. I did not know the area of Dieppe, where the Germans, it would seem, mistakenly expected us to attack, for that was where the English Channel was narrowest. Not being familiar with the northern coastline, I chose Normandy instead, simply because I knew the region. But I purposely avoided the beach resorts I had stayed in—Cabourg, Deauville, Trouville. And so, quite arbitrarily, I selected for my descriptions the very region, somewhat to the east, where unbeknownst to any of us the invasion would be launched—somewhere between Caen, Bayeux, and Carentan. By an even greater element of chance, I pointed with my rod to the precise areas that were to be known as Utah and Omaha Beaches. I even mentioned the little town of Vire, which I did not know but fancied I could construct in my imagination. Some of the bitterest fighting was to take place nearby. When my teammates and the officers to whom I spoke found out where they were going to land, they refused to believe that I had not been secretly briefed. But then, as with much military intelligence, a lot of guesswork is involved. Sometimes it's accurate.

I enjoyed preparing my talk. In my fictional construct of a "typical" French town, I let myself be inspired by an unlikely mixture of stories by Maupassant, Marcel Pagnol (who wrote not about that region, but about the south of France), and Jules Romains, as well as by films featuring Raimu and Fernandel, who were prototypes of the very distant region of Provence—a jarring collaboration of models indeed. My chief concern was to achieve a high degree of local color, no matter how untrue to the Norman realities. The details of my presentation were thoroughly stereotyped. It was all literary and cinematic. There were the predictable types and sites: the mayor, the pharmacist, the local doctor, the priest, the baker and the baker's wife, the church, the school building and the schoolmaster, the town square and the town hall with the tricolor flag. And there I stood in the officer's mess hall, pointing with my rod to the exact area between Vierville-sur-mer and Colleville where "Hell on Wheels" was to land several weeks later. What strikes me in retrospect is not so much my totally fortuitous choice of the actual landing terrain, nor the derivative nature of my presentation. It is the heady sense of control I derived from organizing my disparate materials, setting down my notes, and then delivering my remarks as though talking without a text in front of me. I could not know then that this assignment was a professional initiation.

One day, in late May, all leaves were cancelled. We understood that the moment of the invasion had come. We proceeded to staging and marshaling areas, as they were called. I see us in endless, slow-moving convoys, between half-tracks and other armored vehicles, on our way to Southampton. Children in villages were waving to us, and adults too. During the frequent stops when we were caught in traffic jams, ladies in Red Cross outfits offered us coffee and doughnuts. When we reached the port of Southampton, it was an altogether different spectacle from the one I remembered seeing during our summer school excursion in 1938. There was a huge flotilla of boats and landing craft, and above them a barrage of balloons attached to solid wires to protect the boats from low-level air attacks. It all looked incongruously festive. Of the embarkment itself, I remember only that it took long hours to get the vehicles aboard, and that we were given seasickness pills that made some of us very drowsy, which was probably a good thing.

⟨Ɔ⟩

"HELL ON WHEELS" landed on Omaha Beach on D-Day + 2, the first armored division to land. It was supposed to give support to the 1st and 29th Infantry Divisions, which had landed in the early hours of June 6th and had suffered heavy casualties. Our assembly area was to be near Mosles, on the road to Bayeux. When we managed to get our jeeps onto dry land, the beachhead was not yet entirely secure, nor was it continuous. But the coastal batteries had been silenced, the pillboxes had been stormed, and the road in the immediate vicinity of the seashore was in our hands. The beach was strewn with debris, covered with wooden poles, cluttered with wrecked vehicles, equipment, and abandoned ammunition belts, and near the shore we could see stranded or half-sunk landing craft. The German defense system was also visible: the beach obstacles, the V-shaped antitank ditches, the pillboxes with their powerful gun emplacements. The weather was foul, the light was dirty, the landscape ugly. The site itself seemed hostile, with its natural defenses. After the strips of sand, quite extensive at certain hours, there were sand dunes, a strong sea wall, rock and shingles, and then a steep bluff. I was driving one of our jeeps. When I reached the plank covering the sand, I had to concentrate to stay on that improvised roadway and not get stuck in the sand. I drove tensely all the way from the pontoon to the plank, then on the hard sand, and then on a slow, bumpy path up the bluff to the plateau close to the village of Saint-Laurent-sur-mer. I was dazed by fatigue, by the sea crossing, by apprehension. Certain images remain precise: the overturned landing boats, the poles in the water that supported the Teller mines, the mired trucks, the metal beach defenses aggressively pointed toward the sea. We were impatient to reach an area where we could de-waterproof our vehicles. One image stands out. It is that of a wounded GI, with a large bandage covering his head and hiding his face, leaning against the sea wall. He had only slits for his eyes. A large tag was attached to one of his buttonholes. His eyes could not be seen. But his entire body spoke of dejection and bewilderment.

It was on that plateau beyond the bluff that I fell asleep after de-waterproofing the jeep. Without bothering to dig a foxhole, I had settled near the edge of the field, wrapping myself in a blanket. It was there on the damp ground that a German plane strafed us under the bright light of a flare, and I made that promise to myself to love life no matter what, and never to complain.

The rest of my first night on French soil was quiet, unless I slept through it. When I woke up, my body stiff and chilled, I felt in a rather positive mood. I shaved, using my helmet to wash off the shaving cream. Then, to my own surprise, I felt the need to polish my muddied boots. Was it that I remembered my grandmother's injunction to keep up decorum, if only for oneself? "Especially when you are alone"—those had been her words. My teammates, who watched me working with my brush on the muddy Norman field, cracked some jokes. All of us, it turned out, had our ways of maintaining a sense of dignity.

Soon we were moving again, this time to the nearby assembly area from where our division was to be quickly deployed. The mission of the 2nd Armored Division was to advance as soon as possible to the Cerisy forest, and from there to drive full force toward Saint-Lô, a crucial road center. But the first serious engagement came sooner than expected. The Germans had launched a major counterattack in the area of Carentan, and elite Panzer units threatened to split the troops that had landed at Utah and Omaha. "Hell on Wheels" tanks routed the Germans, inflicting on them their first major defeat in Normandy.

Landing more than forty-eight hours after the first assault waves, we had been spared the worst. But we got a clear picture from several survivors, engineers from an infantry division whom we encountered as we quickly moved back and forth in the Cerisy area trying to gather information from frightened and often reluctant civilians about German defenses further inland. What we heard from the engineer noncoms was unsettling: how they were unable to clear the obstacles in the water near the beach because the infantrymen, under heavy fire, used these obstacles to take cover; how some of them were paralyzed by fear and refused to move; how the wounded disappeared under the surf;

how many of those who waded ashore were mowed down; how very few vehicles made it to the top of the plateau; how it all came close to a disaster. As I now think about what I saw firsthand and the stories I heard on the spot, I have some difficulty believing what an article I read recently would have had me believe—namely, that the way men fight can have not merely a spirit, but a soul. It did not take me long to appreciate During's ironic comment about the "virus" of my earlier war enthusiasm. From that point on, I kept telling myself, let's win the war, but without loving it.

THE CALVADOS HINTERLAND, with its countless hedgerows, posed special problems for military operations. Those thick and bristly hedgerows, on top of mounds of earth and sometimes built on elevations of solid rock, typically serve to enclose the small fields and apple orchards of that part of Normandy. Here and there, the fields are separated by a double hedge and sunken roads. The nature of the terrain determined the tactics in the early stages of the campaign. The hedgerows were difficult to breach and the sunken roads were treacherous. It was excellent terrain for defensive purposes. There was little open space, and therefore limited opportunity for tank deployments. On the other hand, it was perfect sniper country. Hidden machine-gun nests pinned down our soldiers on the move, who then came under very precise mortar barrage. Our tanks at first had much trouble advancing through those hedgerows. From the narrow roads between the hedgerows, they could not disperse into the nearby fields when they came under artillery fire. Solutions had to be found. They came in the form of bulldozers that crashed through the hedgerows and special blades attached to our armor. Such hedge-cutting tanks were nicknamed Rhinoceros.

The *bocage* countryside of farms, clusters of hamlets, and walled fields made for weeks of frustrating, close-quarter fighting. Everybody, especially in the armored outfits, was eager to break out into more open terrain. Sniper country meant trouble of all sorts, not to mention mines, booby traps, and even wire strung across narrow roads to decapitate the

occupants of open vehicles. We were forced to install vertical wire-cut-
ters with sharp teeth in front of our jeeps. The thick hedges lent themselves to ambushes while limiting the vision of troops trying to move
forward. Infantrymen learned to use their rifles to raise their helmets
above the hedgerows in order to attract enemy fire. Many a life was
saved by a helmet thus shot at. Against airbursts, however, there was little protection. They came suddenly, and there was hardly an orchard or
cattle enclosure where one did not come across dead animals and dead
figures in uniform. The German dead were easily identifiable, if only by
their hobnailed boots. One image remains fixed like an old snapshot one
keeps staring at, expecting that it will, at any moment, come to life: a
very young German, lying under an apple tree next to a dead cow, with
his mouth wide open as though about to snore.

The Cerisy forest, one of our early objectives, may in normal times be
a fine place for walks and picnics. It seemed hospitable enough and did
protect our units from air observation as they prepared for a major
assault. But we were not immune from random artillery barrages.
The tree bursts—shells exploding upon contact with treetops—were
especially deadly. Lying on the ground, even in a slit trench, exposed one
even more to shrapnel showering down. It was early on the second day
that I heard sharp crackles and then loud shrieks and repeated cries of "O
my God! O my God!" We rushed out of our tent. In a tent close by,
someone had been hit in the head by shrapnel from just such an airburst.
The bloodied victim was promptly evacuated. It made an impression.
Other casualties confirmed that the forest was decidedly not a picnic area.

In the meantime, our divisional G-2—Colonel Parkins, I believe,
was his name—got our team involved in a rather mad project. He
decided that the troops directly facing us, including many very young
and inexperienced recruits, were ready to surrender. All they needed,
he opined, was some encouragement to do so. He therefore ordered
us—were we not an intelligence team and at home in foreign languages?—to address the enemy troops in German over loudspeakers
right at the very outposts. "Get yourselves there, and do your job."
There were trained Psychological Warfare Units available. They
drafted leaflets composed by refugee writers such as Stefan Heym and
then broadcast them, in between snatches of familiar German music,

from special trucks equipped with amplifiers. But these large trucks could not easily come up to the front lines. At any rate, our colonel decided that we could do better. And so, by fiat, he transformed his military intelligence team into a combat psychological warfare unit. The Signal Corps people were ordered to hang loudspeakers in trees near the German lines during the night. A signal corps GI was killed in the process. Only two members of our "French" team spoke fluent German—Sergeant Andrew and myself. It thus fell principally to us to get down to regiment headquarters, from there to battalion and company headquarters, and from there, on foot, moving forward cautiously and bent over, near the outposts, to a point beyond which we had to crawl along a sunken road, past helmets lying on the ground with ominous holes in them. Three times a day on two successive days we went on this expedition to deliver our message to the Germans, cajolingly. Three times a day we crawled along the sunken road, past the pierced helmets. Always with the same response from the other side: mortar shells whistling down on us. Not a single German surrendered.

Colonel Parkins's foolhardiness soon became even more evident. He was a cavalry officer with only limited interest in military intelligence and a nostalgia for cavalry action. It was reported by those who entered the G-2 tent at night that he would stand with a tall glass of bourbon in his hand and stare at the situation map. Occasionally he would approach the map with a lit flashlight in his other hand and examine it carefully. "Where is the lost platoon?" he would mutter repeatedly, becoming increasingly agitated, until he sent for his jeep and driver. Not forgetting to take his flashlight with him, he set out "to look for the lost platoon," as he put it. Several nights in a row, he apparently went to look, until one night, as we were told, neither he nor his driver returned. I felt particularly sorry for the driver, who probably had little appetite for those nocturnal expeditions.

Our own frustrations had nothing to do with lost platoons; they derived from the difficulty of obtaining any kind of accurate information from the local peasants. They were stubborn, often confused, at times uncooperative or willfully misleading. Some of them were overzealous, tried to please us and told us what they thought we wanted to hear. Which is the path that is mined? Where in the next village is the

German machine gun? "You to take road to right"—and the hand would point to the left. Our trust was limited; we always asked two or three different persons, as we had been instructed. Even then you had to be skeptical if you wanted to survive. Indications and directions were contradictory. We learned all about the unreliability of testimony. And the answers always came in elliptical French. No matter how hard I tried, loud and clear, to display my Parisian intonations, I could not get across the idea that I spoke French as well as, if not better than, they did. "You to go there, you to turn left, you to see big house." They were mesmerized by my uniform. I was an American, and could only be spoken to in infinitives.

We sensed a lot of resentment in the population. On the surface, there was enthusiasm for the "liberation." The Germans, after all, were *les Boches*. But liberation by the Americans brought with it considerable destruction. Towns were heavily damaged, often by indiscriminate high-altitude bombings. Calvados is a rich region, valued for its cattle, excellent dairy products, cider, and the applejack that goes by the name of the region. This Calvados brandy when consumed to excess could easily lead to the field infirmary and to rumors that the Norman peasants were trying to poison American troops. Calvados's prosperity had not at all suffered under the German occupation; because of the severe shortages in other regions, the black market here had flourished. Now, business had fallen off. Behind outward signs of friendliness, there were all sorts of less friendly undercurrents. Yet almost everyone claimed to have engaged in some form or other of resistance against the Germans. Entire villages, if one was willing to believe what one heard, had been members of the FFI, the underground resistance movement known as the French Forces of the Interior. And with all this came a veritable epidemic of denunciations. Neighbors denounced neighbors, merchants denounced other merchants, for having been pro-Nazi collaborators. It was disheartening, to say the least.

I was saddened that the German occupation had not diminished France's internal strifes. If anything, they had become more acute. The sense of humiliation had exacerbated old scars. Shame was never far from anger. Very soon indeed old and new accounts were to be settled in the period of so-called *épuration*—the cleansing or purging that took place all over France, often leading to summary executions. Women were being exposed to public scorn, and at times brutalized, for having been promiscuous with German officers or soldiers. Because of our constant interrogations of civilians, we seemed to attract these unsavory denunciations, motivated by personal and ideological animosities. But we also benefited from local resources. We quickly learned the art of securing more or less comfortable lodgings in abandoned farms, and we knew where to find supplemental food more palatable than the ordinary K-rations and powdered eggs provided at chow time. Once I even fried a juicy slice of calf's liver in my mess kit and on one occasion I enjoyed a real feast with a local farmer, his daughter, son-in-law, and two Parisian refugees who were their paying guests. A picture that was taken on this occasion does not show, however, to what extent the quantities of Calvados consumed made me vague and wobbly.

Ordinary chow, in tents out in the fields, was a more sober affair. We had to clean our tin cups and mess kits, before and after meals, by dipping them into separate large cans filled, one with hot suds, the other with clear, hot water. It was hygienic enough, I suppose, but the unpleasant smell always reminded me of KP. No wonder that in my letters back home I repeatedly asked for chocolate bars, cans of Del Monte fruit cocktail, and even cans of sardines. Personal hygiene was another matter. It was at best that of camping, something for which I have never felt much enthusiasm. Helmets were used for rudimentary sponge baths, and slit trenches filled with lime served as latrines.

There were lighter moments, especially between military operations, when the division was resting or being refitted. We were endlessly entertained and astonished by the antics and buffooneries of Sergeant Andrew. Partly German, partly Polish, but largely unidentifiable in terms of any background, Andrew was loquacious, exuberant, and enigmatic. We did not know much about him, but his reckless, prankish presence made itself felt at all times. Broad-shouldered, disheveled, effusive, moving his head rapidly from side to side while looking at everything with the exaggeratedly open eyes of a clown, Andrew could at times be brutal in speech and behavior, and I recall him later violently kicking his girlfriend under the table of a Broadway cafeteria. Had he been a political militant, a communist agitator? From certain remarks, we guessed that he had been in the Spanish Civil War. He often sang a civil war song of the Thälman Brigade volunteers fighting against Franco, with words set to a well-known Spanish folk song:

> *Madrid und deine Tränen*
> *Die werden wir rächen . . .*

> Your tears, oh Madrid,
> We'll avenge them . . .

Another song ended with words to the effect that one's home is not necessarily where one was born:

> *Nein, wir haben die Heimat nicht verloren,*
> *Unsere Heimat steht heute vor Madrid . . .*

> No, we have not lost our fatherland,
> Our fatherland is now in front of Madrid . . .

When we broke through at Saint-Lô and the way seemed clear all the way to Paris, Andrew ceaselessly sang a parodistic couplet to the tune of the old Communard song "*Vive la Commune de Paris*," with words of his own invention:

> *Avec de Gaulle à Paris,*
> *Avec de Gaulle à Paris,*
> *Nous s'rons encore plus mal foutus,*
> *Nous s'rons encore plus mal foutus . . .*

> With de Gaulle in Paris,
> We'll be even more fucked up. . .

He would slap his thigh in rhythm and at the end of his song would literally roar with laughter. It was at the same time droll, mordant, light-hearted, and politically loaded. Andrew's ebullient spirits did not abandon him, not even during the hell of the Saint-Lô offensive.

Soon indeed things turned grim again. Saint-Lô had to be taken. A German strongpoint near the Vire valley and an essential crossroads, Saint-Lô was the key to a major offensive in the direction of the Cotentin Peninsula to the west and Paris to the east. Its capture would allow us to escape from the closed-in hedgerow country. A break-through would quite literally mean a breakout. But the Germans had some elite troops in the region, and they held fast. "Hell on Wheels" was eventually to lead the attack. At that point, I was attached to the 82nd Reconnaissance Battalion on the assumption that, in a mobile situation, I should be able to gather precious information ahead of the main body of the troops. I was thoroughly alarmed at the thought of racing ahead, and at times roaming between or behind enemy lines. I felt utterly exposed to enemy fire on this reconnaissance half-track—an armored vehicle propelled by caterpillar threads in the rear and a pair of wheels in front. I wondered why I had been picked as I took the full measure of my lack of courage. But I saw no way of not complying with the orders I had received. We proceeded on our mission. I don't know how successful I was in hiding my fear from the nice guys in the recon-naissance unit who seemed to be doing just a very ordinary job. They did not make me feel uncomfortable. They were friendly in a quite nat-ural way, even though they knew full well that I was not one of them.

Before long, we were ordered to halt and wait for new instructions. Something big was in the offing under the code name of Cobra. Bad weather delayed the ominous event for a couple of days. We were posi-tioned at the edge of a wood within a few miles of Saint-Lô. Suspense grew with each hour. Then, early one morning we heard an extraordinary rumble. Next we saw what I had never seen before. The sky was dark with squadron after squadron of heavy and medium-sized bombers—not hun-dreds, but thousands of them. Wave after wave they came and dropped their bombs. We saw them spiral down. The noise was ear-shattering. The landscape gradually disappeared. I felt constant pressure against my head. This was carpet bombing, saturation bombing, and its purpose was to clear a corridor several miles wide. In a flash, I thought of what it must feel like to the Germans just ahead of us. As the bombs came down, some of them fell short, killing not a few of our own troops. Visibility had decreased because of the enormous amount of smoke and dust.

Then there was silence. When we got the signal to move forward, we had to cross stretches of lunar landscape covered with craters. Roads and landmarks were hardly recognizable as part of the human habitat. When at long last we reached Saint-Lô itself, it was a shambles, some heaps burning, some of them smoldering. Hardly a building was left standing. The saturation bombing had been effective: the Panzer Lehr Division was no longer operative as a cohesive fighting unit, its soldiers shell-shocked. I myself felt rather shaken when I joined the other five members of my team on the outskirts of Saint-Lô and took stock of the remains of this "liberated" town: gutted buildings with black smoke bellowing out of empty window frames, collapsed or caved-in walls of dwellings with masonry and furniture spilling out like oversized entrails. The roads outside of town, and the streets inside, were littered with broken-down vehicles and corpses. It was not entirely safe to enter the town, as isolated snipers and stubborn resistance nests persisted.

At that point Sergeant Andrew almost got us into serious trouble. He had done his own intelligence work and came back with the information that in one of the cellars in town—he claimed to know the exact location—there was a cache of superb wine. He was determined then and there to go "liberate" some of the best bottles and wanted our help to make the expedition worthwhile. We tried to dissuade him, mentioning snipers and possible booby traps. Sheer madness, and without any military purpose. Far from dissuading him, it was we who were finally persuaded by his husky pleas to follow him. Not all of us went. But those who did were disappointed by the find. There were a few dust-covered bottles in that cellar, but the cache was far from a treasure. We returned safely, though a few shots were fired at us as we climbed over obstacles in the street. It occurred to me later, as we tasted a sweetish Vouvray, that our exploit was not so different in nature from Colonel Parkins's search for his lost platoon. Perhaps such quixotic madness was contagious.

OPERATION COBRA WAS quite literally a pivotal military operation. This breakthrough at Saint-Lô was the turning point of the Normandy campaign. It opened the way toward Argentan and the sweep to the

River Seine. Various local engagements still gave us concern, but on the whole, during the next four weeks, except for a brief period of rest and maintenance near the Mortain forest, our advances were rapid and steady. Not even pockets of resistance delayed us. We simply bypassed them, leaving to others the task of reducing them. The forward thrust of the 2nd Armored Division was such that much of the time was spent on the move, in our haste to trap the retreating enemy units. On certain days, we covered several dozen miles. Occasional counterattacks did occur, sometimes coming from the rear, which is often the case in mobile warfare. We were put on alert, ordered to wear our helmets at all times, and strictly prohibited from sleeping in our vehicles. Weapons had always to be within reach. The population in the villages and small towns we crossed was decidedly warmer than in Normandy. Their enthusiasm was spontaneous, judging by the cheering crowds, the smiling faces, the embraces, the kisses and flowers that were thrown. Everywhere we were greeted with generous libations, though not everyone was reassured by our arrival. I remember a woman crying hysterically and pleading with us—in vain, I am afraid—because one of our units had set up an artillery piece next to her farmhouse. She was terrified, convinced that her house would become a target. She begged us to move the gun elsewhere, and ourselves with it.

And move we did, not to please her, but carried along by our forward thrust. Our immediate objective was the Seine. Our columns forged ahead so fast that the detailed military maps we used were frequently no longer relevant. In addition to expressions such as "make contact," "seize," "hold ground," "seal off," "pull back," and "pin down," we now most frequently heard terms belonging to the glossary of mobile warfare: "pursue," "cut off," "withdrawal," "seal off," "outflank," "push on," "spearhead." Many of our waking hours were spent in our vehicles. We joked about satisfying our appetite for tourism, and how we would, after it was all over, relish a sedentary existence.

In the meantime, huge contingents of the German army were trapped by a vast pincer movement between Falaise and Argentan. In this "Falaise pocket," the Germans experienced a disaster second only to Stalingrad. Entire units were annihilated. Our division moved forward at the southern edge of the pocket, and we therefore did not find ourselves at the epicenter of their calamitous retreat. But what we did see was impressive enough: countless burned and wrecked vehicles, dead horses still in their harnesses, heaps of dead German soldiers lying in incongruous poses, identifiable as always by their hobnailed boots.

For a while the Germans held on to Elbeuf on the southern bank of the Seine. But "Hell on Wheels" soon captured the town, cutting off all escape routes from the Falaise pocket. We had advanced with lightning speed. This was our own blitzkrieg, and if anything it was more devastating than the German offensive of May 1940. I had lost all sense of time and place, until our division halted for rest and maintenance at Mantes-Gassicourt before crossing the Seine. I suddenly realized that we were only some 30 miles away from Paris, which was said to have been abandoned by the Germans. But American troops were not to enter the city. Out of respect for French pride, it was left to the French units under General Philippe Leclerc to liberate the French capital. However, I could not bear halting so close to Paris and not being present at the time of its liberation. I knew that our division was to remain in bivouac near Mantes-Gassicourt for a couple of days. And so I proposed we take off on our own, in one of our jeeps. Technically speaking, it meant being AWOL, which is a punishable offense. Two members of my team joined me on this expedition, though I do not recall specifically who they were.

I DO RECALL, however, that we gave a ride all the way to Versailles to a young Frenchman, a wiry fellow carrying a German rifle who called himself an FFI. He wore a tricolor armband and asked us repeatedly for yet another American cigarette, which he smoked French-style, stuck to his lip, until the lit end almost burned him. He spoke of blowing up railroad tracks, derailing German troop trains, and rescuing Allied paratroopers. He had given himself a martial appearance by wearing an odd assembly of an American field jacket, old ski boots, and headgear that resembled that of the French mountain troops, the *chasseurs alpins*. I had my doubts. The way he held his rifle, it looked more like an emblem than a weapon. In those heady days, one came across many types with late-developing and untested vocations for patriotic resistance. I felt relieved when he left us near Versailles.

We reached Paris that morning by way of the Porte Saint-Cloud. From that point on, we were in the 16th arrondissement, and I was on familiar ground. Up the rue Michel-Ange, up the avenue Mozart, past the rue de l'Assomption where Jacques Blum used to live. Then a brief commemorative stop at La Muette, where the old gang used to assemble. From there, along the narrow commercial rue de Passy, and then a left turn into the rue Eugène Manuel to look at the windows of our apartment, through which I had stared dreamily when I was supposed to be preparing for my final examinations. On my way to the place du Trocadéro, I recall stopping for a trivial matter at a dry cleaner. Some buttons on my uniform had come loose; I wanted to make a dignified entrance into the heart of Paris. Never since have I been so warmly received by a Parisian dry cleaner, nor dared to request that a couple of buttons be sewn on while I waited. From then on, everything unfolded as in a dream. I drove down the avenue Henri Martin to the Lycée Janson de Sailly, my old school, where as a boy I played marbles on the sidewalk in front of the Petit Lycée. Next up the avenue Kléber, past the Hôtel Majestic, where before the war my Aunt Liza and her husband, Simon Millner, had lived. And then, past the Arc de Triomphe, I began my triumphal ride down the Champs-Elysées, where my father had taken me to watch the military parades that coincided with my birthday. Paris seemed at the same time vast and intimate. Distances were quickly covered in the jeep; there were hardly any other vehicles, though many people—some wearing tricolor armbands—were gathered in the streets. I sped down the Champs Elysées, past the circle of the Rond-Point, then around the obelisk of the place de la Concorde, up the rue Royale, and then on to the successive Grands Boulevards where my mother used to treat me to the movies after my father had departed for the London auction sale. From there, up the boulevard Poissonnière, near where my father's office used to be—all the way to more popular quarters.

On the place de la République I suddenly had a painfully precise image of Dany. In a flash, her address on the nearby boulevard Voltaire came back to me—an address I could not forget after all the letters I had sent her from Deauville following the summer of my great love. Up until that moment, I see myself alone in the jeep. But when I stopped near the place de la République, I recall asking a companion to wait for me. I rushed up the stairs. A woman with gray hair opened the door cautiously. An even older woman was sitting all shriveled up in an armchair, wrapped in a black shawl that she clasped with her knotty fingers. Where is Dany? "*Déportée*," came the answer in a hollow voice that sounded devoid of any emotion. "Disappeared in a camp, with her child," she added in an equally lifeless voice. *Déportée*—I knew what that meant, though the full horror of the death camps had not yet been revealed to us. I knew what my Harrisburg ladies had not wished to know, what even American Jews at that time refused to believe.

I knew, I understood full well, what had happened to Dany. But I could not take it in, could not accept it. Not on *that* day. I fled the apartment without saying a word. I then drove frantically in the opposite direction—back to the center of Paris. I felt the need to be in the youthful student quarter. As though of its own volition, the jeep carried us full speed down long avenues to the place de la Bastille with its tall column, then along the quais of the Seine to the boulevard Saint-Michel— the Boul' Mich—where twice a year I sold my used schoolbooks. I stopped the jeep at the intersection of the Jardin du Luxembourg, right in front of the grillwork through which one has a view of the public garden. It was a favorite meeting place for students of all ages. On that day, a crowd had collected on the sidewalk. We were offered wine, and then some more wine to joyful cries of *Vive la France! Vive de Gaulle! Vive les Américains!* and *Vive la victoire!* And again *Vive de Gaulle*, who had entered Paris the day before, walked down the Champs-Elysées all the way to the Cathedral of Notre-Dame, while snipers were still shooting from some of the roofs. After yet some more wine (I don't know what possessed me), I was standing on the hood of the jeep, holding forth in French. I have not the faintest idea what I could possibly have said in my harangue, but I do recall the perplexed reactions. It he French? Is he American? Yes, he wears an American uniform. No, he speaks French, he is a French liaison officer with the American army. No, he is an American attached to the French forces. Meanwhile I continued my oration, interrupting myself only to gulp down another glass of wine. I must have talked for quite a while. I do not remember the end of my speech.

I next see myself lying on a leather *banquette* in a café, with my swimming head in a woman's lap. She was stroking my hair. Even before I came to, I could smell the strong scent of her perfume. Another young woman was sitting at the table with a tall, greenish drink in front of her. Both were solicitous. It took me some time to collect myself. How had I gotten to that café? My companions, I was told, would return to pick me up. When they did, we drove with the women to the place Pigalle, where we dropped them off at a bar next to a nightclub. After promising to meet them at that same bar on the following night, we drove back to our division assembled at Mantes-Gassicourt, where we collapsed.

On the following morning, we left again for Paris. But when we returned late on that second day, we discovered that the 2nd Armored Division had left its assembly area and crossed the Seine. We were now considerably worried. Our situation was highly irregular, to say the least. Technically we were AWOL, and now that the division was on the move again, this could mean serious trouble. We had no authorization of any sort to absent ourselves. And certainly we were not supposed to have had any business in Paris.

A race now began. The division was in pursuit of the retreating Germans, and we were racing after our division. When we finally caught up with "Hell on Wheels," it had advanced beyond Beauvais. My memory of the relief I felt coincides with a precise image—that of one of our tanks trying to make it through an arched town gate not quite large enough, and damaging the wall in the process. Nothing seemed to stop us, and a giddy optimism had spread. Everyone up and down the chain of command seemed affected. We did not realize that our supply lines were stretched by our rapid advance, and that we would soon run out of fuel and ammunition. For the time being, we forged ahead toward the northern plains as one town after another fell. The sense of inebriation was not caused by wine alone; we seemed to breathe in the heady air of victory. We had no inkling of what lay ahead.

It so happened that I was among the first to enter Bapaume. On the public square, someone claiming to represent the mayor came up to my jeep and declared that I was made *citoyen d'honneur* of the town, gave me an official accolade, and pinned a Cross of Lorraine on my field jacket. More wine was proffered. He called it the *vin d'honneur*. This Cross of Lorraine, which I continued to wear until an American colonel made me take it off, contributed to further confusion as to my military affiliation. The cross, with its two horizontal arms, the upper one slightly shorter than the other, was the emblem of de Gaulle's Free French forces.

Only a few days later, we reached the Belgian border, which our 82nd Reconnaissance Battalion—the very one I had briefly joined during the Saint-Lô offensive—had been the first to cross. And before we knew it, that same reconnaissance battalion reached the outskirts of Hasselt, a mining town very near the Albert Canal. Though only a narrow canal, it was deep and it represented a temporary obstacle to our further advance. In addition, the retreating Germans had left behind deadly obstacles, notably felled trees that were often booby-trapped.

But the inhabitants of Hasselt were boisterously appreciative of our arrival, welcoming their liberators, as they called us, with seemingly endless beer drinking. It was not a festive occasion for everyone, though. Rowdy groups were manhandling some women accused of having slept with the Germans. They dragged them through the streets, kicking and slapping them, and then shaved their heads—re-enacting scenes that had already taken place in many towns of France and Belgium. Lieutenant Tarasco even claimed that he saw swastikas painted on some of the scalps of the Hasselt women. Some of the most vociferous haircutters seen at work were themselves women. I preferred not to look too closely at this revolting "patriotic" spectacle.

The scene inside the pubs was quite loud and disorderly also, though not in the least hostile. The smell of beer and sweat was powerful, and there was almost uninterrupted bellowing of drinking songs. I quickly joined in the general din, belting out the "*Marseillaise*." The Chaliapinesque intonations I had learned from my parents' old record made an impression on my audience. A woman standing next to me put her arm around my waist. She was broad-shouldered and Nordic looking. She repeatedly hugged me, pressing herself against me. When it became apparent that I was interested, several of the Belgians warned me not to get involved, that she was a "bad woman." But nothing could stop me.

The Flemish beer, the songs, the woman's soft hand, the thrill I felt when our fingers interlocked, made me abandon all prudence.

I followed the woman to her apartment and spent the night with her. I left my helmet on the large table that occupied much of the entry. My carbine I kept on the floor, next to the bed. I was uninhibited after all the beer, but in a rush—every time. I am afraid I was a poor lover and did not satisfy her. "*Tu jouis. Pas si vite,*" I heard her breathe on several occasions. I was too fast.

Early in the morning, when the first glimmer of light filtered through the blinds, there were loud knocks on the outside door. The knocking lasted some time, increasingly insistent, then stopped. Was it her lover? Her husband? I never found out.

The next evening I looked for her house, but I could not recognize it. We left Hasselt a day later.

Chapter 13

FROM THE HÜRTGEN FOREST TO BERLIN

W hen the 2nd Armored Division reached Maastricht, on the other side of the Albert Canal just a few miles away from the German border and the city of Aachen, my team was recalled to Paris. We were now well beyond French-speaking territory; our services as French interrogators and interpreters were no longer needed.

Jubilantly, I concluded that for me the war was over. It was now September. France was liberated, except for Alsace. I saw myself back in Paris, leading a hedonistic existence. We were to report to an intelligence headquarters temporarily installed on the avenue Marceau, in a rather chic Haussman-style building. The avenue Marceau is one of a dozen avenues radiating from the place de l'Etoile, most of which carry the names of generals of the French Revolution and of Napoleonic victories. It is what the Parisians call a *beau quartier*. The large apartment or office space was quite empty of furniture, except for desks in every room. I was familiar with the neighborhood. Our headquarters were close to rue Galilée, where my parents and I had stayed in a hotel upon our arrival in Paris, before finding an apartment on the nearby place Victor Hugo. All this contributed to a sense of coming full circle. There was something of a personal victory about this return, only this time I did not come to Paris from the east, as a child of political refugees, but from the west, as a liberator of a country that was and was not mine.

We were given lodgings not too far from these temporary headquarters, but I was determined to find a private place, and then to find an attractive partner with whom to share this privacy. The frustrating Hasselt experience remained on my mind. Having no specific assignment contributed to an illusion of leisure and freedom. I set out on long walks in search of an adequate rental. I located an agency on the boulevard de Courcelles, near the Parc de Monceau, not far from where, years later, my daughter and my son would attend school at the École Bilingue. The agency, upon hearing of my preference for my old *quartier* of Passy, informed me that there was a studio available on a weekly or monthly basis, payable in advance, on the rue des Vignes, and that I should take a look. The idea appealed to me; I was going to be on home grounds, next to the rue des Marronniers, where we had boxed in Jacques Calse's garage. I took a walk to inspect the place. Many memories assailed me along the way. The rue des Vignes was just around the corner from my grandmother's old flat and a few streets away from where my friends and I used to watch the girls come out of school at the Lycée Molière. A quick look at the studio with its deep-red wall hangings and soft light made its past and future purposes clear enough. I did not hesitate; I immediately paid my first week's rent.

The discovery of a partner was a more problematic affair. I did not have casual pick-ups in mind. I longed for nothing less than a real liaison. That, too, would give my recall to Paris a sense of duration. On the very evening I moved to the rue des Vignes with my bags and carbine, I went for a drink at the bar on the corner of the rue de Boulainvilliers— a name I shall not forget. I was greeted by the typical Parisian bar smells of Gauloise cigarettes, red wine, and hard-boiled eggs. At the bar, sipping coffee, stood a petite, dark-haired woman, at most two or three years older than I, exchanging pleasantries with the bartender. She noticed my uniform. She asked whether I had been in Normandy. She came from Evreux, not far from Rouen. Her name was Yvette, and she reminded me of Maggie, who had reminded me of Edith Piaf. There was something about the folds at the corners of her mouth and the expression of the eyes below her heavy lids and plucked eyebrows that spoke to me of a capacity for love and suffering. From certain comments she made that first evening, I gathered that there was, or had been, someone in her life (husband? *ami?*), but that he had remained in Evreux and that it was all over now. I chose not to ask any questions. We walked to La Muette and sat on a bench in the little park. We talked, holding hands. Our fingers played. I caressed the inside of her palm and kissed the back of her wrist. She inspired me to express my desire in a way I never had before. Yet our deportment remained almost chaste. We did not even kiss that night.

At our first meeting in my tiny, crimson-colored flat, Yvette was late. I had bought some Chartreuse liqueur, which in my impatience I began sipping. I kept looking at my watch, aware that the repeated movement of my arm was like a tic. She was only half an hour late, but it felt as though half of the evening had gone by. I was sure she had stood me up. In years to come, the word "chartreuse," or the pale-green color and syrupy taste of the drink we shared, would often evoke a play of tongues I had not previously experienced. Yvette made me feel other sensations that were new to me, as were my own motions. Could one call them love lessons? It all came so naturally in that softly lit room. Yvette liked to pull the sheet over our bodies, as though to make our sensations still more private. In her moments of intense pleasure, she would quite literally coo—so that, even years later, when the sound of cooing pigeons wakes me up in a room overlooking a courtyard, I like to think I am hearing a couple making love in the room next to mine.

Yvette worked as a manicurist until late in the afternoon. During the long hours I waited for our next meeting, I recall singing to myself snatches of Maurice Chevalier's great pre-war hit, "Valentine":

> *Elle avait de tout petits tétons,*
> *Valentine, Valentine . . .*
> *Elle était frisée comme un mouton . . .*

> She had tiny tits,
> Valentine, Valentine . . .
> She was curly like a sheep . . .

The words of the song were relevant only in part. Yvette's hair was not curly, and she did not exactly remind me of a sheep. But the lightheartedness of the Chevalier song corresponded to my joy. At Yvette's request, I had a picture of myself taken, in my field jacket and nonregulation paratrooper's boots. This same picture I sent to my mother and to my grandmother, never once mentioning Yvette. But I later learned that from the tone of the accompanying letter my mother guessed that I had encountered some *"bonne fortune,"* as she put it—an expression I found irritatingly old-fashioned.

My Parisian euphoria put me out of touch with reality. I became thoughtless, if not irresponsible. I was living in a world all my own during this early fall of 1944, almost forgetting that the war was still on. Every day, I had to report to intelligence headquarters, but that was not much of a hardship since there was nothing else to do. Then, one morning, I was informed that a certain colonel in strategic intelligence was looking for an MII person with special language skills, and that I was to report to him for an interview at his Champs-Elysées office. I gathered that his particular branch of strategic intelligence dealt with industrial targets for British and U.S. long-range bombers, and that my assignment would require weekly shuttles between Paris and London. My poor judgment still astonishes me when I think back to my reaction. How could I have been so silly as to make light of such an opportunity? But the idea of absenting myself from Paris and from Yvette seemed intolerable. And the paperwork involved appeared to me quite unromantic. I decided to sabotage my interview. I carefully hid the fact that I knew Russian, the very language that, I was given to understand, would have been a deciding asset, and made it known that I had only a limited taste for drab office work. The colonel, interested at first, gave up on me. I did not care. Yvette's love sounds were sweet music to my ears.

A few days later, my Camp Ritchie files caught up with me. Someone at intelligence headquarters on the avenue Marceau discovered that I knew German, and that I had also been trained as a front-line interrogator of German prisoners of war. I was assigned to the 28th Infantry Division and ordered to report, together with my new team, to where that division was engaged in fighting near the German border. What wouldn't I have given then to have told the colonel that I knew Russian. I could just hear my parents' vehement reproaches.

Such thoughts came too late. The hardest part was telling Yvette. Everything was so precipitous; we had to leave within a few hours. I had to tell her over the phone. I hear myself in the telephone cabin, trying to sound brave and encouraging. We both had trouble finding our words. I was to see her once again, during a short leave from the front.

What has remained are the letters that I kept, though I rarely looked at them over the years. I felt a certain embarrassment at reading Yvette's fervent sentences. Were it not for the spelling mistakes and grammatical errors, many of her sentences could have been lifted from a book of love letters. Yvette's letters were filled with clichés, but their peculiar grammar rendered them intensely personal. The first of those letters reached me soon after we reported to our new divisional headquarters near the Hürtgen forest.

THERE COULD NOT have been a worse assignment than the Hürtgen forest. The Normandy landing and the Saint-Lô breakthrough had been terrifying events, but nothing could compare in brutal discomfort and senseless sacrifice of lives with what several of our divisions, soon torn to shreds, experienced in the slime, cold, and fog southeast of Aachen—and then a few weeks later in blinding snow, during the Rundstedt counteroffensive in the Ardennes. When we reached the area of Roetgen, where the 28th Infantry Division had set up its supply train, we heard how the 9th Infantry Division had been decimated. We were to take over from them. It was slaughter in the forest. But our generals were determined to have the riflemen fight their way inch by inch through the dense, ominously dark forest. The wooded, accidented terrain was soon nicknamed the "Death Factory." It was in this constantly dripping forest that our 28th Infantry Division acquired its nickname, the "Bloody Bucket"—a reference to the red Pennsylvania emblem on our shoulder patch.

Roetgen itself gave no idea of the hell only a few miles away in that accursed forest. Roetgen is a border town, the first German town to be taken by the U.S. army. It was a succession of bleak houses. We were billeted rather decently; German homes, we found as we occupied them, tended to be clean and functional. I got to know the other members of my new team. One of them was soon to become a casualty, though not to the war. He was a smooth-talking, suave Romanian, with carefully groomed, shiny hair. He struck me as something of an operator. He had all the attributes of a cosmopolitan currency dealer in a spy film, including an attaché case filled with banknotes from different countries. When he heard the story of my interview with the colonel in strategic intelligence, he blamed me for having let slip by such an occasion: between Paris and London, what with currency exchanges, I could have made a fortune, he kept repeating, not to mention the fun of a double life in the two capitals. His own double life as intelligence interrogator and currency dealer came to an abrupt end one morning, when an investigating agent appeared with military policemen and dragged him off, together with his loaded attaché case. We never heard from him again. He was replaced within days by Sergeant Slezak from Milwaukee, who had a nostalgia for good beer and liked to sing tunes from German operettas.

Contrasts near the front can be striking. In Roetgen, within a few miles of the murderous Kall trail, life was bearable. My Kodak Retina had just arrived in a package from home. I have a picture of Sergeant Lukács, our somewhat older, Hungarian-born teammate, cheerfully servicing one of our jeeps. Other pictures of these muddy, sullen days in Roetgen suggest good-humored camaraderie. In one of them, I stand with Lieutenant Howe next to a recently affixed sign: ENTERING GERMANY. Howe was a handsome young man of Central European origin who liked to think of himself as a successful womanizer. A few years later, we were to meet again on the Yale campus where I was already an instructor and he was attending law school. I quickly made friends with all five members of my team. We calculated that between the six of us we spoke fifteen languages. We joked a lot, and occasionally we indulged in horseplay. I have two pictures of all of us, some sitting in one of the jeeps, the others standing next to it. In one of these pictures, Captain Muchnik, who had a seemingly inexhaustible repertoire of Jewish songs and folklore, pretends to read a document, while Lieutenant Howe pretends to type a report on a portable typewriter, and I am hamming it up at the wheel. In the other, I theatrically wave a captured sword or bayonet as though it were a conductor's baton, while Lukács stands caressing a cat, and Sahlmann (whose parents were unable to escape from Nuremberg) sits relaxed on a garden chair, *dolce vita*–style. Muchnik watches the scene through dark sunglasses as though he were vacationing on the Riviera. Except for our uniforms, one would not guess that we could hear the sound of heavy artillery barrages.

In one of the pictures, Lieutenant Howe and I stand next to a captured black Mercedes. We commandeered it, though it was in bad shape and had miserable pickup. But it gave us a thrill to drive a civilian car, especially one that had been used by a Nazi official. An American general, seeing us drive it, ordered us to turn it in, "on the double." The Mercedes was by then covered with mud.

It rained or drizzled steadily. On a rare day when a pale sun made a fleeting appearance, operetta-buff Slezak took a picture of me all dressed up, standing in my shiny boots, posing outrageously, helmet under my elbow, with my captured Luger pistol in a holster under my armpit, my six stripes and the Bloody Bucket insignia clearly visible on my field jacket. One might think that we had nothing better to do in Roetgen than pose for pictures.

Yet the battle of the Hürtgen forest was a ghastly military operation, and we soon got a real taste of it. The Americans were paying for the euphoria we all had felt during the last stages of the French campaign, when the Germans were in disorderly retreat and victory seemed within sight. The rude awakening came precisely in the Hürtgen forest. We were now facing the so-called Siegfried line, the German defense line of concrete pillboxes and steel-plated artillery positions. Though we gleefully sang a tune to the effect that very soon we would be hanging our wash on that same Siegfried line, the German troops, now defending their homeland and reminded by Goebbels's propaganda machine that their cities and their families were being mercilessly pounded by Allied air bombings, seemed to have a renewed, even fanatical determination to fight back. Meanwhile, our general staff seemed determined to push through that remote border forest at any cost, even though it was most unpropitious terrain for deploying tanks, and the weather excluded air cover. There seemed to be a real obsession with taking places like Schmidt and the Vassenack ridge. General Cota, the commander of the 28th Infantry Division, was reputed to have said that he'd "sure as hell take them," even if he had to use every medic as a rifleman. Crossing that forest was in fact a stubborn decision, and the cost in lives was atrocious. It meant yard-by-yard fighting, often hand-to-hand, with grenades—and this across a series of well-defended ridges. Units broke, men ran. Entire regiments were torn to pieces; companies split into fragments of demoralized, battle-fatigued soldiers. Battle fatigue was often a euphemism for the dazed condition and reluctance to continue fighting that affected even officers and seasoned noncoms. Some of the men in the Hürtgen forest, I later learned, deliberately inflicted wounds on themselves, shooting at their feet, toes, or fingers, so as to be evacuated. The losses were staggering. Almost the entire 109th Regiment of our division was wiped out in a short period of time during the month of November.

For our foot soldiers, forest fighting was indeed far more difficult than war in hedgerow country. The setting alone was discouraging: stumps of decapitated trees, seemingly impenetrable rows of somber firs, rutted trails, poor visibility. The trees were very close together. It was dangerous to make a move. This was ideal terrain for snipers and hidden machine-gun nests—not to mention mines. Our riflemen had had no training to prepare them for forest warfare. The Germans, on the other hand, had acquired valuable experience in Russia. But even they suffered enormous losses in the Hürtgen forest. It was a bitter, almost static war, where a few hundred yards were gained, lost, gained again; where hills, patches, crossroads were taken, abandoned, taken again—all while the soldiers spent days and nights in waterlogged foxholes. Even the names of the villages and ridges were menacing. I jotted down some of them: Vossenack, Riffelsbrandt, Richelskeul, Todtenbruch—the last one carrying the word for "death" embedded in its very name.

Muchnik was a hard worker—but we would have been hard at work in any case. Our team interrogated not only prisoners of war but German civilians as well, who were less communicative. We had some close-up views of battle damage. (Some of the toughest moments occurred during my brief stay at an army hospital a comfortable number of miles to the rear of the front.) When we visited a few of the more exposed units, we were made aware of the huge gap between divisional headquarters and the lower echelons of regiment and battalion, down to the heavily engaged companies. In the battle of the Hürtgen forest, communications between headquarters and the line units proved to be troublesome. If one remained at headquarters or in a field hospital, it was hard to imagine what a chaotic retreat such as the one at Kall trail was like, with the mired or disabled tanks, the wounded trying to keep up, the need to crawl in the mud, the danger of being crushed by one's own vehicles. We interrogated not only civilians and prisoners, but our own troops in order to get a picture back to headquarters—even though we were not always believed.

A talkative medic described some of the forest fighting to us in ways I can't forget: the vicious house-to-house combat in the villages; the tree bursts caused by special shells, against which lying prone was no protection; the impossibility at times of evacuating the wounded; the men too tired or too scared to leave their foxholes, even to relieve themselves; clothes and limbs blown up into the branches by exploding mines; the horror of raking mortar barrages. The Germans occasionally booby-trapped their own dead. It was hard on the inexperienced replacement troops. Men cracked up. The toll on officers and noncoms was especially heavy.

The army finally crossed the forest, but only after months of defeats and the withering of a number of divisions. One hears a lot about the bloodbaths of the Normandy landing and the trauma of the Battle of the Bulge. The Hürtgen forest was equally bloody, but more erosive. It was a massive hemorrhage that for a long time could not be stopped. The losses in men were such (some divisions lost as many as five thousand men within a few days), and the replacements so frequent, that soon there was a manpower shortage, particularly in the infantry. We were told that a special call for black volunteers had gone out. This was indeed unusual, for blacks were typically put into service and maintenance units. The call for volunteers was presented as a singular opportunity to fight side-by-side with the white brothers-in-arms. The hypocrisy struck all of us in the team. We had no contact with black soldiers; the army was segregated. To be honest, we had not given this much thought—that's the way it was. But now suddenly we were shocked by the hypocrisy of this call for black volunteers, simply because they were needed in battle. Later, shortly after my army discharge, I befriended a black medical student with whom I spent evenings listening to jazz at Café Society in Greenwich Village and who complained—oh, so gently—about his experiences in the great democratic army fighting against Hitler's racism. I tried to persuade him that things were not really so bad after all, but I knew even then that I was arguing in bad faith.

The butchery of the Hürtgen forest, the stories of men shivering at the memory of having stepped on dead bodies in their hasty flight, brought back a literary memory. It was not of one of the antiwar books that my parents made me read. Those books still tended to romanticize the war as a virile and fraternal adventure. What came to mind was a passage in Céline's *Voyage au bout de la nuit* (Voyage to the end of night)—a novel that was far from recommended reading—which describes a scene of World War I in which a character who dreams of deserting watches his fatally wounded captain whimper and piss blood all over himself, and then thinks how wonderful it would be if the soldiers and war-loving captains of all armies could strip themselves of their uniforms, and in their nakedness no longer belong to any army at all.

A similar thought may have occurred to some of the men in or near the Hürtgen forest. Desertion was certainly on the minds of some. The brass tried to counter demoralization and battle fatigue by setting up R&R (rest and recreation) centers with Red Cross "clubmobiles," movies, and USO shows. Even more restorative were the rotating passes to Liège and Brussels, and above all the 78-hour leaves to Paris where some of the men found in the neighborhood of Pigalle, if not oblivion, then a brief respite from screaming meemies and their own panic. Even those of us who were not as cruelly exposed as the riflemen benefited from our generals' calculated concern for fighting morale.

It was one such leave that brought me back to Yvette.

WE WERE THOROUGHLY shaken up inside the truck that carried us on the 250 long miles of bumpy roads from Liège to Paris. We sat, tightly packed, on the hard benches. But I didn't mind. I kept thinking of what lay ahead: the warmth of a bed and the softness of Yvette's body. My only fear was that my desire might desert me. It was very late

in the evening when we met. We found a room in a modest hotel, one
floor above the little café at La Muette that housed the horse-betting
agency. The sheets that Yvette liked to pull over us more than ever shut
out the rest of the world. Yvette asked no questions, and I did not want
to speak of the war. In fact, we spoke very little, even when, the following morning, we sat facing each other in a nearby brasserie, eating a
huge omelet. We watched each other eat and smiled with complicity. I
was struck again by the sadness at the corners of Yvette's mouth. I
recalled the letters and felt ashamed at the thought of my own selfishness and insensitivity. She obviously knew better than I that our story
had no future and no past—certainly no future. Even the present was
ephemeral. But I preferred not to think of time and loss. I cared for the
moment itself.

I had to report to military intelligence headquarters, which had now
been moved to a villa in the residential quarter of Neuilly, close to the
Bois de Boulogne. It was there that a colonel ordered me to take off the
Cross of Lorraine that had been pinned on my field jacket in Bapaume. I
also received my new marching orders. My division, I learned, was
being moved to Luxembourg, where I was to join up with them. I was
pleased that we would be in such an attractive region, not realizing of
course that we would be deployed there just in time to receive the brunt
of von Rundstedt's surprise counteroffensive through the Ardennes,
which came to be known as the Battle of the Bulge. It would seem that
every leave-taking from Yvette preceded a major battle. This time it
was to be a serious threat to the Allied forces.

What stands out of those December days in the Ardennes is mostly a
jumble of white and muffled sensations: the endless snow, the lines of
snow-covered pines with their heavily laden branches, the snowdrifts,
the winding white roads, the military figures in white "spook suits," the
crunching sound of the hard snow under one's boots, and in other
places the feel of stepping knee-deep into piled-up snow—whiteness
everywhere and a sense of void. We moved at night, with our wind-
shields down, covering them with canvas so as to avoid telltale reflections. We drove with our lights out, in the blinding snow and piercing
cold. Our eyes were smarting, the muscles of our faces were paralyzed.
We could hardly see the vehicle in front of us. Driving was partly

guesswork. At any moment we might slide off the ice-coated roads and get stuck where the snow was deep. And everywhere, more of the dead in grotesque frozen postures.

The irony was that the 28th Infantry Division, after its shattering losses in the Hürtgen forest, had been sent for refitting and rest to what was considered a quiet front along the River Our in Luxembourg. The natural beauty and picturesque villages of that region seemed to have been designed as an ideal rest area. In this vacation setting, our units were gradually refitted with vehicles, weapons, and inexperienced infantrymen. These men were still in need of training. But even though the Bloody Bucket division was exhausted, undermanned, and under-equipped, it was given the assignment of covering several dozen miles along the Our, far too extensive a front line for even a heavily equipped division in top shape. Our defenses were too thinly spread, but this did not seem to matter. Was Luxembourg not a rest area? The landscape seemed to confirm the sense of tranquility. The area was hilly, but not forbidding; the many bubbling streams and murmuring brooks could remind one of the wanderer's delight in a typical Schubert lied. Even the few castles looked as though they had been planted in the scenery for the tourist's pleasure.

Wiltz, a strikingly situated small town a few miles east of Bastogne, is where the 28th Infantry Division set up its headquarters. Wiltz is in fact made up of two towns: the historical upper part with its château, and the modern quarters below. We occupied a small house in the lower part. Our team settled into a cozy routine. For a while we kept busy traveling through lovely landscape in the region of the Our in order to interrogate civilians in Clervaux, Hosingen, and Vianden, where we also took a look at the imposing ruins of the medieval castle. We lived in our little house like a family. Captain Muchnik sang old Jewish songs with his cantorial tenor voice. Even in moments of stress, he had a gentle, loving expression on his face—an expression that suggested the patience of ancestral suffering. It occurred to me that "*muchenik*" in Russian means "martyr." I still remember his meticulous handwriting on the drafts of his reports—true labors of love. Slezak, our operetta buff, also sang—though less mellifluously—about a soldier standing guard for his fatherland on the banks of the Volga:

Es steht ein Soldat am Wolgastrand,
Er wachet für sein Vaterland . . .

We had musical discussions. The question was whether music, even without words, could communicate like a language. I recall maintaining that music made repeated statements, that it was engaged in a form of dialogue, in a series of questions and answers. Muchnik supported my view: the others disagreed. But even in our disputations, we felt comfortable with one another. We also made friends with a local resistance leader who presented us with pistols stolen from the Germans—as though we did not already have pistols enough. But I suppose these were his most precious possessions at the time. The gift was to be valued.

Life seemed almost normal. But rumors reached us that soon put an end to our musical discussions and relaxed commerce of friendship with the local patriot. We heard about disquieting German activities beyond the River Our, beyond Sinspelt, in the region of Bitburg. They turned out to be more than rumors. A peasant woman who had crossed the lines and was interrogated several times at different levels of command described unusual concentrations of German troops in the region facing us. Even more disturbing were the masses of equipment, ammunition, and fuel, as well as the river-crossing boats she described. We decided to look at the situation more closely near the outposts and in the villages along the ridge of the Diekirch-Marnach highway, and to see if we could send someone across the lines, possibly near Hosingen. Half of our team settled temporarily in a village inn, a frugal *Gasthaus*. What we managed to find out corroborated the woman's report. It was disturbing enough to make us drive that very evening all the way to 8th Corps headquarters in Bastogne to deliver personally the alarming news. We were received without much enthusiasm by a field officer who looked as weary as he was skeptical. He had already been warned, he said, but in any case there wasn't much that he, we, or anyone else could do about it. Our lines were thin, much too thin. We would just have to sit and wait. Anyhow, at most it was probably a diversionary action.

Somewhat dispirited, we drove back to our village in the uncannily silent night. I rested badly. My sleep was troubled. I was awakened around 5:30 AM by what I thought at first was a thunderstorm—which could not be, since it was December. What I heard was not thunder, even though there were also flashes of lightning; it was the steady rumble of artillery. Sure enough, soon some explosions could be heard in the vicinity. I never dressed in a greater hurry. I gathered my toilet articles and my few belongings and threw them into my bag. In my great haste, I left behind my Kodak Retina. To my lasting shame, while others appropriated German cameras during the war, I managed to lose mine, fleeing hastily and ingloriously from my *Gasthaus* when the shells began to fall. My two companions, even faster than I, were already beside the jeep in the courtyard. In addition to artillery, mortar shells were now coming in. We jumped into the jeep and drove back as fast as was possible in the fog to our divisional headquarters in Wiltz.

This was the morning of Saturday, December 16—a date I won't forget, for this was the beginning of Marshal von Rundstedt's massive counteroffensive, into which more than half a million German soldiers were thrown on a fifty-mile-long front north of Trier. From here on, and for the next ten brutal days, ours was the story of a rout. The 28th Infantry Division bore the brunt of the attack in the region of Clervaux; its 110th Infantry Regiment was badly hurt and compelled to abandon the town. The force of the attack and the boldness of the German plan surprised us. After the war of attrition in the Hürtgen forest, we did not imagine that the enemy had so much strength left. With hindsight, it became clear that the German high command had held on so desperately to its positions in the forest in order to allow its preparations for the Ardennes operation to go undetected.

The German plan was ambitious. The counteroffensive was meant to threaten the entire U.S. army and to split the Allied forces. Specifically, the thrust was intended to reach the strategic River Meuse and, if possible (Hitler was said to be adamant about achieving this aim), to capture the port of Antwerp. It was also a desperate plan. The Germans threw in almost everything available to them (the Russians were pressing them heavily on the eastern front), and the risks were great. They counted on bad weather, not only to make American air detection and air attacks impossible, but also to take advantage of our inexperience fighting in the snow. The great error of our high command was to underestimate German morale and determination and to judge, at least in the early stages, that the operation was only a diversionary sally.

The German resources were impressive. Marshal Dietrich had an entire Panzer Corps at his disposal, made up of reformed Panzer divisions and well equipped Panzer Grenadiers. The much-feared Tiger tanks were seen everywhere. Some of the schemes were quite wild. A task force under the command of the adventurous Colonel Otto Skorzeny was thrown into action. Skorzeny had recruited soldiers with a knowledge of idiomatic American English. Dressed up in U.S. army uniforms, moving in captured American vehicles and even in German tanks disguised to look like American Shermans, they were supposed to cut through our lines, create confusion, appropriate supplies, and seize bridges on the River Meuse. Rumors about this Skorzeny outfit made our men trigger-happy, as my teammates and I were soon to find out. One had better know the password for the day. Some of these daredevil Skorzeny men were eventually captured and shot for fighting in deceptive uniforms.

There was also an especially fierce brigade or regiment known as *Kampfgruppe* Peiper, after the name of its commander, Joachim Peiper, who was already notorious for the atrocities he had committed on the Russian front. This *Kampfgruppe* spearheaded the attack and made deep inroads behind our lines, murdering some of our soldiers who had surrendered. Orders had been given from higher up, it would seem, to instill terror and show no mercy. Massacres of captured Americans took place near Malmédy, somewhat to the north of our divisional units. News spread quickly. The desperate nature of the German offensive should have been evident by the atrocities committed. We only felt the effectiveness of their offensive. Within a few days, the enemy had achieved a "bulge" some 60 miles deep and 45 miles wide and had disintegrated a number of our divisions. Our own 28th Infantry Division, which only recently had been bled in the forest fighting, was this time all but annihilated.

We were unprepared for the magnitude of the German attack, and also unprepared for the weather. We did not have appropriate clothing. For once, I would have welcomed woolen underwear, even if it was itchy. But being cold and wet was not the worst of it. For an entire week, everything around us was sheer confusion. Chaos might be a more accurate word. There were orders and counterorders, orders to withdraw and orders to hold at any cost. Because of the swift movements of the Germans, but also because the fog, the snow, and the overcast sky impeded all air operations, no one knew exactly where the enemy was. Much of the time we did not even know where our own troops happened to be. Lack of information became an even greater hardship because of blocked roads and traffic snarls. Our engineers, when they were available, had to work hard to keep the roads open. Snowdrifts and iced surfaces caused breakdowns and collisions. Vehicles slid off the roads and got stuck in heavy snow. Wiltz was abandoned early on, after a brief but costly defense. Having crossed the Our near Vianden, the Germans penetrated deeply behind our lines, trapping our units or forcing them to flee, together with our divisional headquarters. There were some heroic stands and examples of concerted action, but many companies quickly dissolved. Officers were in search of their men, men were in search of their units. Many of them were dispersed, roaming over the bleak landscape. Commanders were scrounging for troops. One was always in danger of being commandeered by unknown officers. Cooks, MPs, drivers, clerks—anyone could at any point be ordered into combat.

The most extreme confusion occurred at a crossroad called Schumann (there was a café or inn there by that name), a few miles southwest of Wiltz, in the direction of Bastogne. There the most disorganized fighting took place. Only small groups remained cohesive—which was the case of our team. In the general quest for safety or survival, we were all on our own. What counted was resilience, inventiveness, cunning. Having a map and knowing how to read it gave one a distinct advantage. The general message or command—but who gave it?—was "fall back." Where to? What road to take? Two names came up repeatedly: Bastogne and Sibret. The village of Sibret was in fact where our divisional headquarters had moved to. But even that place had to be abandoned very soon. By then we no longer knew where our headquarters had relocated or whether they were still on the move.

We no longer obeyed any orders; there were none. From Schumann on, it was a perilous adventure with tough obstacles and unpredictable dangers—some of them from our own side. Rumors floated of roaming Krauts in U.S. uniforms who spoke English. These were the Skorzeny volunteers who had made forays far beyond our lines. All around us was a real spy obsession, with frequent security checks. One was challenged to provide the password for the day, and one did not always know it. So rapid queries were made—about American geography, the names of state capitals, the names of baseball pitchers. At one point, three of us in one of our jeeps were stopped and asked what is the Windy City. Not one of us knew, for not one of us was a native American. We had all been naturalized recently, and one of us had a heavy foreign accent. I protested our innocence. We were given another chance. Who won the World Series? I suppose it was an easy question, but again we failed the test. This time, it seemed that things were taking a grim turn. We had heard that spies were executed on the spot. I had to do some fast talking. I asked to be taken to their superior officer. It was a close shave.

It was at this point, after General Cota abandoned his temporary headquarters at Sibert, that we found ourselves encircled in a village under heavy mortar fire and rushed down into a cellar occupied by the family who added their wails and loud prayers to the screaming of the incoming shells. A few hours later, at early dawn, at the edge of a sloping field, we came upon grim-looking General Cota himself. He was there, pistol in hand in the early morning fog and snow, ordering the remnants of his division to make a stand. That moment later haunted me, when the German tank swiveled its obscene muzzle and hit our ammunition truck, lighting up the macabre silhouettes of the trees. General Cota had singled me out, together with a few others, to organize the defense. The huge explosion put an end to our stand. Everyone was on the run again.

At first, in the fog and snow, dazed by the explosion, I could not find my jeep. I was afraid someone had driven off with it (our vehicles came without keys; we just turned the motor on). But my comrades had waited for me. Waited? It all happened within seconds after the explosion—half a minute at most.

We were on our own again. I became the acknowledged expert in map reading and figuring out escape routes. My teammates later remembered that I insisted on bypassing the crucial road center of Bastogne, thus saving us from murderous fighting at crossroads in the vicinity. Bastogne itself, encircled by now, held out thanks to the 101st Airborne Division, which had been rushed to the rescue at the last hour. But even if we had tried, we could not have entered the besieged town. We had no choice but to continue our flight to the east. Or was it to the north? I cannot reconstruct our itinerary. I continued studying maps. Partly through luck, partly through instinct, I finally got our team all the way to Awaille. ("A wizard," Lukács years later remarked to Bettina, with his heavy Hungarian accent.)

Awaille lies on the River Amblève, an affluent of the Meuse, which the Germans considered the gateway to the port of Antwerp. This was an important defensive sector on which elements of different badly beaten divisions had converged. It was the headquarters of the 18th Airborne Corps, and a relatively secure place. By the time we reached Awaille, the tide of the battle of the Ardennes was turning. Important forces under the command of General Patton had been hastily shifted to the bulge. The weather had finally cleared, and our planes were able to fly massive sorties. The Germans, by now running out of steam, were pounded. Almost all of *Kampfgruppe* Peiper was destroyed.

In the course of that single week, between December 16, when the counteroffensive was launched, and Christmas, when the Germans were forced to give up Hitler's dream of splitting the Allied forces by crossing the Meuse, we sustained staggering losses. Our entire 110th Infantry Regiment, which had valiantly delayed German advances, was wiped out, most of its officers and men killed, captured, or wounded, and all of its vehicles lost. And ours was only one unit among many. The Germans filmed rows of American prisoners. One such sequence, as I already mentioned, was shown on American newsreels, and my parents—as well as relatives and friends in New York—were convinced that they recognized me among the prisoners. I have kept a still from that newsreel that my distraught parents had obtained. Even I am struck by the uncanny resemblance and would have sworn that the sad, tired-looking face under the tilted helmet was my own. My parents had almost given up hope when they received comforting news in a most unexpected manner.

The good news came from a chance encounter. On the very day I reached Awaille, near a large tent on open ground, I ran into my cousin Ossia, who had played with me when I was a child and taken me to soccer games at the Saint-Ouen stadium. He was in a paratrooper uniform. We fell into each other's arms. He told me that he was with the G-2 Section of the 82nd Airborne Division, and that his specific duty at the time was to prevent and identify infiltration by German saboteurs and spies dressed in American uniforms, and to ascertain that they were not among the retreating U.S. forces. I told him that my division had been decimated, and that I was happy to be alive. There was not much time for conversation. We hugged each other and exchanged good wishes. But on that same day, Ossia found time to send a special army airmail letter to his wife, Ruth, in New York, telling her of our meeting. A phone call from her brought the happy tidings to my parents.

It would seem, however, that they were not totally reassured until they also received word from me. Years later, going through family documents after my father's death, I came across the laconic note I sent my parents on that occasion. It is dated December 25th—probably the day after I reached Awaille. It is written in French, and translates as follows:

> My dear parents—After the tumult of the recent days, I finally found some quiet to write to you. I hope this letter will reach you quickly. Do not worry. I am all right, and I believe that very soon the situation will improve. For the New Year, all my wishes. A thousand kisses. Vitia.

In their happiness to learn that I was safe, my parents probably did not even mind the terseness of my note. There is an interesting postscript, confirming our need for adequate winter clothing: "I have received the package with the warm underwear. It came just in time. Thank you. I need nothing else."

I NEXT SEE us in Alsace that January of 1945, in the town of Saint-Dié, which had been devastated by a terrible fire in the recent fighting. From Saint-Dié we quickly advanced to Sainte-Marie-aux-Mines through dramatically winding roads and views of the Vosges Mountains, with their characteristic rounded summits. After the Hürtgen forest and the Ardennes, we found more pine trees and more snow. We were entering into a historically disputed region. Celts, Germanic tribes, Huns—all had been here. It later became part of France, was lost to Germany after the war of 1870, but was regained after World War I. Hitler had annexed it to the Third Reich after the French defeat in 1940. But its population, despite their Germanic names and the Germanic inflexion of the local speech, was on the whole fiercely attached to France. We were warmly greeted. While stationed in Sainte-Marie-aux-Mines, I was adopted by a couple whose son was a prisoner of war in Germany. They asked me to consider their home as my own and spoiled me with delicious sausages and *choucroute*, which I never liked, but pretended to. *Kugelhof*, packed with almonds and raisins, would appear at the end of the meal. When I had to depart, they begged me to be careful.

To be back on French soil cheered me up. But there was a less cheerful side to our stay in Sainte-Marie-aux-Mines, and again it involved General Cota. It was there, in a courtyard of the town at the end of January, that poor Private Eddie Slovick—a gentle, somewhat mentally disturbed individual—was executed in Cota's presence by a firing squad for having deserted his unit in battle. His execution was supposed to be an example. There had been many other offenders, and some had also been condemned to death. But Slovick is the only one who was executed. Was he a simpleton? It appeared that he had just had enough of the massacre and had fled while the 109th Infantry Regiment bled to death. We learned that his was the first military execution since the Civil War.

My mission at this point was to establish liaison with elements of the contiguous 1st French Army, under the command of General de Lattre de Tassigny. The situation was delicate, and relations with the French were fragile. After the fiasco in the Ardennes, the Germans had decided to threaten the Alsatian front. For strategic reasons, General Eisenhower planned to withdraw to the Vosges range—a better line of defense. This meant abandoning Strasbourg, which had already been liberated. French sensibilities at this prospect became raw, for Strasbourg had a profound symbolic importance. De Gaulle was incensed. I was instructed, together with an American officer who spoke little

French, to discuss improving contact and mutual information with some French officers at their headquarters on a nearby hill. When we arrived, they were having lunch and made us wait. It was clear that they were in no mood to make things easy for the Americans. It took patience, and then some diplomacy. But when I let the French captain know that I had attended the Lycée Janson de Sailly, where he, too, had been a student, he ceased treating me as a lower-rank *américain* or— perhaps worse—as a Frenchman serving in an alien army. We reminisced about life in our neighborhood of Passy and Auteuil, the skating at Molitor and Saint-Didier, and the aromatic *pain au chocolat* that was sold on the rue de la Tour. We rejoiced about the improving military situation: Colmar, the capital of Alsatian gastronomy and vineyards, was in the process of being liberated.

The 28th Infantry Division participated in the reduction of the "Colmar pocket." Early in February, U.S. infantry units reached Colmar itself, but, as had been the case with Paris, it was the French army that officially took possession of the town. My team operated from a charming hotel with an ornate sculpted façade. This charm was marred, however, by regular artillery fire coming at almost predictable intervals from a large gun mounted on a special train hidden in a tunnel somewhere in the direction of the Rhine. The regularity of the shelling only added to our nervousness. I had visions of rails, trains, underpasses, tunnels into which the artillery train withdrew. I had not until then associated long-range guns with the drama and poetry of the trains I so loved. But that train and that gun somehow communicated a sense of momentous solemnity. The heavy, deliberate, monotonous sound of the incoming shells was like a mournful toll announcing the death of Nazi power.

THE REMAGEN RAILROAD bridge, south of Bonn, was soon captured, and the Rhine was crossed. Events began unfolding with incredible speed. Before we knew it, we were deep inside Germany. In April and early May, it became difficult to keep up with the pace of news: the Russian siege of Berlin, Hitler's suicide, the unconditional German surrender. Everywhere we saw towns in ruins. The Germans were not likely to forget the destruction they had brought upon themselves. It would take years to recover. The French defeat of 1940 was nothing in comparison. Some small places we came across remained untouched; the Allied tanks had simply bypassed them. But wherever resistance was put up, or around communication centers, what remained was a heap of rubble. I kept thinking how lucky it was that Paris had been spared.

The war was over, but we had yet to discover the full horror of the camps—the *Lager*. We had to face the problems posed by masses of displaced persons. Civilians continued to endure misery and suffering, and bitter ironies emerged in the attempt to return to normal living. During a brief stay in an evacuation hospital, I witnessed a scene that weighed on my mind for a long time. It was around midnight when four litters were brought into the narrow tent. On those litters were the bodies of four men whose clothes were so blood-soaked that it was at first difficult to tell whether they were soldiers or civilians. They turned out to be Frenchmen in civilian clothes. They were in terrible shape. Acting as interpreter for the medical officer, I approached the one man who was still conscious. With some patience, I got the entire story. They had been prisoners of war in Germany since 1940. When the Allies occupied the town where they had been held, a hundred or so POWs were liberated. Having managed to find some trucks, they had been on their way home to France when a bad accident occurred involving one of the trucks. Eleven of the men on the truck were killed, and the rest were badly mangled. Some died of their wounds a little later. I listened with distress to the laborious speech, interrupted by coughing spells. I knew that death comes to soldiers every day and everywhere, and that death is horrible. But when men have gone through the French campaign of 1940, five years of suffering as prisoners, the destruction caused by the liberating armies, and then get killed in a road accident when only a few days and a few hundred miles separate them from their families, it was enough to make me lose that night's sleep.

I was assigned to work with a task force in charge of "de-Nazification" of the Saarland, a highly industrial region of coal fields that had been of supreme economic and political importance to the Nazis. We were instructed to arrest—if we could find them—the likes of *Kreisleiter* (heads of a region) and lesser Nazi officials. It was an endeavor into which I threw myself with some zeal. We operated from Saarlouis, then from Dudweiler, near Saarbrücken. But we ran into any number of difficulties. Either because of fear or a sense of dignity, the German population was unwilling to give any information or denounce anyone. After considerable detective work (which amused me), and after intimidating some of the people we interviewed, we did manage to make a few arrests. The only trouble was that within at most 48 hours, not only were they set free again, they were put in charge of various town and city administrations. The U.S. military government insisted that the former Nazi officials were indispensable to run things. It was a comedy. We made arrests, while our commanders, more concerned with maintaining law and order and nightly curfews than with the misdeeds of Nazi ideologues, reinstated these "able Germans," and indeed thanked us for having found them in their hiding places. They were needed to ensure that the streets were cleaned, to restore public utilities, and to maintain order. De-Nazification turned out to be joke, as were the rules against fraternization with the German civilians. The black market flourished, and so did more intimate forms of commerce.

Our sense of frustration may help explain a scene of which I am not proud. We had arrested some men, and they were about to mount a truck headed for the local jail. I knew quite well that they were going to be freed within hours and put in charge of the power plant, garbage removal, or some municipal office. Exasperated by the futility of our arrests, I stepped out of my legitimate role of investigator and interrogator. In a nasty mood, I pulled one of the men by his beard across the courtyard while screaming at him, demanding that he answer, yes or no, had he ever heard about the camps. One of my colleagues confiscated a box of pills from another detainee who insisted that he was sick and needed them. I was ashamed of my beard-pulling, but I felt even greater shame that I did nothing to prevent the confiscation of the pills. These are perhaps not what one might call war crimes, but even now, I fail to recognize myself in those moments of anger and vindictiveness. I kept seeing—like a reproach—the gentle face of my father, who was distressed at the mere thought of hurting someone's feelings.

My disgruntlement and indignation were genuine, though—about Nazis given encouragement by our military government, as well as the invasion of bureaucracy and bureaucratic martinets, who seemed to have bred quickly since the fighting ended. These "knights of the wastepaper basket," as I remember dubbing them, were more likely to feel sympathy for the Germans and to be impressed by their neatness and efficiency than were our combat units. I was now in Höchst, very close to Frankfurt, working with upper echelons of the occupation force. It was a new kind of existence. I was no longer working with a small group of friends, enjoying privileges of relative independence. I had become a member of huge organization with regimented office hours, and with nothing to handle but papers and paperwork. Fortunately, some of the documents about Nazi organizations, directives, and propaganda made for absorbing reading. Nowhere else at the time could I have had access to them. My office was spacious and featured my name in large letters. Brass surrounded me. But we achieved very little. There were thousands of refugees and displaced persons, including pregnant women without medical assistance. I felt guilty that I looked well fed or when I was seen carrying PX purchases. Yet in our self-styled "policy-making" body that considered itself so essential, no one seemed to achieve anything. The breed of high-ranking officers who had taken over the world of desks, intricate channels, and red tape never came in contact with real problems and were in no hurry to solve them.

My greatest indignation, early in August, was provoked by the glee with which almost everyone around me at the Control Council greeted the cataclysmic atom bomb that had been dropped on Hiroshima. News reports and editorials gloated. A whole city in ruins! The dead uncountable! Impossible to distinguish between the men and the women. I was offended by the tone as well as by the hypocrisy of the reaction. Not so long ago, we had been outraged by the Germans' use of V-missiles against British cities. It seemed to me that we were now surrendering to the principles of mass destruction and of war against civilian populations that had begun with Guernica and the Luftwaffe's exploits in Poland. I knew that my reactions could be considered "unpatriotic" (the Hiroshima mushroom was supposed to shorten the war in the Pacific and save American lives), but I feared for the future. For once I agreed with the Vatican spokesman who stated that this terrible weapon cast a shadow on posterity. The front line, in future wars, might actually be the safest zone. To this day, I cannot forget that, with all the talk of the horror of a nuclear war, the United States is the only country to have made use of the bomb. And to think that President Truman did not spend one sleepless night over its use—or so he claimed.

Our life near Frankfurt had some lighthearted moments. There was one little shadow: we knew that we would be parting soon. I had hopes of being transferred to the occupation forces in Berlin. In the meantime, we tried to make the most of the time we had together. We even went hunting, but failed to outwit the fox. On one occasion, some experienced hunters took us with them to confront a wild boar. We were a little nervous, having heard that boar hunting—with a history going all the way back to Greek mythology—was not without dangers. We waited all night at our posts, but the animal did not show up for the appointment. In the villa we occupied, we found a roulette game. This became a passion. In the evenings we tried to break the bank. We also made music or listened to records on the old gramophone. I discovered recordings by the baritone Willy Dormgraf-Fassbänder elegantly singing arias from *Figaro's Hochzeit* (the German title) and *Don Giovanni*. It was strange to hear him sing Lorenzo da Ponte's words *"La ci darem la mano"* in German:

> *Reich mir die Hand, mein Leben,*
> *Komm auf mein Schloss mit mir . . .*

It made me long for Ezio Pinza.

I developed a new hobby that was not unrelated to the documents I had to deal with. I tried to learn all I could about Nazi propaganda, their struggle for power, and the conditions that prevailed in Germany before 1933. I was especially impressed by Goebbels's energy, cunning, and revolutionary ideas when it came to molding and orchestrating public opinion. Posters, newspapers, leaflets dropped from airplanes, organized demonstrations, speeches—everything was perfectly harmonized and planned to the smallest detail. It seemed to me that I began to measure the Nazis' singleness of purpose, their successes in the elections, their ways of using and abusing the very freedoms they were quick to abolish once in power. I marveled at the organization of their party, its discipline, the combination of terror and legal parliamentary methods used to attain their purpose. I read and took notes, unaware that what I considered a pastime (I had no practical purpose in mind) was in reality training in scholarly research.

Mine was not, however, an abstract interest. The consequences of the Nazi regime were visible all around us: in the misery of the population, the faces of the children, the houses in ruin, the discovery of barely alive skeletons in the camps, the masses of displaced persons. The plight of the remaining Jews all over Europe was terrible, even though the gas chambers and the ovens were no longer at work. I soon learned more about this when working in Berlin on displaced persons' camps. Surviving Jews who had been freed from the concentration camps, especially if they were stateless, were treated like scum. Nobody wanted them. If they tried to return to their former homes, no one helped them. Their property was gone. Their relatives had disappeared. Except for the very few who managed to live freely through the war years (there were indeed some, even in Germany), the rest were in camps or returning like beggars to their homes. Our own attitudes in the U.S. army were at best ambiguous. We claimed to be horrified by what the Nazis had done, and to have come as rescuers. In reality, the notion that Jews were cowards who managed to get soft jobs, or to stay out of the army altogether, and had pushed America into the war was not uncommon among the soldiers. As for the treatment of the rescued Jews, there were some interesting stories. One of my teammates found his parents and his brother alive in Nuremberg. They were the only ones left of a large family. After having been persecuted for years and forced to live like a hunted animal, my friend's mother was slapped in the face by an American sergeant when she told him in good English that she was Jewish and asked him how she could get in touch with her son, who, she knew, had made it to the States. It was not clear whether the sergeant slapped her because she was German or because she was Jewish.

WE LEARNED THAT our team was to be dissolved, and that we would soon have to part company. We had been together since the Hürtgen forest. We promised to keep in touch once we were back in the States. I was assigned, as I had hoped, to the Control Council in Berlin—specifically to deal with problems involving camps and displaced persons. In that context, I was expected to perform liaison duties with the Soviet authorities. To be assigned to Berlin made the sense of victory more complete for me. Orders for my transfer came at the end of August. Three months had elapsed since Hitler had committed suicide in his bunker and the Soviet soldiers, after a fierce siege, had raised the red flag over the devastated city. By the time I reached Berlin, it was still a disaster area, but the population was emerging from under the ruins. Entire zones were still totally uninhabitable. Many who returned to the city could not recognize their own street.

I was housed with a few colleagues in the modern residential complex known as *Onkel Tom's Hütte* in a relatively untouched area of Zehlendorf. It was green and suburban. It the nineteenth century, Zehlendorf had been a small village outside of Berlin—a popular site for excursions. Apparently an innkeeper by the name of Thomas ran a congenial tavern there—hence the name of *Onkel Tom's Hütte,* an amusing tribute to the fame of Harriet Beecher Stowe's novel. Later, a street went by that name, as well as a subway station and a model residential project for middle-and upper-middle-class families. There were even some opulent villas in the vicinity. The American occupation forces quickly discovered the relative amenities of that quarter and housed their administrative personnel there. Just before my arrival, several thousand apartments had been requisitioned for their needs.

I shared a two-floor apartment with four or five others. The apartment was not spacious, but it was well-ordered and comfortable—typically *kleinbürgerlich,* or middle class. I was surprised to find a rather handsome, leather-bound volume of Verlaine's poems next to an album glorifying the party and Dr. Goebbels. I appropriated both for the duration. Every morning, I had to report to the building of the Control Council. In my naiveté, I believed that here at last I could do something useful to help the plight of the DPs—the displaced persons. But I soon discovered that, even more than at Höchst, this was a fortress of bureaucracy. The long corridors were flanked by large offices. Each section had its own sign. Names appeared, blue on white, in front of all the doors. Colonels and privates, men and women, raced through the corridors, their hands full of documents. Foreign liaison officers—Dutch, French, Belgian, Russian—moved about in a self-important manner. I needed air after hours in this world of "in" and "out" boxes. I had not as yet read Dickens's account of the Office of Circumlocution—but this place was exactly it. Daily business consisted of transferring papers from desk to desk, from office to office, until such time when there was no longer any need to deal with a particular problem. The papers were then carefully filed.

I was also taken aback by the preoccupations of some of the high-ranking officers who seemed to be far less concerned about the conditions in the displaced persons' camps than about finding out what happened to real estate property in Berlin belonging to relatives or friends. In the streets, the spectacle was even less edifying. At many a street corner, American army personnel, including officers, could be seen selling watches to Russian soldiers or engaged in other black-market deals. The climate of callousness and petty gratification repelled me.

My so-called liaison work with the Russians, though it refreshed my knowledge of the language, was even more disturbing. What I saw was not pretty. Conditions in the eastern sector of Berlin were dismal and unhygienic. Horsedrawn carts or lorries could be seen carrying off furniture, appliances, household objects. The Soviets had already dismantled factories and workshops. Electrical plants had been particularly hard hit. But the dismantling and the shipping off were still going on. Even telephone sets and typewriters were confiscated whenever they were found. Relations with Russian officials did have their comical side, if one can find amusement in the sight of a drunken colonel, a *polkovnik* saturated with vodka to the point of literally falling out of his official car. We had interminable discussions about who did what in the war, about Russia's industrial production, about who was the real enemy of fascism. What they envied was American technology and gadgetry. Their leitmotif was the determination to equal and surpass us on our own grounds. It was obvious that the United States was the model. The tone was a blend of exuberant proclamations of friendship, suspicion, respect, and rivalry. But what they admired and wanted to imitate was very far removed from what some of us were most proud of.

In contrast to the Soviet behavior, ranging all the way from official looting to the erection of monuments glorifying the Red Army, the Western Allies in Berlin were genuinely concerned about promoting the arts. Two events remain inscribed in my memory. The first was a totally unexpected opera performance. In the devastated city, where theater and opera houses were gutted or seriously damaged, an opera ensemble was somehow put together in the late summer or early fall. With scant sets and costumes, without much that one would normally consider indispensable, this improvised group managed to give a performance of Beethoven's *Fidelio*. No work could have been more appropriate and more moving under the historical circumstances than this story of tyranny, oppression, and salvation, with its chorus of prisoners thirsting for freedom, its chained political martyr, its tale of loyalty and steadfastness in love, and the ultimate victory of justice. When the chorus appeared singing about freedom, *"Freiheit,"* tears came to my eyes. It was hard not to think of the pale, emaciated, ghostlike figures behind bars and barbed wire in the camps, or packed in cattle cars, or lying prostrate on their tiered bunks, staring at the liberating GIs with their wide-open eyes in which there was hardly a spark of light left. In later years, I would never hear Leonore's strong intonations as she attempts to mobilize her valor (*"Ich habe Mut ..."*) without remembering the extraordinary circumstances of the Berlin performance of 1945. Nor did love ever seem nobler than when Leonore sang about what it can attain:

Die Liebe, sie wird's erreichen

Love will accomplish it . . .

But the most interesting character in this opera, which I had never seen before, was the prison warden Rocco—so weak and so human. He somehow came to represent in my mind what I liked to think was the condition of many "good Germans." Torn between obedience and humaneness, he stands in awe of the governor of the fortress and repeatedly refers to orders that must be obeyed, yet he refuses to murder the prisoner, agreeing at most to be a passive accomplice:

Nein, Herr, das Leben nehmen,
Das ist nicht meine Pflicht

No, sir, to take another's life,
That is not my duty.

Rocco somehow became for me the emblem of surviving decency under the Nazi regime. I kept remembering the train conductor who refused to give us away when asked by the state police whether there were any Jews on the night train that carried us to safety across the Swiss border. I came out of the theater on the Kantstraße as in a trance.

The other unlikely artistic event in the war-ravaged city took place on a late summer evening on the large, sloping lawn of an untouched villa. It was a German version of Shakespeare's *A Midsummer Night's Dream*. The puckish notes of this fairylike poetic work came across beautifully in the German translation. Time stood still as the shades of the late day faded into the night. I kept thinking, through the magic of the evening, that the incidental music composed by Felix Mendelssohn had been prohibited because he was a Jew, and that his statue in front of the Gewandhaus in Leipzig had been taken down early during the Hitler regime.

The performances of Shakespeare and Beethoven in the defeated city were, for me, signals of renewed hope. This hope, I am sure now, was linked to a decision that was so evident, so natural, so much part of me, that it was as though I had made it long ago. Was it not made, in fact, years earlier, when we had stopped at that streetcorner in Princeton and I had glimpsed the university? Perhaps it was not a decision then, but the beginning of a dream to somehow become part of that world of students and studies. I guess the germ of the decision had been planted earlier still, on the *Navemar,* when I heard two of my fellow travelers extol life on an American campus. At any rate, my decision was in place, and it made me oblivious to my irritation and listlessness.

All I wanted now was to get out of Berlin, out of Germany, out of the army. When I was offered a field commission to lieutenant on condition that I remain in the army of occupation for an extra year, I refused. I counted on being discharged soon. I had also become aware of an unusual opportunity—that of attending a special university program offered to qualified American army personnel at Shrivenham, in England. I applied and was accepted.

◌ —

SHRIVENHAM UNIVERSITY, AS it was grandiloquently called, was no university at all, but an American military camp, not far from Oxford, where specially designed courses were offered by volunteer American college teachers sent over for a limited period of duty. I remember Shrivenham mostly in the rain and the fog. I reached it by train, in one of those old-fashioned compartments, each with its own door, to which one had direct access from the station platform. There was no corridor linking the compartments. I had seen such trains in old spy and mystery films, in which the protagonist experiences strange encounters and suspenseful events. But this was a very ordinary journey. The passengers belied the legend of imperturbable British indifference to strangers, for they were talkative and even inquisitive. They asked me about the condition of German cities. When I described the ruins of Aachen, Frankfurt, and Berlin, I could not tell whether they felt sorrow or satisfaction. The streaks of driving rain on the windows prevented me from seeing the landscape.

In the camp at Shrivenham, I saw a number of unmilitary-looking figures in uniform, wearing special insignia I had never seen. These were the American college professors who had been sent over from as far as Wisconsin, Colorado, or Washington State. Some of the paunchier types looked awkward in their regulation army dress. I imagine that they must have felt they were on a kind of adventure. The course of studies was only a few weeks long. The curriculum I selected included voice lessons and modern fiction. But we were not allowed to forget that we were still in the army. Early in the morning, in the chilly fog, we had to "fall out," stand at attention, and be counted before the top sergeant shouted "At ease, men" and made announcements. My knee hurt steadily during these assemblies in the damp weather, and it amused me to think that a twenty-two-year-old veteran of the Ardennes could have developed arthritic joints so soon. As for the voice lessons, they were peculiar to say the least. My voice teacher, who never offered a comment, had me practice the quite arresting spiritual "Sometimes I feel like a motherless child," as well as a Haydn song, with words by Shakespeare about unrequited love:

> She never told her love,
> But let concealment, like a worm i' the bud,
> Feed on her damask cheek . . .

I particularly liked the end of this song, with its image of fortitude in the face of lasting pain:

> She sat like patience on a monument,
> Smiling at grief . . .

The literature class was given by a bearded professor from Lawrence University in Appleton, Wisconsin, who made us read Georges Duhamel's *Civilisation*—stories about World War I field hospitals close to the trenches. Duhamel, who had served in that war as a medical officer, evoked conditions that reminded me of the slaughter in the Hürt-gen forest. I recall writing a paper on this collection of stories, the title of which struck me as an ironic condemnation of all wars. The stories themselves dealt smilingly with the double mystery of violence and compassion. It occurred to me that perhaps the best literature, like the Shakespearean figure in the Haydn song, does indeed smile at grief.

I HAVE MUCH trouble establishing a coherent link between my brief stay in Shrivenham and my return to the States on a warship serving as a troop ship on that occasion. Blanks and discontinuities at times afflict my memories of transitional moments. I traveled at least once to London while in Shrivenham, but the details of the visit seem to have evaporated, except for the frivolous memory of discovering a small restaurant that served lobster salad. My mind was probably already on my reunion with my parents, and on the career plans that by now had crystallized. I began to see the connection between that day in 1941 on Princeton's Nassau Street, when Mr. Slepak had stated so emphatically, "This is where Einstein works," the special assignment on the Salisbury plain when I gave my presentation to officers of the 2nd Armored Division just before the Normandy invasion, and the paper I had written at Shrivenham on literature and war.

My next clear memory has me on a U.S. battle cruiser carrying a large contingent of military personnel back to the States, in late December, in one of the worst Atlantic storms in decades. Hundred-mile-an-hour winds were recorded. The ship, rolling wildly, took twice the normal time to cross the ocean. Many sailors were seasick, which surprised the returning soldiers. But then we did not have to climb up and down from deck to deck on the pitching vessel. I spent most of my time dozing on my bunk, reluctant to get up even at mealtimes. My mind itself was afloat, as it is during bouts of fever. I felt detached, relegated to my seclusion and daydreams.

I always thought that my return from the war would be marked by a series of memorable scenes. Not that I expected parades, fanfares, and confetti, but just as there are blanks and discontinuities in remembered events, so also anticipated and often imagined circumstances, when they finally do occur, can be disappointingly anticlimactic. Trying to describe them in vivid terms would be a form of betrayal. Perhaps the overabundance of sensations results in a form of emotional anesthesia. Certainly my homeward journey was devoid of any epic resonance. Everything unfolded in a commonplace manner: the docking, the final routine at Fort Dix, medical checkups, numerous formalities, taking out a veterans' life insurance policy, the honorable discharge certified by an official document. I now felt vaguely apprehensive about meeting my parents. I feared that everything we said would sound empty, that we could not possibly do justice to what we felt or wanted to feel. For a full twenty-four hours, I delayed returning home. I feared the precise moment my parents would fling open the door and embrace me. For that moment, I knew, would be followed by an unavoidable letdown, by a lapse into quotidian concerns. I spent the night in a hotel in Trenton. I wallowed in the double bed and took repeated showers—this time with no one in sight.

The next morning, feeling somewhat guilty toward my parents because I had delayed coming home, I took the train for New York. My arrival in the city was another disappointment. It was all so ordinary, so predictable, so frustratingly banal: the taxi ride, the sight of the streets obstructed by delivery trucks, the familiar corner drugstores, the lobby of our apartment house, where I caught a glimpse of our grouchy janitor. When I reached the tenth floor and stepped out of the elevator dragging my duffel bag, the apartment door did fly open as I had imagined. My father was coughing with excitement, much as when he thought he was choking on a fish bone. My mother's smile had a slight twitch to it. Their hugs, their exclamations, their remarks about how thin I had gotten, were exactly what I remembered from other slightly irritating homecomings. It was as though nothing unusual had happened to me or to them during my long absence. And then, pell-mell, all sorts of subjects came up that I had also anticipated. What would I do, now that I was back? Whom did I want to see? What did I plan to do with my savings? My parents spoke of losses on the stock market, of friends who were ill, of the big party my uncle was giving on New Year's Eve. I was admonished to call him before I even unpacked, or he would be offended.

It took only a few hours before I felt an insidious desire to be elsewhere. A famous sixteenth-century poem about a happy return to one's home ironically came to my mind. It was Joachim du Bellay's evocation of Ulysses's homecoming to Ithaca that a teacher at the lycée—the one who restlessly walked up and down the rows of students—had inspired me to memorize:

Heureux qui, comme Ulysse, a fait un beau voyage . . .

Happy he who, like Ulysses, has been on a beautiful voyage . . .

Somehow, I did not feel like celebrating the coziness of settling into the bosom of the family. I preferred Tennyson's more romantic version of the warrior's return, for his Ulysses, no sooner is he back on his tiny island than he finds that it is dull and yearns to be off again, "to strive, to seek, to find, and not to yield." Not that I had the slightest desire to pass beyond the Pillars of Hercules and expose myself to further perils. And as for not yielding, that was a notion—if I had ever entertained it—that I had given up some time ago. But my resolution to enter through the portals of some university was now firm, as was my determination to learn and to teach. I had heard about the GI Bill of Rights, and I meant to make good use of that unexpected opportunity.

During the New Year's celebration that preceded the arrival of 1946, my uncle, who was giving the party, encouraged me to flirt with a former mistress of his, a glossy-haired Russian who had also lived in Shanghai. But the considerable amounts of vodka and champagne I had absorbed made me an indifferent conversationalist, and I was not used to the banter of such social occasions. Besides, my mind was on my academic plans and on the university I intended to visit. During all the forced laughter, clowning, hollering, tin trumpet sounds, and loud rattle noises that lasted late into the night, I could not forget that within a few days I would be on a train again—this time to seek admission to a world that for a number of years I had longed for without quite knowing it.

Epilogue

OTHER TRAINS, OTHER STATIONS

O
n the train to Boston that sunny January day in 1946, I thought of my parents' friend Mr. Slepak, who had done research at Harvard Law School in the months preceding Pearl Harbor. It was probably because of him that I had decided to visit Cambridge and the university's admissions office. I had visions of myself—a twenty-two-year-old freshman in a lecture hall listening to eloquent luminaries and taking notes. I vaguely blended the image of ivy with that of the ivory tower, viewing the latter as an exalted citadel of meditation and intellectual friendships. I was now impatient to get started. More than five years had elapsed since the summer of 1940, when, fearing the imminent arrival of the advancing German army, and ill-prepared in almost all my subjects, I presented myself for the *baccalauréat* examination in Bordeaux.

As the train was speeding toward New England, I was struck once again by how different railway travel felt on the two sides of the Atlantic. Only recently, between London and Shrivenham, I had journeyed locked up in a narrow compartment, with no way of escaping from the confined space once the train was rolling. Here on the New York–New Haven–Hartford line, as it was then called, all of us were facing forward, anticipating our destination—all of us together in the same big coach, yet very much by ourselves in our individual seats. And there was no way of stepping into a side corridor as on the modern continental trains I loved so much, to face the shifting landscape as it raced by. The large car with its passengers seated in rows felt more like a bus on rails. It was a public conveyance, democratically cancelling class distinctions. Yet there was only minimal contact between the passengers, even between the ones seated next to each other. Occasionally, there was the awareness of a sneeze followed by the ritualistic "Bless you," or the half-curious, half-indifferent side glance at the book one's neighbor was reading. The trip was punctuated by the stentorian voice of the paunchy conductor announcing the next station as he moved down the central aisle in his ill-fitting uniform.

I missed the huffing locomotive, the steam playfully imitating clouds, the privacy of the compartment, the expectation of brief encounters. I missed the specific allegretto rhythm of European rails, the old familiar sound of doors slammed shut, of probing hammers and clashing buffers. But the cradling motion was there, as was the lullaby of the train. And there was also, undiminished, the joy of the train ride as spectacle, the steady revelations of an animated backdrop rapidly unrolling with the fleeting magic of a film.

In between the Eastern seaboard stations announced by the conductor—Stamford, New Haven, New London—I thought of the passage of years and the many stations I had known. What a distance I had already covered between the Hauptbahnhof in Leipzig and the Gare de Lyon in Paris, between the rue de Provence and the street in Hasselt where the women were brutally beaten and shorn, between the snows of the Ardennes and the gutted opera house in Berlin. I was aware of distances, but also of a sequence that seemed to carry me forward as if by necessity.

But then I thought that mine was not just an ineluctable movement forward, in a single direction. The trains of my memory shuttled back and forth. Even in their deviations and diversions, they spoke to me of repetitions and returns. Must there in fact be a direction, a destination, a point of arrival? I never really wanted my trip to end. The little boy, I remembered, had dreams of an endless journey.

The shuttle of memory: Is it the high point one remembers, or is it the repeated act of remembering? As I look at old snapshots, I ask myself whether it is the event or the picture I see. After a while, I am no longer sure which comes back to me first, preserved over the span of time—the moment itself, or its image. Even the train journeys I recall with nostalgia are transmuted by the act of recall, embellished by the aura of remembrance, purified of their imperfections and of the boredom and anxieties that accompanied them.

The image of the shuttle also seemed to apply to my relations with the books I read and remembered. At a certain point, it proved hard to determine which had priority in my consciousness, the lived experience or the experience of reading. Between the two, there was no gap, no clear line of demarcation. The connective link was in part determined by the books I happened to read, but what I read and retained was also determined by what I was no doubt in need of reading. Perhaps it is true that I always required the mediation of art—whether novels, movies, paintings, or poems—to make real contact with what we call "life."

The repetitive to-and-fro movements of memory made me reflect on the woven texture of lived and remembered events. The threads of a life's warp are fashioned by recurrence. This was not the first time that I thought about the meaning of the word "train," with its connotation of pulling, connecting, and carrying. What we ourselves carry along with us is our own mental baggage, including the resonance of uttered words as well as the weight of the unspoken ones. As the train raced through New England, I became gradually more apprehensive. Though eager to enter college, I was also painfully aware that I was about to start a totally new chapter, and I did not know yet how it would connect with what came before.

I RETURNED FROM Boston two days later. The interview at Harvard had been disappointing. I had been found admissible but was told that I would have to wait until September—eight months—to enter the freshman class. I could not imagine what I would do during those long months before the beginning of the fall term. On the train to New York, to distract myself from my frustration, I kept staring at the flat landscape, now unwinding in the opposite direction. After a while, the gliding and prancing shapes I watched through the window became associated in my mind with musical phrases. I surrendered to day-dreams and began humming and then singing softly in an undertone various Mozart arias, imagining in the private theater of my daydreams that I was at the same time singer, conductor, and audience. At one point, as I had launched sotto voce into Leporello's catalogue aria, I heard a distinct "Bravo!" I did have a public. The woman seated next to me repeated her "bravo." She loved opera; she had a brother, she told me, who was an opera singer, Nicola Moscona. Yes, indeed, I had heard him. He sang bass roles at the Metropolitan. He was a very competent Colline—the philosopher—in *La Bohème*. We began talking about opera careers and the difficulty of reaching the top. We talked about temperamental conductors and impossible colleagues.

As we talked, I became aware that the train had stopped in the New Haven station for what seemed an unusually long time. Suddenly, it was like the visceral sensation of almost missing a turnoff while driving. I reminded myself that there was another university here: Yale. Without taking leave of the opera singer's sister, without even remembering that my parents were expecting me for an early dinner on 72nd Street, I did what I had never done before, but had dreamed of doing all my life. I got off the train on an impulse, as it was about to pull out of the station. I told the cab driver to take me to Yale's administration building, naively thinking that there was only one. We drove past an extensive grassy lawn on which three old-looking churches stood parallel to one another. We arrived a few minutes before 5:00 PM in front of a modern Gothic structure. It was Strathcona Hall, at the intersection of College and Grove Streets. A sign saying "Veterans" pointed upstairs. Before I knew it, with the uncanny ease one experiences in dreams, I was sitting in a small cubicle talking with someone in charge of veterans' admissions. A few preliminary questions: my school transcripts, my career ambitions, my army experience. The latter, I believe, did it. My interviewer had also been near Bastogne. Shrapnel in the head.

A few days later, a letter arrived informing me that I had been accepted at Yale, and that a special beginning term had been set up for March to accommodate the entering veterans. Without hesitating one moment I accepted the Yale offer.

The impulse to get off the train in New Haven led to many good things. But the single most important one was that I fell under the spell of the prestigious scholar and charismatic teacher Henri Peyre, who chaired Yale's French Department and was already a legend well beyond the confines of the Yale campus. He was something of a French cultural ambassador in the United States, and a most influential figure in the humanities. Henri Peyre became my mentor and my model. On my first day at Yale, I was urged to consult him on my course of studies, and there I sat in his office. He immediately teased me, made me feel comfortable, heard me—before I even spoke—outlined my entire undergraduate program, opened up vast possibilities, entered into specifics, and was already planning my future career. Since I wanted to teach French literature, with which I already had some familiarity, he advised me to major in English before proceeding to graduate school. And all the while, he was answering the phone, which did not stop ringing. I am pretty sure (but here I may be influenced by the legend) that he was also dashing off a note at the same time.

I stared at him and stammered a few words. I had never encountered such rapid comprehension, such an intense presence, such speed of mind and of words, so much immediate concern and generosity—not in my school days, and certainly not in the army. He radiated confidence, but the confidence he radiated was in the abilities of the very unproven, self-conscious, and apprehensive beginner he was talking to.

Soon I was to see him in action in the classroom, where I remember sitting next to Bill Coffin, the future Yale chaplain and civil rights activist. Peyre taught a wide range of subjects—French classicism, avant-garde poetry, the tradition of the *moralistes,* the modern French novel—interlarding his scintillating presentations with references to Greek mythology, American sex habits, Russian soul-searchings, French gastronomy, Machiavelli's political theories, and extensive forays into English Romanticism, about which he knew more than many specialists in the field. He had written books, among many others, on the Hellenism of the philosopher Ernest Renan and on Shelley's reputation in France. I came to love him, as we all loved him, somewhat awed by him, somewhat afraid to be teased by him, yet enjoying his benevolent teasing because it was clear that he took an interest in every one of us. We had no words to describe our elation. His fervor, his knowledge, his resplendent digressions, his sunny voice, his endless verbal resources, his ability to synthesize broad currents of intellectual history were a heady feast.

I understood then that to teach meant not so much to impart factual knowledge and hand down ready-made opinions as to provoke, incite, perplex, and even disturb one's students, and to encourage them, not to imitate and repeat, but to discover their own voices. It took me twenty-five years—and at that only well after Peyre had retired and left New Haven, and I myself had succeeded him as chair of the department—before I could even consider leaving Yale myself. Leaving any earlier would have felt like apostasy. By a long-range turn of irony once more involving the Eastern seaboard train, I ended up not in New England but in Princeton, which was in reality not so much an arrival as a return. For it had been in Princeton, in the fall of 1941, shortly after I reached the United States as a refugee from Vichy France, that I had my first brief vision of an American campus and felt invaded by the desire—a desire I secretly carried in me throughout the war—to belong one day to the university world that I had glimpsed as I stood in front of Nassau Hall on that September day—a wide-eyed adolescent, almost a boy still.

I OFTEN WONDERED if it is because I recognize the child in me that I find it so hard to take myself seriously. Sometimes I tease myself into believing that mine is a case of arrested development. But if seriousness means acting grave and important, then I am not ashamed to have been able to make fun of my occasional *esprit de sérieux*. The imp of pretentiousness should be thwarted. I laugh every time I remember Montaigne's wonderful observation that even on the loftiest throne one is still only sitting on one's ass. No, I resist taking myself seriously, except perhaps in my deeper allegiances and fears.

It has been said that one cannot be courageous if one has not known fear. I have certainly known fear, though I am not sure that I have ever really been courageous. Fear of death has not prepared me to face it. The more I fear losing life, the more I love it; the more I love it, the more terrible its loss appears to me. There is no use remembering the promise I made to myself on the bluff above Omaha Beach. I have learned that harrowing moments can come in the most unexpected and trivial ways, as when on one occasion an alarming medical report was given to me over the phone at the same time as the new bed for our guest room was being brought into the house.

I have learned to live with a sense of reprieve. Even more than in my childhood, I have learned to appreciate the beauty of convalescence, when every leaf, every flower, every snowflake gives detailed pleasure. Like many other students, I studied Keats's sonnet "When I have fears that I may cease to be . . . " The poem speaks of solitude and loss, but it also speaks of the irreplaceable beauty of the present moment, "the fair creature of an hour." Whenever similar fears assailed me, I understood that there was no time to be lost, though I was not always able to put that thought into practice. I knew that it was high time, or as the Germans say—resorting to a railway metaphor—*höchste Eisenbahn*. The image of the train about to leave—perhaps the last train—also made me think that better ones than I had to go.

If I have always feared inevitable loss, even of that which I never truly possessed, it has helped me prize those privileged moments that provided a sense of duration. Mozart has surely given me some of the most intense joys—and so has music in general, that intangible and invisible construct. Perhaps I should not hope for joys greater than that. The absolute has always daunted me. In Toronto, in the Chinese collection of the Royal Ontario Museum, I read some lines titled "*Zhao hun*" ("Calling Back of the Soul"), in which the poet-philosopher warns his soul not to climb to the heaven above, where tigers and leopards are ever ready to rend the mortal flesh. I believe that the Greek poet Pindar, the bard of the athletic games, expressed a similar loyalty to the finite when, in one of his odes, he exhorted his soul not to aspire to immortal life, but to make the most of the realm of the possible.

As I listen to the familiar sound of the Dinky that plies tirelessly between Princeton Junction and Princeton, I now often think of mortal flesh, of violence and death, and of the human impulse to inflict pain and humiliation. I think of those women in Hasselt and in so many other places who were dragged through the streets, beaten, and then shorn. They had slept with German soldiers, and the Germans were the enemy. But they were perhaps better than the neighbors who broke their ribs and brutally cut off their hair. Those women may never have denounced anyone nor been responsible for anyone's deportation. The same could not be said of some of their neighbors.

Lately, I do not know why, I have been listening more intently to the reassuring yet nostalgic wail of the Dinky as it returns to the home station. Almost every night I wait for it and welcome its sound, always surprised by how far its monotonous lament carries after nightfall. And it seemed only fitting that when my colleagues, not long ago, were about to present me with the traditional testimonial watch, they decided, remembering my love of trains, to give me a gold-plated train watch. It has the words "Great American Train Watch" engraved on its back. The little hand that normally indicates the seconds on the dial is replaced by the miniature silhouette of a locomotive pulling a tender and three coaches with people at the windows. Every second, the train, covering half of the circular rails, advances one notch. When I press a button on the right side of the cover and hold the watch to my ear, I can hear three brief whistles, followed by the chugging of a locomotive and the repeated sound of a bell, and then a dozen iambic cadences produced by a train's wheels on railroad tracks—a mini-example of *musique concrète*, that poetic language of sounds based on tape-recorded noises. If I press the sound button inadvertently, or if my watch gets caught in a sleeve, the sound of the bell can be heard faintly across the room. I cherish this toy. It reminds me of the child I was and have remained, of that same child who stayed awake all night in the sleeper so as not to lose one exciting moment of the journey.

Victor Brombert's parents left Moscow at the outbreak of the Revolution in 1917. After a brief period in Denmark and a year in London, they moved to Germany and finally settled in Paris in 1933, where the author grew up and attended the lycée. His adolescent experiences and political education took place during the turbulent years of the Nazi threat to Europe, while France was torn by social and ideological conflicts at the time of the Popular Front and the Spanish Civil War.

As late as July 1941, when all of Europe seemed to have succumbed to Hitler's power, and Jews were increasingly persecuted, Victor Brombert and his parents managed to escape to the United States by way of Spain, on a banana freighter overcrowded with refugees. After Pearl Harbor and America's entry into the war, Brombert served in U.S. Army military intelligence, landing on Omaha Beach with the 2nd Armored Division. He participated in the Normandy campaign, the liberation of Paris, the Battle of the Hürtgen Forest, the Battle of the Bulge, and then, in occupied Berlin, dealt with the problem of displaced persons' camps. Upon his return to the United States he entered Yale, the class of 1948, under the GI Bill of Rights.

A holder of undergraduate and graduate Yale degrees, as well as honorary doctorates from the Universities of Chicago and Toronto, the author has been professionally active as a literary critic and professor of French and comparative literature. He chaired the Department of Romance Languages and Literatures at Yale University before accepting an appointment at Princeton University, where he became chair of the Council of Humanities. A former president of the Modern Language Association, he is a member of the American Academy of Arts and Sciences and the American Philosophical Society. He has taught and lectured in numerous universities and institutions in the United States and in Europe, including Columbia University, New York University, the University of California, Johns Hopkins University, the University of Puerto Rico, the University of Bologna, he Scuola Normale in Pisa, Italy, and the Collège de France in Paris.

DATE DUE
